Identity Work in the Contemporary

EDUCATIONAL FUTURES
RETHINKING THEORY AND PRACTICE

Volume 67

Series Editor

Michael A. Peters, *University of Waikato, New Zealand*

Editorial Board

Michael Apple, *University of Wisconsin-Madison, USA*
Miriam David, *Institute of Education, London University, UK*
Cushla Kapitzke, *Queensland University of Technology, Australia*
Simon Marginson, *University of Melbourne, Australia*
Mark Olssen, *University of Surrey, UK*
Fazal Rizvi, *University of Illinois at Urbana-Champaign, USA*
Susan Robertson, *University of Bristol, UK*
Linda Tuahwai Smith, *University of Waikato, New Zealand*
Arun Kumar Tripathi, *Indian Institute of Technology, Mandi, Himachal Pradesh, India*

Scope

This series maps the emergent field of educational futures. It will commission books on the futures of education in relation to the question of globalisation and knowledge economy. It seeks authors who can demonstrate their understanding of discourses of the knowledge and learning economies. It aspires to build a consistent approach to educational futures in terms of traditional methods, including scenario planning and foresight, as well as imaginative narratives, and it will examine examples of futures research in education, pedagogical experiments, new utopian thinking, and educational policy futures with a strong accent on actual policies and examples.

Identity Work in the Contemporary University

Exploring an Uneasy Profession

Edited by

Jan Smith
Durham University, UK

Julie Rattray
Durham University, UK

Tai Peseta
University of Sydney, Australia

and

Daphne Loads
University of Edinburgh, UK

SENSE PUBLISHERS
ROTTERDAM/BOSTON/TAIPEI

A C.I.P. record for this book is available from the Library of Congress.

ISBN: 978-94-6300-308-7 (paperback)
ISBN: 978-94-6300-309-4 (hardback)
ISBN: 978-94-6300-310-0 (e-book)

Published by: Sense Publishers,
P.O. Box 21858,
3001 AW Rotterdam,
The Netherlands
https://www.sensepublishers.com/

Cover image by John Wheeler

Printed on acid-free paper

All Rights Reserved © 2016 Sense Publishers

No part of this work may be reproduced, stored in a retrieval system, or transmitted in any form or by any means, electronic, mechanical, photocopying, microfilming, recording or otherwise, without written permission from the Publisher, with the exception of any material supplied specifically for the purpose of being entered and executed on a computer system, for exclusive use by the purchaser of the work.

TABLE OF CONTENTS

Preface: Mapping the Terrain of Identity-Work Research   vii
Jan Smith and Julie Rattray

Part I: On Conceptualising Academic Identities Work

1. From Professional Educational Values to the Satisfaction of Psychological Needs – A Sequence of Ideas   3
   Charles Neame

2. Forging Academic Identities from within: Lessons from the Ancient World   17
   Susan R. Robinson

3. A Labour of Love? Curiosity, Alienation and the Constitution of Academic Character   33
   Paul Sutton

4. The Mechanics of Identity Formation: A Discursive Psychological Perspective on Academic Identity   45
   Neil McLean and Linda Price

Part II: On Researching Academic Identities

5. Uneasy Academic Subjectivities in the Contemporary Ontario University   61
   Sandra Acker and Michelle Webber

6. On the Conduct of Concern: Exploring How University Teachers Recognise, Engage in, and Perform 'Identity' Practices within Academic Workgroups   77
   Tai Peseta, Giedre Kligyte, Jan McLean and Jan Smith

7. Finding a Tūrangawaewae: A Place to Stand as a Tertiary Educator   91
   Dorothy Spiller and Pip Bruce Ferguson

Part III: On Writing Academic Identities

8. Writing of the Heart: Auto-Ethnographic Writing as Subversive Story Telling – A Song of Pain and Liberation   105
   Simon Warren

TABLE OF CONTENTS

9. Doctoral Induction Day: An Ethnographic Fiction on Doctoral Emotions 117
   James Burford

10. Doctoral Supervisor and Student Identities: Fugitive Moments from the Field 129
    Barbara Grant, Catherine Mitchell, Edward Okai, James Burford, Linlin Xu, Toni Ingram and Vanessa Cameron-Lewis

11. Toil and Trouble: Professional and Personal Expectations and Identities in Academic Writing for Publication 143
    Gina Wisker

Part IV: On Supporting Academic Identity Development

12. Creative Research Strategies for Exploring Academic Identity 157
    Virginia King and Jennie Billot

13. Recognising Ourselves and Each Other in Professional Recognition 169
    Daphne Loads and Brigid Collins

14. The Metanoia of Teaching: Translating the Identity of the Contemporary Academic 181
    Karla Benske, Catriona Cunningham and Sam Ellis

Epilogue: Continuing the Conversation 195
Tai Peseta and Daphne Loads

Notes on Contributors 203

Index 211

JAN SMITH AND JULIE RATTRAY

PREFACE

Mapping the Terrain of Identity-Work Research

Despite the well-documented pervasiveness of audit culture (Strathern, 2000) and the neo-liberal ethos of our university contexts, many academics are still able to 'carve out' space for cherished research agendas (Clegg, 2008). The tension between corporatist management styles and academics' personal values is represented by the 'unease' of our title, and this volume therefore foregrounds the increasing interest in the affective dimension of academic work.

A very real strength of research into academic identities is its diversity, drawing on a wide range of conceptual lenses and methodological approaches. This diversity is present in our contributions to the current volume, its richness deepened further by work from authors across four continents, each with its unique configuration of university life. Finding an organising device that can capture such diversity is something of a challenge and no categorisation will be perfect. The four themes we have chosen to structure the book will, we hope, capture and reflect the multiplicity of inquiry practices our authors have adopted in this instance; we do not suggest that these are the only ways of conceptualising academic life, academic practices and, importantly, academic identities.

ON CONCEPTUALISING ACADEMIC IDENTITIES

Identities are complex phenomena (Lawler, 2008) and in contemporary Western thought, not a property of individuals, instead being understood as fluid, negotiated and performed in many different contexts. Through prior investment in their specialised disciplinary study, all academics come to a view of identity-work that reflects and respects these affiliations. As both work and personal contexts evolve, opportunities arise for identity-work research, especially affective work where the prevailing culture of higher education seems currently to be disrupting what Margaret Archer calls the 'continuous sense of self' (2000:77). Many tools can be brought to bear on this exploration, and in Part I of the book, our authors draw on philosophical and Marxist thinking and social psychology, to theorise the development and maintenance of academic identities. These are not empirical pieces; they are attempts to draw out some fundamental and usable conceptualisations of how identity-work research may be undertaken.

Each of these chapters aims to explore the relevance of existing theories, and relate these to the current conditions of academic work, and thus academic identities, in UK and Australian settings. We are shown how the authors' chosen frameworks inform explorations of what it means to participate in university life in different settings. Sutton, uniquely in this volume, applies his framework to teaching undergraduates to highlight the danger of the increasing commodification of university life that accompanies corporatisation. The influence of the audit culture on staff is troubled by the timely philosophical and moral explorations of Robinson and Neame, who remind us that at the heart of academic life are some treasured values. The potential erosion of such values in a race to be 'competitive' in an instrumental sense is brought to the fore by these authors, who show the benefit of exploring beyond the writings traditionally associated with identity-work. Moving from the wider environmental focus of these contributions, McLean and Price consider not the cultural dimension but the agentic, using the lens of discursive psychology to highlight the performance aspect of individuals' identities. The implications here are explored further in Part III of the book with its concentration on representation through writing.

All research needs a sound conceptual base and the choices made by authors here show just a subset of the diversity of tools and schools of thought that can be brought to bear on identity-work research. What is clear is that choices can come from disciplinary affiliations, student and/or community engagement, or concern for the wider environment in which the academy operates. No useful meta-narrative of identity-work research seems to emerge, and this raises an important challenge to the totalising discourse of audit culture.

ON RESEARCHING ACADEMIC IDENTITIES

In Part II, the focus moves to the 'doing' of identity-work research, and its outcomes. Whilst all four chapters here are theoretically informed in this part, they are less about the initial conceptualisation of research into identity-work and more about lived experiences. The empirical nature of the chapters gives us an insight into how individuals respond to their daily working life routines. The contributions here show the value academics place on doing rewarding work, whether in the potentially more benign environment of Canada (Acker and Webber), as part of a team in Australia (Peseta, Kligyte, McLean and Smith) or as individuals in New Zealand (Spiller and Ferguson). Identification as part of a wider enterprise is clear to see amongst those who volunteered evidence, connecting well to the values-base established in Part I.

The messiness of identity-work research is also apparent in these contributions. All of the authors in this part take on the challenge of collecting and interpreting narrative data, mostly, it could be argued, from a more sociological turn of thought. Culture-clash is in evidence: a variety of factors in academic life intrude on personal biographies and expectations to induce feelings of uncertainty and powerlessness. As Watson (2009) has observed, there is a pervasive culture of demoralisation in the UK system of higher education, but if we dig further, he noted, we find that individuals remain passionate about their work. However satisfied with those elements that individuals can control (teaching, research), a sense of unease surrounding corporate culture infuses these accounts.

It can be argued that the UK has moved furthest towards a 'measured university' (the theme for the next Academic Identities Conference in Sydney in 2016) through imposition of the RAE/REF and soon a 'TEF' – a teaching equivalent. Many of these policies are exported over time to other jurisdictions, which so far in the Anglophone world, only Canada seems to have resisted to a degree, so the accounts in this part of the book illuminate some very important aspects of identity-work in the contemporary university: given their geographical dispersal, it raises the question of how the variability in national and institutional contexts shape experiences currently, and leads us to ponder when and where convergences may appear.

ON WRITING ACADEMIC IDENTITIES

Little in academic life is so fraught with challenges to identity as writing for publication. Kamler and Thomson (2006) explicitly link academic writing with identity-work, a valuable proposition that shows how early in a putative academic career writing and identity become so high-stakes. The 'publish or perish' mantra is evident in many HE systems that employ either direct measures of 'outputs' like the UK, Australia and New Zealand, or in those which set the bar high for tenure or performance management (USA, Canada, Thailand, Hong Kong). These systemic expectations ignore the personal investments made in writing and devalue what Warren terms *'disruptive and evocative texts'*. Contributors to this part of the book show, through their chosen formats and modes of expression how producing identities through academic writing actually *feels*.

All of the contributions trouble the notion of 'sterile' academic writing and foreground how choice, variability, identification and identity are challenged and re-affirmed through the process of writing. Some contributions are personal and autoethnographic (Warren, Burford), showing the power of affect as a key issue in academic 'being' and how this is constantly (re-)negotiated for new and more experienced colleagues alike. Internally-driven writing desire can easily come into conflict with corporatist risk aversion exercised through the imposition of targets such as the production of a timely and acceptable thesis (Grant, Mitchell, Okai, Burford, Xu, Ingram and Cameron-Lewis) or REF-able publications (Wisker).

These contributions seem laden with the notion of power in the Foucauldian sense, showing how those negotiating their academic identities have internalised the discipline of writing, whilst rebelling in some ways through the forms of writing they produce. Is writing one of the spaces where, out of the reach of corporatisation, we can find Clegg's 'principled personal autonomy' (2008:343)? The delight in compiling a volume on identity-work research has been the celebration of an eclectic mix of contributions, a very public statement of asserting our academic identities in the face of unease.

ON SUPPORTING ACADEMIC IDENTITY DEVELOPMENT

Initial and ongoing professional development are important activities in academic life, especially with regard to the development of a teacherly identity. This final part concentrates on creative approaches to professional development, showcasing the benefits of providing space and activities that enable thinking outside of the strictures and structures documented elsewhere in the book and linking well to the previous part by legitimising such personal explorations. There is also a loop back to Part I, as Academic Developers research those of their practices that support colleagues to develop their own values and identities as academics. The value of this work can be seen in its potential to encourage freedom and creativity, negating what Land (2004) called the 'domesticating' agenda of some universities' policies.

Particularly striking amongst the three contributions is the emphasis on both artistic work and metaphor to reveal: the power of inducing a different mode of expression leading to representations that may not have been immediately obvious even to their creators, let alone those interpreting the artefacts produced. King and Billot document the benefits and potential pitfalls of analysing metaphorical or visual data, that Loads and Collins and Benske, Cunningham and Ellis also address in the use of more artistic techniques: the sensitivities that can be revealed in such productions need encouragement and affirmation. Freed from linear thinking-writing processes that characterise much of academic life, identity-work can be explored very effectively in safe spaces supporting more expressive and therapeutic perspectives (Loads and Collins) and the humanities-focused (but unusually, team-based) close-reading of 'confessions' (Benske, Cunningham and Ellis). Undertaking such activities proves liberating for colleagues who welcome the opportunity to think differently about their work environments.

The encouragement and space to think differently, however, can manifest itself in uncomfortable realisations which reflect the stories of the writers in Part III and the interviewees of Part II. The importance of the values-base established in Part I comes full circle in expressive development activities, and the academy is often found wanting. Sometimes, the exercise of agency is such that the corporatising environment of the contemporary university is rejected, its opaque practices proving less than amenable. Contest, conflict and paradox infuse the accounts in this volume: a timely reminder that the unease of our title is very real but that identity-work is also open to negotiation through creative acts and principled writings.

* * *

USING THIS BOOK

Those actively engaged in researching academic identities will, we hope, find much of interest in this volume. Each chapter is self-contained, and the book can be navigated in any fashion of the reader's choosing. Those new to the field, given the diversity of perspectives on offer, may find the following brief chapter summaries beneficial as they characterise the nature of a contribution: its theoretical, methodological or disciplinary roots, and aims to orientate readers less familiar with the field.

In Part I, Chapter 1, Charles Neame explores the benefits of an interrogation of personal values. He highlights the difficulties that can arise when others seek to impose a value set on academics. Philosophical in orientation, this contribution challenges us to articulate our own values as practising academics. Susan Robinson uses key principles from classical philosophy in Chapter 2 to construct an argument from Stoical thought that could be applied by the contemporary academic in considering how to deal with the many pressures involved in practising their profession. A reading of Marxism underpins Paul Sutton's contribution in Chapter 3 and its concern with undergraduate students' lack of curiosity. He foregrounds the dominance of exchange-value over use-value of a contemporary higher education experience and thus the need for change. In Chapter 4, Neil McLean and Linda Price draw from the discipline of social psychology, in particular the performative role of discourse and its importance in identity positioning to analyse how academics can portray their experiences in context. Our hope is that this part of the book provides insight to the many disciplinary perspectives that can be taken when it comes to researching identity-work in the contemporary university.

To open Part II, Sandra Acker and Michelle Webber explore in Chapter 5 how even the lightly regulated Canadian higher education system is now producing policy and structures that shape academic work. In an empirical investigation within the sociological tradition, their findings contrast well with other contributions where regulation is far more powerful. In a departure from most work in this volume, Tai Peseta, Giedre Kligyte, Jan McLean and Jan Smith consider aspects of identity-negotiation as part of a teaching team in Chapter 6. Rather than focusing on individuality, the poststructuarlist analysis contained therein gives a sense of (not) fitting within particular cultures and team-working environments. In Chapter 7, Dorothy Spiller and Pip Ferguson, based in New Zealand and Ireland respectively, interrogate interviews and written portfolios from a reflective sociological stance, to draw conclusions about the benefits of initial professional development to give space and support to the identity-work enterprise. Empirical work gives rise to powerful stories which, whilst highly-situated as the authors acknowledge, can travel the globe and be recognised.

Many of the contributions in Part III of this volume draw from literary and autoethnographic traditions. In Chapter 8, Simon Warren offers us a poetic take on serious academic issues: those of pressure, burnout and depression, connecting a powerful personal 'Me' story to wider conceptual resources to summon an 'Us' story showing the value of different forms of representation. This is followed by another autoethnographic contribution in Chapter 9 from James Burford, based in Thailand, that explores the pressure to conform that is placed on new doctoral students and how indifferent the current performative university now is to those who constitute it. In Chapter 10, Barbara Grant works collaboratively with some of her doctoral students – Catherine Mitchell, Edward Okai, James Burford, Linlin Xu, Toni Ingram and Vanessa Cameron-Lewis – to trouble a range of supervisor/supervisee relations: power, fear, dominant culture, collegiality, reminding us that academic life is never a comfortable space whether we are new or established. We close this part with Chapter 11, by Gina Wisker who draws on a range of research studies, merging some literary readings with social scientific practices to foreground the affective dimensions of writing for publication and the personal investments involved.

The importance of encouraging and supporting identity-work is the focus of Part IV of the book, with an emphasis on creative approaches that have the potential to defeat the more performative culture evident in earlier chapters. In Chapter 12, Virginia King and Jennie Billot draw on both narrative and visual data produced in professional development contexts to show the liberating power of metaphor for individuals coming to understand their relationship with the academy. To continue the theme of 'undoing' ingrained academic practices in development work, in Chapter 13, Daphne Loads and Brigid Collins show how engaging with arts-enriched approaches can help us to break out of habitual and guarded modes of communication. Chapter 14 is a contribution from Karla Benske, Catriona Cunningham and Sam Ellis who describe a collaborative take on the frequently solitary Humanities activity of close-reading of texts, in this case '*confessions*' from colleagues regarding their teaching practices, productively analysed from a range of perspectives. These authors foreground the importance of safe and creative spaces to support identity development work and ways that the artefacts produced can usefully be analysed.

WAYS FORWARD

This preface has aimed to tame an unruly beast: to find some organising device for an eclectic mix of disciplinary and methodological approaches to doing identity-work research in the contemporary university. We hope that both the sketching of the themes that inform the parts of this work and the Chapter Summaries directly above, serve as a useful orientating device whether you are new or experienced in the fields of identity-work or higher education more generally. Putting these contributions together has been enormously rewarding and interesting as the editors have sought to appreciate the breadth of research available in the area. The diversity that characterises the field, as noted above, is both challenging and rewarding. We hope there is something of interest for academics globally, no matter the stage of their career.

Whilst this introduction necessarily focuses on the text that follows, with each chapter contributed by active researchers from across the globe, we have tried to highlight the particular to give voice to some powerful stories. Each conceptual lens or methodological approach has something to contribute, and the context-specificity of identity-work research is key: biography, geography, policy and disciplinary culture each have something to add to a fascinating field. Researching their intersections – a task we have attempted to begin with this volume – should provide fertile ground for a satisfying research agenda long into the future. Demoralised accounts of academic labour can, as the late Sir David Watson noted, so easily dominate the narrative of the corporatised university. We hope there is hope – and in the accounts presented here there is evidence that even where disempowerment is felt, there is still resistance to the excesses of performativity – and it appears that through creativity and writing, the self-realisation of which Clegg (2008) writes, remains possible. To close this work, we provide an Epilogue which look outwards, to explore the implications of the fruits of identity-work research in university contexts internationally.

REFERENCES

Archer, M. (2000). *Being human: The problem of agency*. Cambridge, England: Cambridge University Press.
Clegg, S. (2008). Academic identities under thread. *British Educational Research Journal, 34*(3), 329–345.
Kamler, B., & Thomson, P. (2006). *Helping doctoral students write: Pedagogies for supervision*. Abingdon, England: Routledge
Land, R. (2004). *Educational development: Discourse, identity and practice*. Buckingham, England: SRHE/Open University Press.
Lawler, S. (2008). *Identity: Sociological perspectives*. Cambridge, England: Polity Press.
Strathern, M. (2000). *Audit cultures: Anthropological studies in accountability, ethics and the academy*. Abingdon, England: Routledge.
Watson, D. (2009). *The question of morale: Managing happiness and unhappiness in university life*. Maidenhead, England: Open University Press.

Jan Smith
School of Education
Durham University, UK

Julie Rattray
School of Education
Durham University, UK

PART I

ON CONCEPTUALISING ACADEMIC IDENTITIES WORK

CHARLES NEAME

1. FROM PROFESSIONAL EDUCATIONAL VALUES TO THE SATISFACTION OF PSYCHOLOGICAL NEEDS – A SEQUENCE OF IDEAS

INTRODUCTION

The origins of this paper lie in my observations of a set of departmental reviews presented by heads of department in one particular institution in the UK, and in subsequent discussions with some of those colleagues. Listening to them set out their passionate visions of curriculum prompted something akin to Baxter-Magolda's (2004) idea of 'moments of epistemological transformation' (p. 31). What was particularly striking was hearing some of these department heads use a humanist language of care, in a very practical context, to describe and evaluate the instrumental notion of curriculum (which was the brief given to them for the review). Ashwin (2014) has noted that higher education 'research has tended not to examine the relations between knowledge and curriculum in higher education' (p. 123) yet the experience described above by heads of department seemed to be precisely connected with that relationship. It was not about knowledge codified into learning outcomes, nor about knowledge categorized scientifically as an output of empirical research; but it was about knowledge in the form of understandings about the development of students through engagement with learning communities and processes. It was also about curriculum as a site for the development of relationships between people and their worlds.

This chapter considers how curriculum, when it celebrates and is explicitly informed by clearly articulated intrinsic values, contributes to the identity formation of students and their teachers – but especially the latter. Specifically, the chapter invites reflection on how a values-based approach to curriculum on the part of teaching staff can influence the development of their professional identity. I draw on several ideas from different literatures to link the notions of educational values, professionalism in higher education, and the academic identity of teachers in higher education (HE). The final such idea brings into play the connection between values-based identity development and wellbeing.

The first idea is that curriculum can be determined in one important sense by reference to values rather than to content; and furthermore, that defining curriculum as content in the absence of an ethical framework is an insufficient condition for worthwhile education to take place. This is a values-driven idea which is not empirical but derives from the convictions of educators who develop curriculum from this particular moral position.

The second idea concerns the role of values in identity formation and arises from a logical analysis of the definition of 'a value'. This is indeed a contested term (Himmelfarb, 1995) but common to many definitions is agreement that a value typically represents an inner, or intrinsic conviction of some sort (e.g., Nussbaum, 1990), or an indicator of commonality that binds the perspectives and behaviours of a particular community (e.g., Sayer, 2004). In other words, values are intensely associated with identity. Any attempt by an outside agency (such as an employer or a professional body) to impose values is arguably an attempt to manipulate identity. Without ascribing moral weighting to one education system over another (although readers are free to do so), a system that subscribes to the manipulation of identity is very different morally from one which refutes such manipulation. I suggest that many colleagues who strongly support the values sets presented by institutions such as the Higher Education Academy (through the UK Professional Standards Framework) would simultaneously reject the notion that they approve of identity manipulation; in which case either my argument is flawed, or there is disagreement or ambiguity over the nature of values and their relationship with identity. Illich (1973) put it in more vehement terms:

> … the institutionalization of values leads inevitably to physical pollution, social polarization and psychological impotence: three dimensions in a process of global degradation and modernised misery. (p. 9)

The third idea is connected to the second through the issue of identity manipulation. I consider two competing metaphors for curriculum: 'trajectory' and 'ecology'. I suggest that the well-meaning trajectory metaphor ('launching' students onto a successful career 'pathway') is actually manipulative because it casts the student as an object to be directed according to the agency of institutions. The relative merit of the ecology metaphor (Barnett, 2011; Jackson, 2014) is contrasted with this, whereby curriculum is seen as an ecosystem within which teachers, learners, and institutions co-exist interdependently, sharing agency for cooperation on the one hand, and independence on the other.

Following from this, the fourth idea proposes that a simplified model of self-determined values helps to articulate how we as educators 'profess' our academic identity, and thus lay claim to 'professionalism' in our teaching practice. If values are not to be imposed extrinsically but are still recognised as a force for social cohesion when shared, they have to be shareable. I propose that the simpler they are, the more readily shareable they are, and the better they work as a lens through which we can recognise, acknowledge and respond to the values of others.

And finally, out of these considerations of the relationship between professional values and academic identity, and prompted by self-determination theory as hinted at above (Ryan & Deci, 2000a), comes a link to the satisfaction of psychological needs. The three basic psychological needs of competence, relatedness and autonomy

(Ryan & Deci, 2000a) can be associated with conceptions of educational values, in the sense that a professional stance shaped by those values can directly influence the satisfaction of all three needs, with an associated increase in wellbeing.

An integrated model of these ideas, then, posits that curriculum should be informed by the intrinsically generated values sets of its participants – including those who teach it – and that teaching this kind of values-based curriculum contributes both to the satisfaction of the teacher's psychological needs and to their confidence in professing an academic identity. This, in turn, enhances the teacher's wellbeing.

The chapter follows these ideas in sequence – although some of the later ideas look back in acknowledgement to the earlier ones before moving on. They are not equally sized bricks in a conceptual wall; some are weightier than others, and some serve as links or scene setters, rather than stand-alone proposals. The first two ideas are flags or markers for those that follow, and the scope and emphasis of the following sections varies accordingly.

IDEA 1 – CURRICULUM: VALUES VERSUS CONTENT

Barnett (2000) marked the excitement of the new millennium suggesting that the new role for the university is:

> to help us comprehend and make sense of the ... knowledge mayhem [*of a supercomplex world*]; and to enable us to live purposefully amid supercomplexity. (p. 409)

This might be interpreted at face value as acknowledging the performative imperative of universities, producing knowledge measured by its use value. But the roles Barnett (2000) actually proposes for the university are 'built around personal growth, societal enlightenment and the promotion of critical forms of understanding' (p. 411). As he would go on to say some years later in his book *A will to learn* (Barnett, 2007: 6), 'ontology trumps epistemology'. For the curriculum and those who experience it, this is essentially a contrast between values and content. It may be helpful to keep the idea of curriculum open, as something that is not fixed but which acts for each of us as a representation of the things that matter to living in higher education.

IDEA 2 – VALUES, KNOWLEDGE AND IDENTITY

Drawing on Bernstein's (2000) characterisations of knowledge-as-research, knowledge-as-curriculum and knowledge-as-student-understanding, Ashwin (2014) suggests that these offer us

> a powerful way of gaining a sense of the transformative power of higher education because it brings into focus the ways in which higher education transforms students' understanding and identities. This involves developing a

deeper sense of how students' engagement with knowledge and curriculum can transform their relations with themselves and the world. (p. 124)

The colleagues in my opening anecdote seemed to have unconsciously formed a variation on '*knowledge-as-curriculum*' in a category of '*knowledge-as-"being in the world"*'. As Levinas (1996) says in his discussion of Heidegger's thought, the question: 'How does knowledge correspond to being?' is a more profound formulation of the problem of knowledge" (p. 12).

In a complex world where education is about becoming, many scholars have proposed ideas about personal epistemology and transformational learning. One of the most powerful of these ideas is Baxter-Magolda's (2008) notion of self-authorship. She writes that:

The majority of my longitudinal participants [*in a 20 year study*] entered college dependent on external authorities for what to believe, how to identify themselves, and how to relate to others. Over the course of their college experience, multiple perspectives among external authorities and the societal message that young adults should take responsibility for themselves led participants to rely less on external sources and consider relying on their own internal voices. It was not until after college, however, that most were able to bring their voices to the foreground to construct their own beliefs, identities, and interdependent relations with others. (p. 48)

Higher education, then – the '*college years*', as Perry (1970) puts it – is an extraordinarily significant transformational period for many students. Baxter Magolda (2008) defines self-authorship as reflecting 'the ability to internally define one's beliefs, values, identity, and social relations' (p. 53). This is not solely a description of a process of identity formation but a skill required in order to achieve it in a self-aware and intrinsically directed manner. And it is not a skill development process confined to students either. If teaching, for empathetic teachers, is an iteration of reflecting on the development of students, on one's own influence on that development, and on the implications for oneself, then self-authorship must feature as an ongoing dimension of teacher identity also.

IDEA 3 – TRAJECTORY VERSUS ECOLOGY

The metaphors for personal development are potentially many, and many of these relate to the notion of step-wise transition. Perhaps taking their cue from *As You Like It* and Shakespeare's thoroughly 'glass-half-empty' view of the seven ages of man, there are many images of development that describe stages (especially in psychology) starting with Erikson's stages of psychosocial development (Rosenthal, Gurney, & Moore, 1981), and including Piaget and others. Perry (1970) proposed nine 'positions' of epistemological growth in his scheme of intellectual and ethical development, and it is inevitable that many models, of whatever sort, use some system of discrete categorisation as a basis for simplifying the particular features of experience that they are intended to explain.

A popular alternative is an evolutionary form of metaphor which reflects the lived experience: development as a journey, or pathway… the river of life, and suchlike. Indeed, the word curriculum is Latin for 'course' (hence a course of study), and we still express our professional and other achievements as a 'curriculum vitae' – the course of life.

Jackson (2014) uses two competing metaphors. He talks of trajectories of development as

> a story of creation in which people create or co-create new knowledge and understanding in order to develop along the trajectories they have chosen for themselves or have been determined by others. (p. 3)

But in the same paragraph he introduces the rich notion of ecology where development is

> an ecological story in which personal and professional development emerges in an organic and often unpredictable way from the contexts and circumstances of people's lives. (Jackson, 2014: 3)

Yet in the context of higher education, the metaphor of the 'career trajectory' seems to have gained in popularity since governments decided that education was a function of economic success, rather than of personal development and social growth (Leitch Review, 2006). A simple exploration of institutional messages that incorporate the notion of 'trajectory' is informative. One institution, for example, exhorts students to: *Amplify your career trajectory. There is power in knowledge.*[1] Another offers: *Tips for Boosting Your Career Trajectory*[2] while a third cites an academics' area of research interest to include the *Inter-relationships between career trajectories, socialisation and identity*.[3] And there is more. The University of Colorado has carried out research into trajectories: *Faculty Career Trajectories and the Institutional Factors that Shape Them: Comparative Analysis of Longitudinal Faculty Interview Data*[4] while elsewhere, a distinguished academic offers a presentation entitled: *Life After Schaeffer: The Academic Career Trajectory*.[5] At the University of Oxford, its research career guidance document, advises that: 'an early discussion to identify the researcher's aspirations and likely career trajectory should take place';[6] and the University of Manchester's promotions criteria guidance notes declare that:

> Decisions on promotion will be based on merit, with the expectation of significant evidence of both the appropriate level of performance and future career trajectory.[7]

Academics seem to be content with the trajectory metaphor – both for themselves and for their students. In the examples above, it is associated with ideas of power and energy, aspiration, achievement and performance. The trajectory metaphor is also used to frame research performance too.

Staying with the territory of metaphor, the problem with the notion of 'trajectory' (apart from the unfortunate inevitability of the career parabola that 'what goes up must come down'), is its inherently inanimate association. The Oxford English Dictionary gives exclusively physical definitions, such as 'of or pertaining to that which is thrown or hurled through the air or space' (OED online[8]). We could not choose a metaphor better placed to suggest an absence of self-determination, were we to search for some time.

An aficionado of the trajectory metaphor might argue that this hardly matters: *'you know what I mean'*! The whole point of metaphor, however, is to encapsulate meaning, not take it for granted. This particular metaphor is so problematically loaded that it simply will not do for many philosophies of education. Becoming a 'trajectoid'[9] – the 'object' that follows a trajectory determined by a combination of its physical properties and the impetus applied to it by some other mechanism – is not a satisfactory summary of the human achievement that arises from our educational experiences.

The alternative metaphor identified earlier – curriculum as ecosystem – already proposed in an educational context by Barnett (2011) and Jackson (2014), opens up a different philosophical position with significant implications for academic identity. The differences between the two metaphors are many: a person is moved along a trajectory but lives within, and as part of, an ecosystem; mapping the trajectory focuses on the individual whereas the ecosystem may be mapped as a network of interdependence between individuals and the diverse features of their environment; the trajectory is linear but the ecosystem is multidimensional; the trajectory has limited outcomes and is dependent on a number of key inputs, while the ecosystem is a set of boundless possibilities; the curriculum is one factor in determining the trajectory whereas in the second, the curriculum is the ecosystem, and the ecosystem is the curriculum.

This last point is worth expanding. It requires a notion of curriculum which is more than content: it is the totality of educational experience. The distinction between formal and informal learning becomes blurred, as do identifiers such as student or teacher. Pat phrases such as *'learning for the real-world'*[10] evaporate into their own tautological meaninglessness when we garner respect for the entirety of life's educational value.

In terms of its relevance for identity formation, we can play out the ecosystems metaphor through the ecological notion of curriculum as a landscape, in and of which teachers are stewards and students their apprentices; both dependent on the same resources, and both doing the same work, albeit with different and constantly developing roles. This contrasts rather nicely with the more traditional 'shepherd-flock' analogy of the pastoral tradition of education, where students are given the role of dumb animals to be cared for by a different species (not, we hope, in this metaphorical instantiation, destined for the dinner table of the latter).

Jackson (2014) hints at the importance of the parallel development of students and their teachers in his reference to what he calls the *wicked* developmental problem facing universities:

> Nested in this challenge is the developmental problem of how teachers, learning advisors or professional educational developers develop *themselves* so that they can support and enable their students to develop themselves so that they can act effectively in the future worlds they will inhabit (*my emphasis*). (p. 2)

The idea of stewards and apprentices working with, and dependent on, a shared network of knowledge resources fits with Barnett's (2000: 415) 'multilayered character of knowing-in-the-world'. In a view of curriculum as ecosystem, we can reconcile Barnett's model of conceptual supercomplexity with an ecological model of systems complexity. Emphasising that supercomplexity is not to be confused with a postmodern absence of explanatory frameworks, he characterises supercomplexity as consisting of 'a surfeit, an embarrassment, of frameworks; and some pretty large frameworks at that' (Barnett, 2000: 416). He then asks 'is knowledge a matter of contemplation or of action? Is it a force for controlling the world or for communicating with it?' (p. 416).

Ecosystems are also super-complex; an ecosystem is a meta-framework of multiple, possibly infinite sub-frameworks, each functioning according to its own rules of tension and balance, and each surviving or failing, depending on its compatibility with the meta-framework. Our capacity for thriving within such systems depends not on our ability to explain and control them, but to adapt systemically within them. Curriculum as a knowledge world comes to be about knowledge-as-being, as the form that one's identity takes within a knowledge ecology. Indeed, '*being* overtakes knowledge as the key epistemological concept' (Barnett, 2000: 418).

These two metaphors of 'trajectory' and 'ecology' are fundamentally competitive in grammatical and philosophical terms. Consider the grammar of development first. The first metaphor, 'trajectory', invokes an image of the student without agency: an object launched into its future by a benevolent institution populated by benevolent teachers. 'Development' here is used in a transitive sense; that is to say, the verb 'develop' governs a direct object. The student as 'trajectoid' has no agency in the image: it (and as an object it loses even the human problem of gender; at least we don't need to struggle with the 'he/she' problem in this grammatical construction) ends up where we think it should end up, depending, of course, on the accuracy of our aim. Anecdotally, one UK vice-chancellor was reported as talking of his students as being the arrows the University fires from its bow! Intended as an uplifting 'into the future' energetic image, no doubt, it appears fundamentally paternalistic and disempowering, nonetheless.

The second metaphor – ecology – is profoundly different, both in its grammatical and philosophical implications. These philosophical implications, incidentally, have a direct bearing on pragmatic issues of learning and teaching. The ecology metaphor implies development as part of an organic, interdependent system. Here, the vice-chancellor and his students are inextricably interconnected. The VC *cannot* fire his students from his[11] bow because he does not have that agent-object relationship with them. Neither, of course, do the worker bees in his classrooms and laboratories – the teaching staff. In this metaphor, development is cast in an intransitive sense, grammatically speaking. The verb 'develop' does not carry an object, but is descriptive of the change experienced by the subject. In this case, students (and their teachers, as fellow parts of the ecosystem) are themselves developing; they are not 'being developed'.

The philosophical implications flow readily from the grammatical analysis: student as object, or student as subject? Or rather, because this developmental experience applies to teachers and students alike, we ought perhaps to substitute another word – maybe as simple a word as 'people'. The relationship between people and the 'contexts and circumstances' (Jackson, 2014: 3) in which they learn is at heart a philosophical issue. Our sphere of interest here is 'people in education', by which we mean people whose lives and identities are influenced by education, whether as students, teachers, or others. In this chapter, I am interested in 'people in education like me'. That qualification is deliberately provocative: surely, recognizing our struggle for becoming, following Barnett's (2007) Heideggerian 'ontological turn' in an infinitely diverse world, to look for 'people like me' is to close my mind to diversity and to shackle the potential for growth and development through engagement with difference. To appreciate difference, we need to know what something or someone is different *from*. We can then ask questions such as '*why are you as you are*?' and '*why am I as I am*?' These questions about identity are central to curriculum.

Education is teleological. It deals with ends, and therefore with means, and is value-laden as a consequence. What are the ends, purposes, or goals of education? These are not given (although our acceptance of a particular set of goals may well be influenced by others), but depend very much on the personal values that each of us holds in respect of education. Elsewhere (Neame, 2014), I have addressed the context of resisting the imposition of values sets which are mandated by such external agents as professional bodies, however well-meaning they may be. Yet, adopting the ecological metaphor does not require us to set aside the idea of development as step-wise progression completely. On the contrary, ecology fundamentally involves growth and transition. Baxter Magolda (2008) explained how one of her respondents ('Dawn') 'described sorting internally what she believed in order to refine the essence of her identity'. Dawn talked of:

> stepping into that realm of not judging people, treating them with compassion, acting in my life without judging and with compassion. (p. 55)

This is a beautiful developmental and transitional metaphor which not only illustrates the 'becoming' of a person who has achieved a capacity for empathy, but which uses a language of transformation vis-à-vis the world. Dawn 'steps' into a non-judgmental, compassionate relationship with others, almost as a symbolic arrival in a new state of being. Indeed, she describes it as a 'realm', using a word traditionally meaning 'kingdom'.[12] Ironically, like the animal kingdom, there are no kings in this state of nature; regulation (another word derived from the language of kingship) is achieved through the balance of mutual and competing interests, where those like Dawn choose to pursue mutuality rather than competition. In other words, it is an ecosystem[13] where relationships based on mutuality sit alongside, and around, relationships based on competition.

IDEA 4 – VALUES AND PROFESSIONAL IDENTITY

If metaphors allow us to conceptualise the nature, process and environment of developmental identity formation, the question of values and how they are shaped, remains. The need to produce and articulate my own personal 'set' of values was prompted by a reaction to externally articulated values statements. Paradoxically, I came to argue that values statements should be intrinsically generated by each of us, yet I found myself largely dependent on reactions to the statements of others in the production of my own values statement. I was struck (and somewhat confused) by the distinctions in emphasis, conceptualisation, and even grammatical construction put forward by different bodies claiming professional authority over the values basis of their members' and affiliates' engagement with higher education. In reaction to that, I produced the simplest model of personal professional values that I could. The result, after much iteration, was to claim that what I value as a professional educator, is the transformation of communities and their members through scholarship. This has everything to do with identity because it governs how I see my relationship with my professional communities. It is professional in the sense that this is how I 'profess' my identity as an educator. There are three values (three essential 'things that I value') within this simple values statement:

- Transformation (which captures the *purpose* of education);
- Community (which captures the entirety of our relations with other *people*, and which is thus the source of the important psychological need of relatedness – (e.g., Ryan & Deci, 2000a, 2000b); and
- Scholarship (which captures the *process* whereby communities and their members engage in education to achieve their own transformation and to support that of others).

Being able to 'profess' a clearly articulated set of values in this way offers one simple notion of 'professionalism'; by professing values which are self-determined (that is to say, they are defined and selected by an intrinsic process of ethical consideration, in contrast with values which are mandated by institutions), they become an intrinsic part of one's professional identity.

IDEA 5 – PROFESSIONAL IDENTITY AND SELF-DETERMINATION: SATISFACTION OF PSYCHOLOGICAL NEEDS

McLean (2012 and in this volume) identifies the connection between the disciplines of education and psychology, and a surprising lack of psychologically-based research in the academic identities literature. A key connection lies in a shared perspective that within these disciplines identity is co-constructed. Identity develops out of a continuous engagement with the interaction, or discourse, between a person's intrinsic values and the extrinsic values expressed by the communities to which that person belongs or aspires. In this sense, McLean (2012) argues, we adopt identities in order to '*claim group membership*'. On the other hand, we reject association with groups to which we do not aspire, perhaps because the values of those groups are not consonant with our own intrinsic values. On this argument, we retain agency in our values-based identity formation. On the other hand, we may maintain our membership of groups with dissonant values sets from our own, if our ability to leave those groups is constrained by economic or social factors. We may not be able to afford to leave a job with an organisation of which we disapprove, or we may not wish to because our friendship groups are tied up with it. With that caution in mind, there is another set of psychological theories which illuminates the relationship between identity formation, group membership and agency. Self-determination theory (SDT) explains the role of the three essential psychological needs of competence, relatedness and autonomy (Ryan & Deci, 2000a, 2000b). SDT seeks to explain the distinction between action that is intrinsically motivated and that which is extrinsically motivated. Intrinsic motivation derives satisfaction directly from the engagement with the action itself, whereas extrinsic motivation represents reasons for action, or psychological influences on it, which are external to the individual. These influences may include pressure to conform to social, family, or professional convention, for example. Much of the research which draws on SDT as an explanatory psychological theory reflects a positivist theoretical perspective (e.g., Wilkesmann & Schmid, 2014). At the same time, the theory offers an interpretivist framework for exploring the relationships between individuals' worldviews and their sense of wellbeing. Within an ontological frame of reference for education, we can connect the development of a teacher's professional identity – marked by increasingly confident articulation of personal and professional values – with the satisfaction of the psychological needs that leads to wellbeing.

If we consider the three values model introduced above, we can make a direct connection between each value and a corresponding psychological need. As indicated earlier, these fundamental needs are for relatedness, autonomy, and competence. My argument here is that we value community (the 'people' part of my values set above) because it allows us to reify the notion of relatedness in a sense of connection with other people and social groups. We may each have different sets of community connections, and feel inclined to engage with them in different ways, but for each of us it is the need for relatedness, in some form, that we satisfy through those connections.

The value of transformation – our educational 'purpose' – is that it satisfies our need for autonomy. Autonomy is not the opposite of relatedness; it is instead the sense of gaining control over our need to depend on others. Autonomy helps us to define our relatedness, and gives us the self-confidence to profess an identity. Autonomy is the mark of successful self-authorship. The final psychological need, for competence, is satisfied professionally through scholarship (the 'process' part of my values set). Scholarship (its contested nature itself the subject of an extensive literature) captures the idea of a 'proper process' for transformation through education. It encompasses a whole raft of notions – including those of reflection, rigour, reliability, validity, care, and openness – which characterise effective education.

CONCLUSION

In the final analysis, my argument might be construed to mean that values are adopted for selfish reasons, even though they have the appearance of determining a morally right approach to life. We adopt values that satisfy our psychological needs, and which thereby improve our wellbeing. The discussion (it turns out) is basically Aristotelian. The education of trajectory is about poeisis: developing skills (techne) to lead to useful products. The interdependent, ecosystemic education on the other hand is about phronesis: developing a 'practical wisdom' guided by a moral disposition. The resulting praxis involves engagement with community to achieve ethical ends. Identifying an intrinsic values set enables such ethical ends to be identified and pursued through education. The engagement with community, the reflective interplay with knowledge through scholarship, and the goal of transformation interpreted in ethical terms, are what satisfy the psychological needs of relatedness, competence and autonomy respectively. Education based on self-determined values represents a virtuous circle of identity formation, wellbeing, and – in the representation of a curriculum that embodies, not a trajectory, but the infinite possibilities of life – an enhanced potential for education itself.

NOTES

[1] Olin Business School: course information page http://www.olin.wustl.edu/EN-US/academic-programs/specialized-masters-programs/Pages/default.aspx
[2] Regent University faculty blog http://blogs.regent.edu/faculty/2012/10/16/mentoring-matters-tips-for-boosting-your-career-trajectory/
[3] Reading University: staff member's public web page. http://www.reading.ac.uk/education/about/staff/alan-floyd.aspx
[4] http://www.colorado.edu/eer/downloads/LEAPtrajectoriesReport2007.pdf
[5] http://clas.uiowa.edu/files/history/denial%2C%20flyer.pdf
[6] Oxford University: http://www.admin.ox.ac.uk/media/global/wwwadminoxacuk/localsites/personnel/documents/policiesandcops/RSCoP.pdf
[7] University of Manchester: http://documents.manchester.ac.uk/display.aspx?DocID=473 (1–7 all accessed 30th April 2015).
[8] http://www.oed.com/view/Entry/204477?redirectedFrom=trajectory#eid (accessed 5th March 2015)
[9] "No dictionary entries found for 'trajectoid'." OED online (12th March 2015).

[10] Source: the website of almost any university in the Western world.
[11] "Just 14 per cent of UK vice-chancellors are women" (Grove, 2013).
[12] Derived from old French 'reaume', or in modern French 'royaume'.
[13] Ecosystem: From Greek 'oikos' – house or habitation; and 'systema' – an organized whole, compounded of parts.

REFERENCES

Ashwin, P. (2014). Knowledge, curriculum and student understanding in higher education. *Higher Education, 67*(2), 123–126.

Barnett, R. (2000). University knowledge in an age of supercomplexity. *Higher Education, 40*(4), 409–422.

Barnett, R. (2007). *A will to learn: Being a student in an age of uncertainty*. Maidenhead, England: Society for Research into Higher Education & Open University Press.

Barnett, R. (2011). The coming of the ecological university. *Oxford Review of Education, 37*(4), 439–455.

Baxter Magolda, M. B. (2004). Evolution of a constructivist conceptualisation of epistemological reflection. *Educational Psychologist, 39*(1), 31–42.

Baxter Magolda, M. B. (2008). The evolution of self-authorship. In M. S. Khine (Ed.), *Knowing, knowledge and beliefs: Epistemological studies across diverse cultures* (pp. 45–64). New York, NY: Springer.

Bernstein, B. (2000). *Pedagogy, symbolic control and identity: Theory, research and critique* (Rev. ed.). Oxford, England: Rowman & Littlefield.

Grove, J. (2013, August 22). Why are there so few female vice-chancellors? *Times Higher Education*. Retrieved from http://www.timeshighereducation.co.uk/features/why-are-there-so-few-female-vice-chancellors/2006576.article (Accessed March 12, 2015).

Himmelfarb, G. (1995). *The demoralisation of society: From Victorian virtues to modern values*. London, England: Institute of Economic Affairs.

Illich, I. (1973). *Deschooling society*. Harmondsworth, England: Penguin.

Jackson, N. (2014). Creativity in development: A higher education perspective. *Lifewide education*. Retrieved from http://www.creativityindevelopment.co.uk/uploads/1/3/5/4/13542890/chapter_1.pdf (Accessed on March 12, 2015).

Leitch Review of Skills. (2006). *Prosperity for all in the global economy: World class skills*. Norwich, England: HMSO. Retrieved from http://webarchive.nationalarchives.gov.uk/20130129110402/http://hm-treasury.gov.uk/d/leitch_finalreport051206.pdf (Accessed on March 12, 2015).

Levinas, E. (1996). Martin Heidegger and ontology. *Diacritics, 26*(1), 11–32.

McLean, N. (2012). Researching academic identity: Using discursive psychology as an approach. *International Journal for Academic Development, 17*(2), 97–108.

Neame, C. (2014). *Scholarship as educational process and scholarship as educational value: A model of values-based education*. Conference paper: Educational Development in a Changing World. International Consortium for Educational Development (ICED), June 17, 2014. Stockholm, Sweden: Karolinska Institutet.

Nussbaum, M. C. (1990). *Love's knowledge: Essays on philosophy and literature*. Oxford, England: Oxford University Press.

Perry, W. (1970). *Forms of intellectual and academic developments in the college years*. New York, NY: Holt, Rhinehart & Winston.

Rosenthal, D. A., Gurney, R. M., & Moore, S. M. (1981). From trust to intimacy: A new inventory for examining Erikson's stages of psychosocial development. *Journal of Youth and Adolescence, 10*(6), 525–537.

Ryan, R. M., & Deci, E. L. (2000a). Self-determination theory and the facilitation of intrinsic motivation, social development, and well-being. *American Psychologist, 55*(1), 68–78.

Ryan, R. M., & Deci, E. L. (2000b). Intrinsic and extrinsic motivations: Classic definitions and new directions. *Contemporary Educational Psychology, 25*(1), 54–67.

Sayer, A. (2004). *Restoring the moral dimension: Acknowledging lay normativity.* England: Lancaster University. Retrieved from http://www.lancaster.ac.uk/sociology/research/publications/papers/sayer-restoring-moral-dimension.pdf (Accessed June 19, 2015).

Wilkesmann, U., & Schmid, C. (2014). Intrinsic and internalized modes of teaching motivation. *Evidence-Based HRM: A Global Forum for Empirical Scholarship, 2*(10), 6–27.

Charles Neame
Centre for Excellence in Learning and Teaching
Manchester Metropolitan University, UK

SUSAN R. ROBINSON

2. FORGING ACADEMIC IDENTITIES FROM WITHIN

Lessons from the Ancient World

INTRODUCTION

Recent changes within the globalised enterprise university have led to a 'de-centring' of the academic from many of the traditional core functions of the academy. This chapter draws upon ethical teachings from the Hellenistic era, the period spanning the death of Alexander the Great (c.356 – 323 BCE) to the founding of the Roman Empire in 31 BCE, to provide insights into the problems academics face, as they struggle to (re)formulate their identities within the contemporary academy. In particular, three schools of philosophy are explored: Cynicism, Stoicism and Epicureanism. The Hellenistic schools were offering different formulae for realising self-sufficiency (*autarkeia*) on the road to overcoming perplexity or psychological turmoil. It is argued that, of the three schools, Stoicism may provide the richest psychological and intellectual resources for educated individuals coping with changing job requirements in the enterprise university. The ensuing discussion uses Ancient lessons regarding *autarkeia* and social responsibility to reinterpret the traditional academic values of autonomy and collegiality.

HIGHER EDUCATION DURING A TIME OF CHANGE

Academics' individual and collective identities are being undermined by increased workplace pressures, as Western universities respond to national educational policies that are attuned to the forces of globalisation. This chapter argues that, with universities 'diversified, expanded, globalised, internationalised, borderless/ edgeless, marketised, technologised, and neo-liberalised' (Morley, 2012: 354), recent decades have seen a 'de-centring' of the academic from the core functions of the academy, with significant consequences for academic identities.

The 'de-centering' of the academic within the academy is vividly illustrated in the widespread adoption of technology-enhanced instruction (Rhoades, 2007). 'Challenge, variety and autonomy', qualities academic seek and value in their work (Bryson, 2004: 54), may all be curtailed under the roll-out of ICT-rich education. The knowledge society encourages the reduction of knowledge to information 'consisting of objectified, commodified, discreet, decontextualized representations'

(Tsoukas, 2007: 827). Of course, all information revolutions serve to 'commodify' and democratise knowledge (Sharrock, 2004: 269). What is new, in the move to technology-enhanced instruction in higher education, is the presence of a large course team or 'virtual assembly line of instructional production' (Rhoades, 2007: 6), with a relatively small proportion of the participants (the 'content providers') on academic contracts. Course content, which was formerly determined by a department of discipline-focused academics, may morph into 'learning objects' (Poon, 2006: 97), small packages of stand-alone information to be marketed for institutional profit (Rhoades, 2007). Thus, the task significance of academic work is diminishing, as academics lose ownership and overall control of the process and product of instruction (Poon, 2006). Once 'learning objects' are placed online, institutions may make cost savings by entrusting face-to-face instruction to large cadres of cheaper, less-qualified academic labour (Poon, 2006), further eroding the academic skills profile of the higher education workforce.

In the area of research, academics' understandings of what constitutes significant discipline-relevant enquiry are being decentred by the existence of national competitive research evaluation exercises such as the British RAE/REF, and the Australian ERA.[1] Harley (2002) discovered that academics hoping to score well in these exercises were obliged to chase volume over quality of publications, publishing 'quick and dirty' articles lacking rigour, scholarship and weight. Increasingly, in response to national research audits, it is management rather than academe who decide research foci (Henkel, 2005) as part of institution-wide research strategies.

Today, academics find themselves working alongside a range of colleagues whose roles exceed their job descriptions (Whitchurch, 2008a). The cadres of online and academic developers who contribute to technology-enhanced instruction belong to the emerging breed of workers, whom Whitchurch (2008b) dubs 'blended' or 'third space' professionals: highly educated staff on non-academic contracts, who are likely to undertake extended project work crossing the traditional divide between the academic and administrative functions of the university. Rhoades (2007: 6) notes the tendency of non-academic units to become interest groups committed to expanding their size and influence. This suggests that the 'pure' academic voice is becoming diluted within many higher learning institutions and that increasingly, non-academic staff may be setting the tone for institutional mission statements. The progressive dilution of the academic voice within the academy leads to what Winter dubs 'academic identity schism', as managers and academics disagree in defining job values and roles (Winter, 2009: 122).

Academics today are being asked to develop a range of 'unrelated and non-complementary skills' as they add activities of community service and research consultancies to their working roles (Churchman, 2006). Many so-called 'blended professionals' working in the outreach space of university community participation are Whitchurch's (2008a) 'unbounded professionals'. Exposure to such colleagues may involve taking on new tasks and working with risk in the form of external community associations (Whitchurch & Gordon, 2010). The net result is that academics often find themselves working to somebody else's agenda: the professions, in the area of learning and teaching; with research questions and priorities increasingly dictated by community partnerships and external funding agencies (Smith, 2012; Rhoades, 2007). Smith describes some research-focused academics as 'flexians', engaged in the unsatisfying task of diluting policy messages for key audiences (Smith, 2012: 171). Rowland worries that the academic experience becomes less coherent, the wider the cross section of society the academic tries to service (Rowland, 2002).

Some commentators working in the field of academic identity assume that identities reflect the lived social context of individuals, as these are shaped by social processes within strong and stable communities (Henkel, 2005). Identity is socially constructed over time, and reflects the blending of imagined and real components (Billot, 2010) as part of the 'lived complexity of a person's project' (Clegg, 2008: 329). Under the knowledge society, communities are destabilising as the boundaries between the academic world and the wider community are becoming 'fuzzy, movable and permeable' (Henkel, 2007: 93), in ways that perhaps change our understanding of the nature of the academy.

This chapter investigates the key moral doctrines of the Hellenistic philosophers with a view to providing guidance to modern academics who may need to rethink their core academic values as they pursue careers in the contemporary 'enterprise university'.

WHY EXPLORE THE ANCIENT WORLD?

Like many academics today, Ancient Greek youth were posing the question, 'How can I be a success?' Ancient Greek philosophers were the lifestyle coaches or self-help gurus of their day. Philosophies like Epicureanism were 'therapeutic' in nature, offering practical guidance in the conduct of life. Young persons consulted charismatic philosophers searching for the formula for *arete*,[2] a form of human excellence or 'life virtuosity' (Merlan, 1972: 145). The answer invariably was couched in terms of those virtues or character traits, cultivation of which would lead to *eudaimonia*, human flourishing or success, a notion inadequately translated by the word 'happiness'.[3] For the Epicureans and later Roman Stoics, *eudaimonia* often comes to be identified with *ataraxia*, a form of 'unperturbedness' or 'psychic calm' (Stephens, 2007: 141).

Certain historical developments in the Hellenistic world created resonances with events today, making it appropriate to revisit this era to shed light upon the dilemmas facing modern academics. Two of these developments are described below.

Ancient Greece and the Origins of Higher Education

Adjusting to globalisation. Revisiting debates in the Hellenistic world illustrates that identity issues arising from wider economic and political connections are nothing new. The Hellenistic philosophers were providing intellectual consolation during a period of geopolitical uncertainty, a time when the Greek city-states ceded their autonomy to the empires of Alexander the Great (c.356 – 323 BCE) and subsequently Rome (Garnsey in Rowe & Schofield, 2000; Lillegard, 2003). As minds became fixated upon more-than-local political connections, the Hellenistic period saw the first glimmerings of the concept of 'cosmopolitanism'. Thus Ancient political insecurities bear certain resonances with geo-political changes occurring under increasing globalisation today.

Disciplinary demarcations. Many of the so-called 'Socratic' dialogues of Plato[4] depict confrontations between a character named Socrates and a number of public intellectuals operating from about 460 to 380 BCE, who travelled between the Greek cities lecturing and teaching for fees (Kerferd, 1997). These 'Sophists' were the first recognisably professional teachers (Zeller, 1980), visiting the gymnasia[5] and other sites where young people congregated, where they offered training in public speaking and politics (Waterfield, 2000). The rise of democracy in the city states called for the types of speaking and thinking skills the Sophists provided (Kerferd, 1997; Osborne in Taylor, 1997). In the adversarial legal system of Ancient Athens, individuals could not rely upon professional advocates to prosecute on their behalf or to defend them in court (Brickhouse & Smith, 2004). Training in the art of persuasion became crucial to personal success (Scenters-Zapico, 1993). Robinson (2007) suggests that the Sophists may have played a role in the spread of democracy throughout the Greek world. Plato and Xenophon painted an unflattering portrait of the Sophists as men of 'a spurious cleverness, and a love of cash' (Barnes, 1982: 449), setting the groundwork for the modern pejorative use of the term 'sophist'.[6]

Exploring Ancient philosophies suggests that disciplinary demarcation disputes, and arguments about the nature and composition of academe, are nothing new. Plato's dialogues record one individual's (Plato's) view of a battle between two emergent models of higher education in Greek society: one centred upon the discipline of philosophy, the other upon the discipline of rhetoric. However, this conflict has also been viewed as an internal demarcation dispute within the discipline of philosophy itself.[7] The confrontation between Plato's Socrates and the Sophists perhaps anticipates tensions in the academy today between those who offer a technical, skills-based approach to education, and those who accept Socrates' belief that education performs a serious moral purpose in transforming the personality of the learner (Johnson, 1998). Such tensions are likely to increase now that practice-based disciplines such as health and social work have been brought into the academy (Whitchurch & Gordon, 2010).

THE CONSOLATIONS OF PHILOSOPHY: HELLENISTIC ETHICS

Socrates and the Hellenist Schools

Plato's dialogues form part of a tradition of writings testifying to the historical figure of Socrates. Many modern scholars take the view that the Hellenistic philosophers read the dialogues of Plato to provide insight into the character, behaviours and espoused ethical views of the historical Socrates (469 – 399 BCE), and for this reason, they believe that a close reading of the Socratic dialogues of Plato and Xenophon can inform modern readings of the Hellenistic philosophers.[8] The Hellenistic schools broadly split between those (e.g., Cynics, Cyrenaics)[9] who emulated the personal behaviour of Socrates in their own ethical practice; and those schools such as Stoicism, which owed a debt to Socratic moral doctrines.

Cynicism[10]

Cynicism was a 'missionary philosophy' (Moles, in Rowe & Schofield, 2000: 422), which achieved popularity for hundreds of years.[11] Key early figures included Antisthenes (c.445 – 365 BCE), who became a disciple of Socrates late in life, and Diogenes of Sinope (c.412-403 – 324-321 BCE) who was influenced by the writings of Antisthenes.[12] The story of the first wave of Cynicism, in the third and fourth centuries BCE, derives from much later Roman sources (Branham & Goulet-Caze, 1996). In these written sources, Diogenes became a mythical figure, known through sayings (*chreiai*), pointed anecdotes and aphorisms designed to illustrate key Cynic doctrines (Branham & Goulet-Caze, 1996), but which also serve to illustrate the wit of the man.

Cynicism amounted to an eccentric lifestyle choice underpinned by a philosophical rationale (Irvine, 2008; Branham & Goulet-Caze, 1996). The Cynic lifestyle was intended to mimic the Socrates depicted in Xenophon's *Memorabilia,* a figure celebrated for his frugal habits, endurance of hardship, and indifference to material prosperity (Rich, 1956). The Cynics adopted a form of 'aggressive primitivism' (Trapp, 2007: 191), rejecting the trappings of civilised urban living in favour of a 'natural,' animal-like existence. They enacted their philosophy as performance art, living rough on the streets in the 'uniform' of Diogenes: a crude cloak that could be doubled for warmth, a knapsack or food wallet, and a staff. Lacking all refinements of modern appearance, bearded, shoeless, homeless, the Cynics lived off the land or on whatever they could beg, borrow or steal – generally legumes or lentils – eschewing cooked meat, favouring water over wine (Desmond, 2006). Legend has it that Diogenes lived in a *pithos* or large storage jar. Diogenes was an exhibitionist, performing all bodily functions in public (including masturbation). Thus, he seemed actively to court the apocryphal reputation he eventually achieved (Long, 1996b).

The rationale underlying this shamelessness was captured in Diogenes' motto of 'defacing the currency'. Taken literally, the phrase described the reason for his exile from his native Sinope: the offence of defacing coins (*nomisma*) to put them out of circulation. 'Defacing the currency' also metaphorically described Diogenes' mission to challenge and discredit the *nomos,* the norms and customs of contemporary society (Desmond, 2006; Branham & Goulet-Caze, 1996) including the institutions of marriage and private property. The Cynics used the literary form of the diatribe as a pedagogical tool, hectoring individuals, publicly interrogating their behaviour to reveal hypocrisy and inconsistency (Branham & Goulet-Caze, 1996; Long, 1996a).

Most (1989) has argued that one cherished cultural ideal of the Ancient Greeks was *autarkeia*, a term which describes the autonomy and integrity of the self in the economic, political and even erotic realms. One modern translation of this term would be 'self-sufficingness' (MacCunn, 1904: 192). Greeks would protect their economic 'autarky' by relying upon no one else for their subsistence, and their political 'autarchy' by maintaining freedom from external compulsion. Any sexual threats to the integrity of the self were met by exercising minimal contact with the opposite sex (Most, 1989). The novelty of Diogenes lies in the enthusiasm with which he pursued the ideal of autonomy by paring down his needs to the absolute minimum, as he strove to imitate the self-sufficiency of a divine being (Rich, 1956). The high value Diogenes placed upon *autarkeia* appears in those *chreiai*, where Diogenes objects to praising the generosity of almsgivers, on the grounds that doing so diminishes the dignity and autonomy of the recipient.[13]

Stoicism

The founder of the Stoic school, Zeno of Citium (c.333 – 261 BCE) conducted lessons at the *Stoa Poikile* (Painted Colonnade) at the north-west corner of the Agora in Athens. Prominent Stoics included Chrysippus of Soli (c.282 BCE – 206 BCE), and in the Roman era Epictetus (born c.50 – 60 CE), and the emperor Marcus Aurelius (121 – 180 CE). The doctrines of Stoicism are known almost exclusively through a series of later secondary sources including Diogenes Laertius (second century CE) and the 'doxographers', literary hacks who reported the views but seldom the arguments of the Stoics, often jumbling together the opinions of different generations of Stoics as they described Stoic doctrines with the sole purpose of refuting them. Some recent commentators have been drawn to the discourses of the Roman Stoic Epictetus, which convey something of his pedagogic impact upon students (Long, 2002; Stephens, 2007; Irvine, 2008).

For the Stoics, human flourishing, or mental health, depended entirely and exclusively upon achieving excellence of mind and character (Long, 2002). Thus virtue, and having the right attitude of mind in action, was the only true good. By comparison with virtue, everything else was 'not good', or morally indifferent.

Zeno studied with the Cynic Crates. So it is not surprising that Stoics shared the Cynic belief that to live virtuously was to live 'in accordance with nature' (Irvine, 2008: 36; Stephens, 2007). In Stoic thought, human nature encompasses the physical needs of embodied beings, their intellectual nature, plus their nature as social creatures with social ties and obligations.[14] Stoics readily acknowledged that 'nature' in the sense of a person's bodily constitution, would impel individuals to prefer certain 'indifferents' over others: health and wealth over sickness and poverty. In introducing a second species of value ('preferred indifferents') alongside the only true value (virtue), Zeno seems to be reconciling two mutually contradictory theses attributed to Socrates in Plato's dialogue, the *Euthydemus*.[15]

Chryssipus developed the doctrine of *oikeōisis*[16] a term carrying connotations of 'affinity', 'attraction', and 'appropriation' or 'making something one's own', to show how an organism's original instinct for self-preservation underpins this two-tier value system. *Oikeōisis* is used to describe the moral evolution of a human being, from a pre-rational stage where the infant is driven by instinct to satisfy their bodily needs, through to the age of rational and moral maturity, when the individual realises the importance of social ties, and the duties and obligations these bring. In this way, the notion of *oikeōisis* helps to explain the mixture of self-regarding and socialising instincts in human beings (Long, 2002). According to Epictetus, the mature human being would discover their moral duties by rationally considering their different social roles as children, siblings, parents, employees, and so on (Long, 2002; Stephens, 2007).

The Stoics celebrated the figure of the Sage, a totally enlightened being for whom virtue was the only true good. Being a sage was an all-or-nothing affair, the transition to this state being both instantaneous and decisive (Brouwer, 2007). Relatively few individuals qualified for this status (Stephens, 2007; Irvine, 2008; Long, 2002). When pressed, Stoics like Epictetus would cite Socrates, Diogenes and Zeno as examples of sages (Stephens, 2007). The majority of human beings struggling to achieve human excellence would be classed as 'moral proficients,' persons on their way to becoming sages. The proficient or sage would take a holistic view of the universe and its workings, realising that whatever happened to the individual served the greater good of the whole (Stephens, 2007).

Stoics believed that emotions (*pathē*) were 'disturbances' in the soul, brought about by forming false opinions about reality (Holowchak, 2008; Irvine, 2008). The *apatheia* or relative emotional detachment of the Stoic sage did not mean that the sage felt no emotion. The sage would feel only *eupatheiai*, feelings based upon a rational assessment of the objects of emotions. These 'good feelings' fell into three distinct categories: rational elation, which was a rational counterpart of the non-rational feeling of pleasure; caution or rational avoidance, as the reasonable counterpart of fear; and wishing as the rational counterpart of irrational appetite or desire (Holowchak, 2008; Long, 2002). However, as the sage understands that no present event constitutes a threat to their virtue, they will not feel any rational counterpart to the wholly irrational feeling of distress (Holowchak, 2008).

Epicureanism

The moral theorising of Epicurus (341 – 270 BCE) begins with the recognition that human beings are embodied creatures, and that the happy life is impossible if humans neglect the claims of the body. Consequently, Epicurus identified pleasure as the only good, and securing pleasure as the goal of life.

Today the term 'Epicurean' denotes a person who pursues unusual and refined tastes. This use of the term distorts the message of Epicurus' philosophy. In identifying the good with pleasure, Epicurus was recommending neither a life in search of sybaritic delights, nor one of continual pleasant stimulation. According to Epicurus, humans are motivated less by the desire to experience positive pleasures than the desire to be free from pain. For Epicurus, the real goal of life was to achieve *ataraxia* or peace of mind. Human beings could find peace of mind and contentment by realising, firstly, the true nature and significance of pleasure; and secondly, how simple it is to avoid pain whilst satisfying basic human needs.

Under Epicurus' 'serene hedonism' (Bergsma, Poot, & Liefbroer, 2008: 397), pleasure marks the limit of pain.[17] Epicurus identified the state of lacking pain in the body as an intrinsically pleasant state worth having. However, once pain has dispersed, adding new pleasures does not enhance our happiness (Bergsma et al., 2008). The rational person will not act to avoid every pain. Sometimes, humans will trade off a temporary pain in the hope of greater pleasure to follow.

Epicurus identified three classes of desires: those that were class 1, natural and necessary (e.g., desire for food and drink); class 2, natural but unnecessary, to the extent that failing to satisfy these would not cause pain (e.g., desire for an exotic range of foods); and class 3, desires neither natural nor necessary (e.g., the desire for fame or glory) (Bergsma et al., 2008). Epicurus believed that a wise person would secure their *autarkeia* by pursuing class 1 pleasures, avoiding class 3 and limiting exposure to class 2 pleasures by exercising self-restraint. Epicurus warned against the pursuit of luxury for the same reason as the Cynics and Stoics ahead of him: in the interests of pursuing *autarkeia* (Brenk, 2002–2003).

HELLENISTIC WISDOM AND THE MODERN ACADEMY

Comparison of the Hellenistic Schools

The Hellenistic philosophical schools sought to limit the personal vulnerabilities of individuals grappling with new political complexities. In particular, all three schools offered formulae for increasing the individual's self-sufficient autonomy (*autarkeia*). For the Cynics and Epicureans, this would be achieved by limiting one's bodily needs and by adapting desires to resources (Irwin, 2007): desiring relatively little, and consuming even less. Through the rigid exercise of moderation, the Cynics ensured they were not beholden to any other human being, and thus remained politically independent and free. Like the Epicureans, the Stoics cautioned against forming desires, the fulfilment of which lay outside the individual's control. However, many Stoics were able to reconcile Stoicism with both political and material success, as attested by a number of high-profile Roman public figures, including Seneca the younger and the emperor Marcus Aurelius (Irvine, 2008). The Stoic might pursue the good things of life, including family, fame and fortune, whilst avoiding excessive emotional investment in the outcome, knowing that such morally indifferent things are fragile and can be taken away.

Despite commonalities of thought, there remain notable doctrinal differences across the three schools. The formulae for flourishing and success offered by the Cynics and the Stoics seem both counter-intuitive and paradoxical. In the single-minded pursuit of the individual's integrity or *autarkeia*, Cynicism affirmed 'the worthlessness of everything that life had to offer' (MacCunn, 1904: 192). And Stoicism takes this further, by insisting that the Sage can be *eudaimon* (happy, flourishing, blessed) even under torture. In anchoring *eudaimonia* to the physical body and its states of pleasure and pain, Epicureanism apparently offers a more realistic picture of the foundations of human happiness.

Unfortunately, because Epicureanism has survived as little more than lists of key doctrines, the would-be modern Epicurean is given little guidance in how to achieve the necessary revaluation of priorities and values. In contrast, Cynicism and Stoicism are able to offer practical recipes for achieving *autarkeia*, through a process of *askēsis* or systematic training in self-discipline (Stephens, 2007). For the Cynics, *askēsis* amounted to a form of physical training, exposing themselves to heat and cold and other hardships in an on-going process of mental and moral improvement (Branham & Goulet-Cazé, 1996; Long, 1996a).

The *askēsis* recommended by Stoics such as Epictetus involved mental training (Stephens, 2007). Irvine (2008) suggests some of the forms that Stoic mental training might take, including *negative visualisation*: the imaginative exercise of dispossessing oneself of all one holds dear, contemplating the death of friends and loved ones with a view to showing we can survive such catastrophes (Irvine, 2008; Brenk, 2002–2003). When confronted with adverse events, Stoics like Epictetus might also engage in *projective visualisation*: imagining that unfortunate events are actually happening to someone other than ourselves, and adjusting our emotional reactions to those of a spectator rather than a main participant in events (Irvine, 2008). If nothing else, a Stoic can learn how to 'save face' when reacting to career setbacks in front of their supervisors.

Irvine (2008) contends that anyone, even a homeless person, would benefit from engaging in negative visualisation and for this reason, Stoicism is not a philosophy confined to the affluent or the socially blessed. We can grant Irvine's point that Stoicism is a philosophy with things to say even to the downtrodden, yet still insist that, for those who have experienced real oppression or hardship, Stoicism is unlikely to gain traction.[18] It is one matter to persuade someone who has previously enjoyed some worldly prosperity or success but is now down on their luck (e.g., Diogenes in exile or enslaved) that they can get by without most material advantages. It is a far greater leap for someone perennially engaged in a struggle to survive to imagine how things could be worse. Nor would this person take psychic comfort in being told that their personal suffering benefitted the universe as a whole. However, since few academics occupy the bottom rungs of society, there is no obvious impediment to academics internalising some of the lessons of Stoic philosophy.

A Philosophy for Modern Academics?

Both Cynicism and Epicureanism stress the value of autonomy, but in a way that is unlikely to engage young academics today. Cynicism requires the individual to surrender too many material comforts in the pursuit of self-sufficiency. Worse, Cynicism apparently commits the individual to a form of perpetual rebellion against the norms and conventions of society. Only those academics already enjoying some career success would consider setting their own terms in opting into or out of key aspects of the modern academic role. As previously suggested, what survives of Epicurean philosophy is lacking in actionable practical recommendations. In stressing the pre-eminence of rationality over other human traits, Stoicism perhaps is the Hellenistic philosophy most likely to appeal to intellectuals.

It would be rash to suggest that a majority of academics enjoy sage-like wisdom, simply by virtue of their extensive education. However, the slow intellectual training involved in many academic disciplines foregrounds and imitates the pursuit of wisdom by the Stoic proficient. Like the study to become a Stoic sage, training to teach in the academy encourages the individual to reassess and reprioritise existing values and what is 'appropriate' to oneself as an academic as opposed to a common citizen. This may involve the ability to sacrifice some leisure activities in pursuit of career-enhancing publication and research. The education and training of the academic also develops many of the mental tools appropriate to the Stoic proficient, including powers of critical thinking and reflexivity and with these, the moral imagination to play out scenarios and their likely consequences, before taking action. In her research into academic identities, Clegg (2008) discovered that academics were able to use reflexivity to defy managerial working environments and maintain 'highly distinctive, strongly framed academic projects of the self' (Clegg, 2008: 340). The mental exercises proposed by the Stoics perhaps provide some of the positive content for academics' moral imagination and acts of reflexivity.

Optimists use the example of Whitchurch's new blended university roles to help predict the future composition of academic tasks and careers (Whitchurch & Gordon, 2010; Coates & Goedegebuure, 2010, 2012). The increasing complexity of academic work and roles leads Coates and Goedegebuure (2010, 2012) to predict the future disaggregation or 'unbundling' of academic work (Coates & Goedegebuure, 2010: 21), with some academics becoming teaching-only or research-only specialists. Rather than viewing academic work as a classic 40–40–20 ratio of research, teaching and administration, or increasingly a blend of research, teaching and community engagement, the academic might dip between different functions at different points in the career life cycle, in horizontal rather than vertical career movements (Coates & Goedegebuure, 2010, 2012). It is also predicted that academics will be exposed to leadership and managerial roles at an earlier point in their careers (Whitchurch & Gordon, 2010). Clearly, if they are to negotiate contemporary academia, intellectuals must decide how they engage and invest, both intellectually and emotionally, in new task distributions.

The *eupatheiai* of the Stoics provide clues to the forms of intelligent emotional investment that academics should make in the rapidly evolving academy. As explained above, the Stoic sage avoids feelings that are irrationally strong or ill-founded in fact. For the Stoic, emotional investments should be proportioned to real risks and opportunities. Above all else, the individual should not invest strong feeling in matters which lie outside their individual control. The Stoic replaces 'warm' emotions with 'cool' rational emotions of a kind appropriate to workplace relationships in the modern academy, which might require task commitment minus personally damaging emotional investments. Adopting this cool regard will help the modern academic to select the appropriate balance between teaching/administration/research/community-based engagement, without thereby compromising their personal integrity.

Autonomy versus Collegiality: The Value of 'Cool Regard'

The historical origin of the university in the medieval 'community of scholars' (Harris, 2005: 424) has established two broad clusters of academic values forming part of the traditional academic imaginary. The 'autonomy' cluster encompasses a number of cherished freedoms, including: the ability to select tasks and research projects; time and space for thinking and research; the opportunity to engage in socially useful critique; and self-management within disciplinary departments. The 'collegiality' cluster describes professional relationships based upon trust between equals, both within strong discipline-focused units but also occurring on a wider basis within institutions. Collegiality remains an important value for many academics. Bozeman and Gaughan (2011: 175) discovered that of all the variables they tested, 'believing that one's departmental colleagues appreciate one's research contributions' was the most important predictor of academics' job satisfaction. As noted in the first section of this chapter, academics are being asked to form new relationships within and beyond the academy, in ways that change the meaning of collegiality.[19]

The values of autonomy and collegiality potentially stand in conflict with one another. The more one asserts one's autonomy, the less collegial and co-operative one's behaviour becomes. The socially disruptive behaviour of the Cynics illustrates the dangers of pursuing too much personal autonomy. Clearly, if they are to survive in today's academe, academics need to strike the right balance between the twin demands of loyalty to one's discipline, profession, institution, and wider community on the one hand; and care for the well-being of the self on the other. Again, Stoicism demonstrates how it is possible to prioritise the needs of the self, whilst still meeting a range of broader obligations.

The Stoic doctrine of appropriation (*oikeōisis*) provides an account of the relative ordering of the two values of duty to self and duty to others. Under the doctrine of *oikeōisis*, 'cool' rationally-based other-regard is preceded, developmentally, by 'warm', instinctive, pre-rational regard for the immediate needs of the self. At the same time, 'cool' rational attention to the mental health of the self takes logical precedence over ethically-based relationships with others. Appeal to *oikeōisis* helps to dispel one misrepresentation of the Stoic sage, as fixated upon protecting their own moral virtue, even at the expense of familial and social connections. The Roman Stoic Epictetus did not believe that the Sage protects their virtue at the expense of social obligations. Rather, Epictetus believed that training in virtue, or having the right attitude of mind, was a pre-requisite for good citizenship. Under the doctrine of *oikeōisis*, we need to care for our individual selves, to get our internal constitution or pattern of desiring right, in order to equip ourselves to behave well in our social roles (Long, 2002). This is what it means to say that self-regard logically precedes an ethical attention to the interests of others. However stressed they may feel in the modern workplace, academics should feel empowered to say 'no' to tasks which compromise their personal integrity, on the understanding that maintaining their integrity is the only way they can function well in their roles.

It would be naïve to suppose that appeal to Stoic doctrines and values solves all problems confronted by the modern academic. Academics who find themselves working with Whitchurch's (2008b, 2008a) 'unbounded' professionals in risk-carrying ventures, cannot share Epictetus' confidence that social relationships determine one's duties. The specific duties appropriate to these new social roles will only emerge slowly, over time. Given the complexity of the modern university, some conflicts in duties – between duties to the profession and discipline on the one hand, and to professional and community stakeholders on the other – seems inevitable, at least in the short term.

CONCLUSION

What it means to be an academic remains in a state of flux under the globalised, enterprise university. Writing in 2005, Mary Henkel expressed guarded confidence that despite recent policy changes, the core academic values of the primacy of the discipline and academic autonomy had retained much of their normative power (Henkel, 2005). In the decade since, the ongoing 'de-centring' of the academic from the academy within the corporatised university perhaps makes this assessment look optimistic.

This chapter has delved into Hellenistic moral theories in search of strategies to assist academics who are struggling to adjust to new challenges and opportunities. Shopping for ideas between three Hellenistic schools of philosophy yields the notions of autonomy (Cynicism), mental tranquillity (Epicureanism) and cool self- and other-regard as important considerations in negotiating the prevailing climate of academe. In particular, the Stoic notion of *oikeōisis* points the way to an appropriate relative ranking of cool self-regard versus other-regard, creating a fitting balance between the traditional core academic values of autonomy and collegiality, which remain necessary to personal career success.

NOTES

1. Denoting 'Excellence in Research in Australia'.
2. The term aretē is much wider in scope than the modern word 'virtue' (denoting moral excellence). Following Aristotle, many ethicists assumed that each thing, including a human being, served a particular purpose (telos) or function and possessed its own aretē (virtue/excellence). Aristotle includes in the list of virtues such things as wittiness and the capacity for philosophising. Aretē also denotes features that are in no way human. It would be possible to have the aretē of a knife, a dog, etc. Nehemas (1999, pp. 4–5) proposes that aretē described whatever accounted for an object's 'justified notability'.
3. 'Eu daimon' literally means 'having a good demon/god smiling upon one', and thus carries connotations of being 'blessed' or fortunate. McMahon (2004, p. 7) notes how the modern words for happiness in all Indo-European languages "are all cognate with luck". The term may also carry connotations of good mental health, or maintaining a persisting, sound frame of mind. See Stephens (2007, p. 141).
4. Hippias Major, Hippias Minor, Protagoras, Meno, Gorgias, and The Republic.
5. The uses of gymnasia for both physical and moral training are explored in Hawhee (2002) and Wycherley (1962).
6. For a short but comprehensive list of Plato's objections to the Sophists, see Waterfield (2000, p. xxix ftnote).
7. Sidgwick (1873, 1872) has argued that the term 'sophist' was not fixed in the fifth and fourth centuries BCE and was used indifferently to denote all philosophers as well as a special branch of philosophy. Plato himself used the term in three different ways across his dialogues (Sidgwick, 1873, p. 67). Cassim (2000, p. 106) suggests that the term 'sophist' has functioned as the 'other' of philosophy. Cassim implies that, had these figures never existed, philosophers like Plato would have been obliged to invent them, to help distinguish their intellectual ware from competing options.
8. For conspicuous examples of this style of reading, see Irwin (2007, pp. 57–68) and Long (1996b, pp. 1–34).
9. Lack of space makes it impossible to say anything about this school here.
10. The name 'Cynicism' is related to the Greek word for 'dog'. The name of this school derives, either from their tendency to meet by the Cynosarges (White Hound) gymnasium, or for the Cynic tendency to live the 'natural' life of a dog. See Branham and Goulet-Cazé (1996, p. 4).
11. Branham and Goulet-Cazé (1996, p. 16) claim they have identified over 80 Ancient Cynics.
12. Contemporary scholars query the written tradition which says that Diogenes was a pupil of Antisthenes. For evidence on either side of the debate, see Branham and Goulet-Cazé (1996, pp. 7, 414–415); and Long (1996a, p. 32).
13. The following anecdote (Diogenes Laertius, VI, 2, 62) is typical: When some people commended a person who had given him a gratuity, he broke in with "You have no praise for me who was worthy to receive it."
14. For a description of the different meanings of 'nature' in Stoic thought, see Stephens (2007, pp. 123–124.
15. In the Euthydemus, Socrates apparently states that virtue is the only good; and that wisdom added to certain good things makes these better. For more on this, see Irwin (2007, pp. 57–68) and Long (1996b, pp. 1–34).
16. This term is unusually difficult to translate. For a discussion of the difficulties and some of proposed translations, see Long (2002, pp. 182, 197–198) and Stephens (2007, pp. 124–125). A good classic article describing the doctrine is Pembroke (1996).
17. "For we are in need to pleasure only when we are in pain because of the absence of pleasure, and when we are not in pain, then we no longer need pleasure" ('Letter to Menoeceus', §29, in Inwood & Gerson, Eds., p. 31).
18. In an exception that perhaps proves the rule, it is worth noting that Epictetus himself was a former (educated) slave. It could be argued that Epictetus' espousal of Stoicism came after and not before his personal fortunes improved.

[19] Future higher education research might test the changing meaning of academic collegiality, by surveying academic staff within a number of institutions across different countries, with a view to discovering the extent to which academics are changing their focus from internal to external partnerships and collegial associations.

REFERENCES

Barnes, J. (1982). *The presocratic philosophers* (2nd ed.). London, England & New York, NY: Routledge.
Bergsma, A., Poot, G., & Liefbroer, A. C. (2008). Happiness in the garden of Epicurus. *Journal of Happiness Studies, 9*(3), 397–423.
Billot, J. (2010). The imagined and the real: Identifying the tensions for academic identity. *Higher Education Research and Development, 29*(6), 709–721.
Bozeman, B., & Gaughan, M. (2011). Job satisfaction among university faculty: Individual, work, and institutional determinants. *Journal of Higher Education, 82*(2), 154–186.
Branham, R. B., & Goulet-Cazé, M.-O. (Eds.). (1996). *The cynics: The cynic movement in antiquity and its legacy.* Berkeley, CA & London, England: University of California Press.
Brenk, F. G. (2002–2003). Sheer doggedness or love of neighbour? Motives for self-sufficiency in the cynics and others. *Illinois Classical Studies, 27/28*, 77–96.
Brickhouse, T. C., & Smith, N. D. (2004). *Routledge philosophy guidebook to Plato and the trial of Socrates.* New York, NY & London, England: Routledge.
Brouwer, R. (2007). The early stoic doctrine of the change to wisdom. *Oxford Studies in Ancient Philosophy, 33*, 295–315.
Bryson, C. (2004). What about the workers: The expansion of higher education and the transformation of academic work. *Industrial Relations Journal, 35*(1), 38–57.
Cassim, B., & Wolfe, C. T. (Trans.). (2000). Who's afraid of the sophists? Against ethical correctness. *Hypatia, 15*(4), 102–120.
Churchman, D. (2006). Institutional commitments, individual compromises: Identity-related responses to compromise in an Australian university. *Journal of Higher Education Policy and Management, 28*(1), 3–15.
Clegg, S. (2008). Academic identities under threat? *British Educational Research Journal, 34*(3), 329–345.
Coates, H., & Goedegebuure, L. (2010). *The real academic revolution: Research briefing report.* Australia: H. Martin Institute. Retrieved from http://www.lhmartininstitute.edu.au/userfiles/files/research/the_real_academic_revolution.pdf (Accessed February 14, 2014).
Coates, H., & Goedegebuure, L. (2012). Recasting the academic workforce: Why the attractiveness of the academic profession needs to be increase and eight possible strategies for how to go about this from an Australian perspective. *Higher Education, 64*(6), 875–889.
Desmond, W. (2006). *Cynics.* Stocksfield, England: Acumen.
Harley, S. (2002). The impact of research selectivity on academic work and identity in UK universities. *Studies in Higher Education, 27*(2), 187–205.
Harris, S. (2005). Rethinking academic identities in neo-liberal times. *Teaching in Higher Education, 10*(4), 421–433.
Hawhee, D. (2002). Bodily pedagogies: Rhetoric, athletics, and the sophists' three Rs. *College English, 65*(2), 142–162.
Henkel, M. (2005). Academic identity and autonomy in a changing policy environment. *Higher Education, 49*(1), 155–176.
Henkel, M. (2007). Can academic autonomy survive in the knowledge society? A perspective from Britain. *Higher Education Research and Development, 26*(1), 87–99.
Holowchak, M. A. (2008). *Stoics: A guide for the perplexed.* London, England: Continuum International Publishing.
Inwood, B. (2005). *Reading seneca: Stoic philosophy at Rome.* Oxford, England: Clarendon Press.
Inwood, B., & Gerson, L. P. (Eds.). (1988). *Hellenistic philosophy: Introductory readings* (2nd ed.). Indianapolis, IN & Cambridge, England: Hackett Publishing Company.

Irvine, W. B. (2008). *Guide to the good life: The ancient art of Stoic joy*. Oxford, New York: Oxford University Press.

Irwin, T. (2007). *The development of ethics: A historical and critical study: From Socrates to the reformation* (Vol. 1). New York, NY: Oxford University Press.

Johnson, S. (1998). Skills, Socrates and the sophists: Learning from history. *British Journal of Educational Studies, 46*(2), 201–213.

Kerferd, G. B. (1997). The sophists. In C. C. W. Taylor (Ed.), *Routledge history of philosophy: From the beginning to Plato* (Vol. 1, pp. 244–270). London, England & New York, NY: Routledge.

Lillegard, N. (2003), *On Epicurus*. London, England: Wadsworth/Thompson.

Long, A. A. (1996a). The Socratic tradition: Diogenes, crates, and hellenistic ethics. In R. B. Branham & M.-O. Goulet-Cazé (Eds.), *The cynics: The cynic movement in antiquity and its legacy*. Berkeley, CA, & London, England: University of California Press.

Long, A. A. (1996b). *Stoic studies*. Berkeley, CA & London, England: University of California Press.

Long, A. A. (2002). *Epictetus: A stoic and Socratic guide to life*. Oxford, England: Clarendon Press.

MacCunn, J. (1904). The cynics. *International Journal of Ethics, 14*(2), 185–200.

McMahon, D. A. (2004). From the happiness of virtue to the virtue of happiness: 400 BC – AD 1780. *Daedalus, 133*(2), 5–17.

Merlan, P. (1972). Minor Socratics. *Journal of the History of Philosophy, 10*(2), 143–152.

Morley, L. (2012). Researching absences and silences in higher education: Data for democratisation. *Higher Education Research and Development, 31*(3), 353–368.

Most, G. W. (1989). The stranger's stratagem: Self-disclosure and self-sufficiency in Greek culture. *Journal of Hellenic Studies, 109*, 114–133.

Nehemas, A. (1999). *Virtues of authenticity: Essays on Plato and Socrates*. Princeton, NJ: Princeton University Press.

Pembroke, E. G. (1996). Oikeiōsis. In A. A. Long (Ed.), *Problems in stoicism* (2nd ed., pp. 114–149). London, England & Atlantic Highlands, NJ: The Athlone Press.

Poon, T. S. (2006). The commodification of higher education: Implications for academic work and employment. *International Journal of Employment Studies, 14*(1), 81–104.

Rhoades, G. (2007). Technology-enhanced courses and a Mode III organisation of instructional work. *Tertiary Education and Management, 13*(1), 1–17.

Rich, A. N. M. (1956). The cynic conception of Autarkeia. *Mnemosyne* (Fourth Series), *9*(1), 23–29.

Robinson, E. W. (2007). The sophists and democracy beyond Athens. *Rhetorica: A Journal of the History of Rhetoric, 25*(1), 109–122.

Rowe, C., & Schofield, M. (Eds.). (2000). *The Cambridge history of Greek and Roman political thought*. Cambridge, England: Cambridge University Press.

Rowland, S. (2002). *The enquiring university*. Maidenhead, England & New York, NY: Open University Press.

Scenters-Zapico, J. (1993). The case for the sophists. *Rhetoric Review, 11*(2), 352–367.

Sharrock, G. (2004). Rethinking the Australian university: A critique of Off course. *Journal of Higher Education Policy and Management, 26*(2), 265–278.

Sidgwick, H. (1872). The sophists. *Journal of Philology, 4*(7), 299–307.

Sidgwick, H. (1873). The sophists – II. *Journal of Philology, 5*(10), 66–80.

Smith, K. (2012). Fools, facilitators and flexians: Academic identities in marketised environments. *Higher Education Quarterly, 66*(2), 155–173.

Stephens, W. O. (2007). *Stoic ethics: Epictetus and happiness as freedom*. London, England & New York, NY: Continuum International Publishing.

Taylor, C. C. W. (Ed.). (1997). *Routledge history of philosophy: From the beginning to Plato* (Vol. 1). London, England & New York, NY: Routledge.

Trapp, M. (2007). Cynics. *Bulletin of the Institute of Classical Studies, 50*(S94P1), 189–203.

Tsoukas, H. (1997). The tyranny of light: The temptations and the paradoxes of the information society. *Futures, 29*(9), 827–843.

Waterfield, R. (Trans.). (2000). *The first philosophers: The presocratics and sophists*. Oxford, England: Oxford University Press.

Whitchurch, C. (2008a). Beyond administration and management: Reconstructing the identities of professional staff in UK higher education. *Journal of Higher Education Policy and Management, 30*(4), 375–386.

Whitchurch, C. (2008b). Shifting identities and blurring boundaries: The emergence of third space professionals in UK higher education. *Journal of Higher Education Quarterly, 62*(4), 377–396.

Whitchurch, C., & Gordon, G. (2010). Diversifying academic and professional identities in higher education: Some management challenges. *Tertiary Education and Management, 16*(2), 129–144.

Winter, R. (2009). Academic manager or managed academic? Academic identity schisms in higher education. *Journal of Higher Education Policy and Management, 31*(2), 121–131.

Wycherley, R. E. (1962). Peripatos: The Athenian philosophical scene – II. *Greece & Rome, 9*(1), 2–21.

Zeller, E. (1980). *Outlines of the history of Greek philosophy* (13th ed.). New York, NY: Dover Publications.

Susan R. Robinson
School of Management
University of South Australia, Australia

PAUL SUTTON

3. A LABOUR OF LOVE?

Curiosity, Alienation and the Constitution of Academic Character

One loves that for which one labours, and one labours for that which one loves. (Fromm, 2003: 73)

PROLOGUE: SITUATING MY ACADEMIC IDENTITIES RESEARCH

This chapter extends research undertaken for the 2012 (Auckland, New Zealand),[1] & 2014 (Durham, UK) Academic Identities conferences. Researching for the Auckland conference lead to my 'discovery' of the work of the Marxist thinker and psychoanalyst Eric Fromm. This discovery was precipitated by a footnote in Freire (1985) referring to Fromm's (1964) explanation of the terms biophily and necrophily. Curiosity piqued, I began reading Fromm's work. A one-time leading light of the Frankfurt School, a public intellectual *avant la lettre*, Fromm was the author of populist works that sold millions world-wide. Today, in the UK, Fromm is at best relegated to academic obscurity, and at worst forgotten (McLaughlin, 1998).[2] Perhaps this is because his brand of accessible critical theory is dismissed as 'Frankfurt Lite' (Brookfield, 2002: 97) and, therefore, unworthy of serious academic consideration. For me, however, Fromm's synthesis of the humanism of the early Marx, and post-Freudian psychoanalysis, provides a fruitful explanation of the ways in which character (identity) is the product of social structure, culture, and human agency. This I explored in my Durham conference presentation. Participation in this conference lead to another important discovery: contemporary Marxist analyses of labour, (for example Holloway, 2010). Engagement in both conferences prompted this chapter – a reflexive attempt to understand the academic identities of the students I teach, through the language and conceptual tools of Marxist humanism. In doing so, it has significantly re-shaped my own academic identity as a university sociology teacher.

INTRODUCTION: A QUESTION OF FROMM

The question that engendered this chapter is: 'In a university system wherein knowledge is so easily and extensively acquired, why do so many students appear to lack curiosity?' I am baffled and troubled by this apparent lack as, for me, curiosity is the *sine qua non* of academic life. No, more, of being human. It signifies an intense interest in the world, an enlivening of perception, without which we become less than fully human. My ruminations on this question were shaped by the following passage from a much loved novel. The central character, a veteran school history teacher, laments:

> Nothing is more repressive than the repression of curiosity. Curiosity begets love. It weds us to the world. It is part of our perverse, madcap love for this impossible planet we inhabit. People die when curiosity goes. People have to find out, people have to know. (Swift, 2010: 207)

This led me to think that my students' ostensible lack of curiosity was not a simple case of lack of interest in knowledge. Rather, it was a more deep-seated problem of repression: a repression that separates students from the academic world; a repression of the love that characterizes human connectedness. As Swift (2010) states, something in people dies when the drive to know the world ceases, when curiosity is repressed. The repression of curiosity, then, is both an ontological and epistemological problem. Losing the will to know kills something of our human being. But what causes this repression?

My answer to this question lay in the theory of alienation contained in the work of the early Marx, and popularized by the now largely overlooked Marxist-psychoanalyst Eric Fromm. He argues that the mechanism through which the repression of curiosity takes place is fear. According to Fromm (1962: 126), 'the most powerful motive for repression' is 'the fear of isolation and ostracism': fear of aloneness, fear of separateness. Or in other words, a fear of being curious, where curious is defined as 'exciting attention by being strange or odd' (Hoad, 1990: 109). It is as if by being curious about the world, about knowledge, students fear they will become curious people, separated from their peers and their world. I think Fromm deployed what may be called a 'social-relational ontology of emotion' (Lyon, 1998: 48). The origin of the emotion of fear lies in social being, not within the individual. In such an ontology, emotions such as fear have a 'foundational role in social relations' and social relations are 'foundational in the genesis of emotion' (Lyon, 1998, pp. 53–54).

In my view, the fear that causes the repression of curiosity is a product of wider socio-economic and cultural shifts that have reshaped the social relations of learning. Learning has become increasingly characterized by 'automaton conformity' (Fromm, 1960, 1963). The world has become increasingly globalized, economically, politically and culturally. Life is increasingly characterized by complexity, uncertainty and rapid change. Students today, just as they did in the past, find a refuge from uncertainty and complexity in conformity. As Brookfield (2002) observes, the automaton conformist credo dictates one must not be different or peculiar in any way: one must adjust to prevailing realities rather than question them. Curiosity is antithetical to successful adjustment to the prevailing reality of global neo-liberal capitalism, and a corporatized higher education increasingly focused on preparing students for employment.

But why is this fear of being curious so strong? Fromm (2003) argues that its power is rooted in the peculiarity of the human condition. Humans are a part of, and set apart from, nature. Our reason and self-awareness existentially separate us from the world and burden us with the awareness of that separation. Reason has the capacity to transcend instinct but generates aloneness. This creates a need to restore connectedness between the self and the world, and manifests as the need to be in active relation to our fellow human beings. Humans must satisfy their basic natural needs for food shelter, clothing, and their social need for human relationships (Fromm, 2003). Both needs, what Fromm (1978) call the existential modes of 'having' and 'being', require satisfaction, and both are necessary to human existence. But when 'having' dominates 'being' then alienation and destructiveness follow. Moreover, capitalist society is based upon the exploitative appropriation of labour power in commodity production. This fosters the domination of 'having' over 'being' and the repression of curiosity follows. Repression of curiosity, and the having existential mode, are necessary for the reproduction of capitalist social relations. Thus, the emotion of fear links structure and agency (Barbalet, 2002). The lived experience of fear is produced by the macro-social economic positionality of students, and their meso-social positionality within the institutional learning culture. Fear constrains agency and limits humans' freedom to realize their potential to become fully human (Fromm, 1960).

The repression of curiosity is a continual and chronic process. People fear 'seeing more than society allows' as 'the truth would compel people to experience their own irrationality or powerlessness' (Maccoby, 1995: 77). Repression is socially and psychically structured in order to prevent people from becoming aware of their own disempowerment and alienation. Such repression, Fromm argues, prevents people from realizing their freedom to explore other more humane modes of being in the world. Repression of curiosity is, in my view, an integral dimension of the socially structured conditions of student performance in contemporary corporatized universities.

The discovery of Fromm's work supplied me with the theoretical tools to persuasively connect the subjective and objective, and agency and structure in my own sociological thinking. In Fromm's socio-psychoanalytic exploration of the Romantic Humanism of Marx (Morrs, 1996), lay the dialectical solution to my troubling question. Absence of student curiosity was the product of alienation. Such alienation emerged from the fear of potential estrangement caused by the development of a critical academic character. Curiosity tends to produce a social character at odds with the dominant neo-liberal social character of 'having' rather than 'being'. The automaton conformity of adjusting to the exigencies of the world, rather than changing that world, tends to repress curiosity. It is this relationship between alienation, academic labour, and social character that I now want to unravel.

ALIENATION, ACADEMIC LABOUR & SOCIAL CHARACTER

In contemporary universities, rather than enacting an identity of the scholar motivated by curiosity and a love of learning, many students appear to adopt the identity of consumers motivated by a neoliberal cost-benefit calculus. Academic work is simply a means to the end of getting the qualification necessary for a professional job. This identity is consolidated by the tendency for higher education institutions to operate as corporate universities (Roggero, 2011), oriented to servicing the economy, and producing docile but useful workers. The result, I argue, tends to be the both the alienation of academic labour and the repression of curiosity.

For Marx, alienation was a 'necessary phenomenon' and was 'inherent in human evolution' (Fromm, 1962: 57). Following Marx, it can be argued that students' academic labour, like alienated labour in general, has four dimensions: first, alienation from the product of labour (assessment); second, the process (learning/teaching); third, self (learner identity); and finally, the other (peers/teachers) (Fromm, 2011; Mann, 2001; Ollman, 1976). Alienation from product, process, and others alienates students from themselves such that they become objects to themselves. Through alienation the social relations of learning and teaching are reified. A relation between people – teacher and student, student and student, etc., – is turned into a relationship between objects, and between things: assessments, grades and degree certificates.

Fromm was interested in the linkage between alienation and what Marx (2011) called 'social character'. Social character became Fromm's signature concept. He defined social character as a specific type of relatedness to the world. It is through our social character that we relate to others, the world and ourselves. Social character develops from living in a shared culture, from shared lived experience and lifestyle. The function of the social character is to shape and direct human energy to ensure the social and cultural reproduction of capitalism (Fromm, 1963). Indeed, by adapting to capitalist conditions of existence humans develop those traits that make them desire to act in ways they have to act. Human desire and human need are powerfully shaped by capitalist social relations. The function of character is to enable people to do what is socially and psychologically necessary and to derive satisfaction therefrom. Fromm (1962: 243) recognised that 'social character internalizes external necessities, and thus harnesses human energy for the task of a given economic and social system'. Furthermore, education is 'the means by which social requirements are transformed into personal qualities' (Fromm, 1962: 245). Higher education then, reproduces the kind of personalities or character necessary for the continued reproduction of capitalism.

Fromm posits a dialectical relationship between internal psychic life and external conditions (social structure and culture). In humans character displaces instinct and shapes the drive for survival and relatedness. It is developed through the socialization process: first in the family and then in school, but it continues throughout life. For Fromm, 25 per cent of human behaviour was the product of genetic factors; 25 per cent the product of early childhood experiences; and 50 per cent the product of social character (Maccoby, 1995).

Social character is the way capitalist societies shape behaviour by channeling human energy in particular ways. It is the 'transmission belt' (Fromm, 1962: 78) between the economic infrastructure and the ideological superstructure. There is a dialectical relationship between economic structure and social character. Fromm's (2003) analysis shows how types of social character evolve under corporate capitalism. The dominant type he termed the 'marketing orientation', and the subordinate type the 'productive orientation'.

These two forms of social character are examples of what Weber (1949) called 'ideal types'. They are methodological constructs that bring together, and simplify, the general characteristics of complex phenomena, in order to develop an analytical model. Actually existing reality is then compared to this model. Weber (1949: 90) is quite clear that ideal types are not value judgments, and that they are not present in empirical reality; rather, they are developed to analyse that reality. Ideal types are a 'one-sided *accentuation* of one or more points of view' synthesized into an *'analytical* construct' (Weber, 1949: 90 emphasis in original). As heuristic tools they crystalize the essential qualities of the phenomenon being analysed.

Fromm's ideal types of social character were developed to analyse the ways in which corporate capitalism in post-second world-war USA formed identity. However, I think they are useful constructs for analysing tendencies within student academic identity in twenty-first century corporate universities. This said, I am aware that actually existing student identities are diverse and complex, and that the danger of reifying these tendencies must be avoided. Nevertheless, Fromm's analytical constructs do make possible insights into student alienation, and lack of curiosity. It is to the dialectical relationship between the two major types of social character, the marketing and the productive character orientations, that I now turn.

The Marketing Character Orientation

The marketing orientation is a mode of social relatedness in which people experience themselves as things, as commodities. Capitalist societies not only transform things into commodities to be exchanged in the market place, they also transform people into commodities. And the value of a person, like the value of a commodity, is dictated by their exchange value in the 'personality market' (Fromm, 2003). Higher education has become as much a means of commodifying the self for exchange in the jobs market as a means to the end of the pursuit of truth. Fromm's marketing character draws on the pivotal relation Marx (1946) established between the use and exchange value of labour.

As stated above, under corporate capitalism labour is characterized by alienation from self, other, process, and product. So learning as alienated student labour (and the knowledge produced) is not considered to have an intrinsic use value, only extrinsic exchange value. The social relations of corporate capitalism position students in such a way that they think of both themselves, and knowledge, as commodities. As Ollman (1976: 183) argues:

> In capitalism no commodity is a use value for the workers who make it. A worker does not produce what he (sic) wants, but what will earn him sufficient

money to buy what he wants. He produces use-value for others ... his product becomes a use value only after it has been exchanged.

Exchange value is both the expression of alienation and the condition of its existence. So for students, the product (an assessment) only has value when it has been exchanged for a grade, which itself only has value when it has been exchanged for a degree. This in turn is only valorized when it is exchanged for a job. Indeed, '[t]he whole process of living is experienced analogously to the profitable investment of capital, my life, my person being the capital which is invested' (Fromm,1963:148). This statement certainly resonates with my own experience of learning and teaching in contemporary higher education. Students appear to perceive me as their financial fund manager, and bestow upon me the responsibility of generating a good return (in the currency of the UK a 2:1 degree classification) on their three year investment (tuition fees).

Fromm (2003) argues that people fashion themselves to conform to the kind of personality most in demand. That is, students are dependent on the vagaries of the invisible hand of the 'personality market'. This causes deep insecurity. A character dominated by the marketing orientation experiences their own agency as a form of alienation, a commodity. The real nature of humanity is masked because agency is not used creatively for the purpose of self-realization, but rather to sell the self. Both human agency and the products thereof, become estranged.

The use-exchange value nexus expresses the alienation inherent in the social relations of corporate capital. Through alienated academic labour students are alienated and turn themselves into commodities. The social relations of learning and teaching – relations between people – are turned into relationships between objects, between things. Through this inversion the student becomes a 'self-conscious and self-acting commodity', a 'human commodity' (Marx, 2011: 111). In corporate capitalism:

> We produce not for a concrete satisfaction but for the abstract purpose of selling our commodity; we feel we can acquire everything material or immaterial by buying it, and thus things become ours independently of any creative effort of our own in relation to them. In the same way we regard our personal qualities and the result of our efforts as commodities that can be sold for money, prestige, and power. (Fromm, 1960: 226)

The neoliberal marketing orientation engenders a necrophilious reification of thought, action and feeling (Fromm, 1964, 1973; Freire, 1998). Fromm (1960: 158) links necrophilia with Freud's death instinct, and its dialectical counterpart biophilia, with the life instinct (eros):

> Life has an inner dynamism of its own; it tends to grow, to be expressed, to be lived. It seems that if this tendency is thwarted the energy directed towards life undergoes a process of decomposition and changes into energies directed towards destruction. In other words, the drive for life and the drive for destruction are not mutually independent factors but are in a reversed interdependence.

However, unlike Freud, Fromm argued that psychic energy is not biological or libidinous in origin (Bronner, 1994). Rather, psychic energy flows from the socially created human need to love and be loved. The origins of psychic energy lie not within individual being, but within social being. We have a social-relational predisposition to love life. We are biophilic.

Fromm (1973: 365) defines biophilia as 'the passionate love of life and all that is alive'; the desire to grow and cultivate the growth of others. It is the ability to influence others through the power of reason and love, through example rather than force (Fromm, 1964). Biophilia embraces the uncertainty and complexity of life, and the biophilious person envisions the world as a structuralized whole that is more than the sum of its parts. The ability to adopt such a structuralized worldview is essential if learners are going to become critical thinkers (Brookfield, 2002). Without this worldview reality becomes an unconnected collection of fragments. Here we see the thoroughness of Fromm's dialectical approach: the world is a complex web of interpenetrating phenomena, with each phenomenon relationally contained in others. To understand the parts you must understand the *sui generis* nature of the whole.

Thus, for Fromm, there is a dialectical relationship between life (creativity) and death (destructiveness): necrophily emerges from unlived life, from the frustration of not being able to love and be loved, and results in a destructive predisposition. In necrophilious social relations academic labour becomes dead labour: a form of 'living death' (Dinerstein & Neary, 2002: 11). It is not valued in itself, but only in relation to what it can be exchanged for in the market: a job and money. In the marketing character orientation curiosity is repressed. Thinking is reduced to 'grasping things quickly so as to be able to manipulate them successfully' as 'all that is necessary to know is the surface features of things, the superficial' (Fromm, 2003: 55). Knowledge becomes a commodity, thinking and knowing are instruments to produce grades which are a means to the end of certification. The main incentive for learning is not interest in the subjects taught, or the pursuit of truth, but 'the enhanced exchange value knowledge gives' (Fromm, 2003: 56). Truth then becomes an 'obsolete concept' (Fromm, 2003: 55) that has no exchange value. This engenders student resistance[3] to, and skepticism about, the pursuit of truth, and thus represses curiosity. However, this necrophiliac marketing character orientation is not an ineluctable fate. It exists in a dialectical relationship with the productive character orientation.

The Productive Character Orientation

Before I address the nature of the productive character orientation, it is first necessary to elaborate further Fromm's Marxist-humanist theory of dialectics. From a dialectical perspective, the world is a complex web of interpenetrating phenomena, with each phenomenon relationally contained in other phenomena. Dialectics tries to capture something of the continual process of change in social reality. It is a 'theoretical apparatus for viewing reality' (Ollman, 1976: 60). This theoretical apparatus posits four principles of social development. First, quantity becomes changed into quality:

for example, the pursuit of grades becomes displaced by the pursuit of truth. Second, opposites mutually penetrate each other: the marketing and productive character orientations are intrinsically related. Third, change comes through contradiction or negation: the alienation of the marketing orientation is negated by the engagement of the productive orientation to learning. Lastly, change is spiral not linear: it turns back on itself. Even though the marketing orientation may be superseded, its potential still exists and may manifest again in an altered form. In short, these dialectical developmental principles attempt to penetrate beneath the surface appearance of social reality in order to grasp its essential relations.

In his dialectical research into social character, Fromm sought not only to interpret the human condition but also to change it: to transform the alienation of the marketing character into the creativity of the productive character. The productive character orientation is the positive pole, or antithesis, of the marketing orientation. It is the negation of the negation. Furthermore, the productive orientation is a positive mode of social activity that shapes all aspects of human experience (Fromm, 2003).

Fromm defines the productive orientation as a form of non-alienated activity, in which people experience themselves as subjects rather than objects. It is 'a process of giving birth to something, of producing something and remaining related to what I produce. This also implies that my activity is a manifestation of my powers, that I and my activity are one' (Fromm, 1978: 91). As stated above, Fromm's (1978: 105) thesis is that through our unique blend of 'minimal instinctive determination and maximal development of the capacity for reason' we have 'lost our original oneness with nature'. However, to avoid the possibility of utter separateness (and thereby insanity), the human species must, of necessity, create new forms of unity with each other and the world. This desire for unity, for relatedness is for Fromm one of the most important motivations underpinning human behaviour. In the productive character orientation alienation and repression are dialectically transcended (Fromm, 1978).

A productive character type is both rational and critical, and is an active relationship with the world, where thinking penetrates beneath surface appearances. Productive thinking is structuralized thinking. It is a process of understanding the relationship of the whole to its parts. Productive thinking is also objective. Fromm's notion of objectivity is a singular one. It does not signify detachment but rather intense interest, or what I call curiosity. Objectivity then is a form of connectedness; an active dialectical process between the knower (the subject) and the known (the object). Through this activity meaningful relationships between self, other and the world are created. And for Fromm, this activity is first and foremost, animated by the feeling of love.

Fromm defines love as a feeling of connectedness with others and with nature that does not negate a person's independence and integrity. Love 'implies a syndrome of attitudes; that of care, responsibility, respect and knowledge' (Fromm, 1963: 33).[4] The essential characteristic of love is labour: it is a caring activity oriented to the cultivation of growth. For Fromm, this necessitates the responsibility to actively respond to the world. Respect signifies the ability to know the world as it is, for example, to see a student as a unique individual not an abstract category. Love, however, can only be developed in a dialectical relation to reason, to unsentimental critical thinking (Fromm, 1978). The labour of love then enables alienated learning to be transcended through active relatedness.

Fromm (2003), like Freire (1972),[5] acknowledged that the word love is problematic, as it is saturated with bourgeois sentimentality. I continue to struggle to think through such sentimentality, to re-appropriate the word love, and I continue to find the notion of teaching with love troubling. However, my understanding of what Fromm meant by love, and especially the notion of teaching with love, was deepened through reading a novel about academic identity. The central character, an English professor, realizes late in life that love is an on-going process not a fixed state, and that love:

> …was a passion neither of the mind nor of the flesh; rather, it was a force that comprehended them both, as if they were but the matter of love, its specific substance. To a woman or to a poem, it said simply Look! I am alive. (Williams, 2012: 259)

Teaching with love means teaching with a passion animated in ways that transcend mind and body. It is a recognition of the quality of the aliveness in our students and ourselves. Love is the signifier of the life force that animates both the human and non-human worlds. Love, therefore, is the foundation of Fromm's humanist ethic of biophily, and biophily is the leitmotif of all of his work (Horney, 1992).

Epistemological Alienation and Epistemological Curiosity

Academic labour for Fromm must above all be a labour of love.[6] In the marketing orientation, academic labour is loveless, simply a means to an end, a commodity to be exchanged. Therein lies its value, and therein lies the alienation that characterizes much student activity.

But as Marx (2011: 179) writes, 'alienation has a positive as well as a negative significance'. Even in the productive character orientation wherein academic labour is a labour of love, alienation still exists but in a positive form. Indeed, the positive moment of alienation is a necessary dimension of engaged learning as it is the foundation of critical thinking. If students are to think critically, they must cultivate the ability to estrange themselves from their commonsense, taken-for-granted knowledge of the world. Critical thinking involves making the familiar strange. It involves an epistemological alienation, that is, knowing the world in an unfamiliar fashion. The dialectical relations of learning are characterized by a spiral movement in which the familiar becomes the alien, and then turns back on itself to become the familiar once more. In dialectical learning, epistemological alienation is transformed into a non-alienated productive thinking.

Epistemological alienation is a key moment in the development of 'epistemological curiosity' (Freire, 2005: 54). Epistemological curiosity is a form of knowing that involves an intense interest in objects of investigation that enables the unveiling of their deeper meanings and relationships. But epistemological curiosity also involves acknowledging that knowing may involve fear; a fear of the difficult, of being unable to comprehend: a fear of failure. This is what another dialectician, Bachelard (1994: 111), called the 'fear-curiosity complex'. People are afraid to know the world anew and yet also desire to do so. The dialectical relationship of fear and curiosity 'is the perceptible threshold of all knowledge upon which interest wavers, falters and returns' (Bachelard, 1994: 110).

Freire (2005: 52) argues that a way of enabling learners to live with this tension between fear and curiosity is to encourage them to develop 'intellectual discipline'. Through educating and disciplining fear, rather than dismissing it, what were once objects of fear become objects of curiosity, objects of learning. Part of the process of developing intellectual self-discipline requires teachers to guide students into an exploration and refinement of their curiosity. To achieve this, teachers need to learn from their students the most effective ways to engage, and re-engage curiosity. Thus, when students' interest wavers and falters, teachers can help facilitate its return.

CONCLUSION: STRAYING AFIELD OF THE MARKETING CHARACTER ORIENTATION

> As for what motivated me … it was curiosity … not the curiosity that seeks to assimilate what it is proper for one to know, but that which enables one to get free of oneself. After all, what would be the value of the passion for knowledge if it resulted in a certain amount of knowledgeableness and not … in the knower straying afield of himself (sic). (Foucault, 1992: 8)

I have used Fromm's ideal type constructs of the marketing and productive character orientations to explore the ostensible lack of curiosity in the students I teach. This lack I have argued is a product of student alienation that emerges from a fear of being different, and results in the repression of curiosity. Nevertheless, this fear can be transformed through a dialectical form of learning that 're-absorbs alienation into itself' (Marx, 2011: 188). In this way it is possible to transform the student's social character. The dead labour of the marketing academic orientation wherein learning is subjugated by exchange value, is transformed into the living labour of the productive academic orientation, wherein learning is characterized by use value. Through stimulating epistemological curiosity alienation can become transformed into 'creative self-activity' (Fromm, 1964: 53). Such a transformation requires teachers to situate themselves 'in-against and beyond' (Holloway, 2010) the commodification of knowledge that characterizes much student learning in the contemporary neo-liberalising, corporate university. This transformation also requires students to stray far afield of their marketing character, to cultivate a passion for knowledge, and to become productive characters. However, as Fromm argues, this will only be possible if the academic labour of both learner and teacher is a labour of love.

NOTES

[1] See Sutton (2015).
[2] McLaughlin (1998) demonstrates in the USA during the 1960s and 1970s, and during the late 1980s in the UK, that Fromm's sociological reputation declined rapidly.
[3] Resistance is, however, a necessary part of the dialectics of teaching and learning. This is eloquently expressed by Swift (2010: 239) when commenting on the purpose of education: "It's not about empty minds waiting to be filled, nor about flatulent teachers discharging hot air. It's about the opposition of teacher and student. It's about what gets rubbed off between the persistence of the one and the resistance of the other. A long, hard struggle against natural resistance". See also Permumal (2008).
[4] See also hooks (2003:131) who defines "love as a combination of care, commitment, knowledge, responsibility, respect and trust".
[5] Interestingly, Freire (1972) cites Che Guevera. True revolutionaries, Che argued, are guided by love. Freire (1972: 62, footnote 4) writes: "The distortion imposed upon the word 'love' by the capitalist world cannot prevent the revolution from being essentially loving in character, nor can it prevent the revolutionaries from affirming their love of life." Freire is here extolling the virtue of biophily.
[6] It is significant that L. J. Friedman's (2013) intellectual biography of Fromm is entitled *The Lives of Eric Fromm Love's Prophet*.

REFERENCES

Bachelard, G. (1994). *The poetics of space*. Boston, MA: Beacon Press.
Barbalet, J. (Ed.). (2002). *Emotions and sociology*. Oxford, England: Blackwell.
Bronner, S. E. (1994). *Of critical theory and its theorists*. Oxford, England: Blackwell.
Brookfield, S. (2002). Overcoming alienation as the practice of adult education: The contribution of Eric Fromm to a critical theory of adult learning and education. *Adult Education Quarterly*, 52(2), 98–111.
Dinerstein, A. C., & Neary, M. (2002). *The labour debate: An investigation into the theory and reality of capitalist work*. Aldershot, England: Ashgate.
Foucault, M. (1992). *The history of sexuality: Vol. 2: The use of pleasure*. London, England: Penguin.
Freire, P. (1972). *Pedagogy of the oppressed*. Harmondsworth, England: Penguin.
Freire, P. (1985). *The politics of education: Culture, power, and liberation*. South Hadley, MA: Bergin & Garvey.
Freire, P. (1998). *Pedagogy of freedom: Ethics, democracy and civic courage*. Oxford, England: Rowman & Littlefield.
Freire, P. (2005). *Teachers as cultural workers: Letters to those who dare to teach*. Boulder Colorado, CO: Westview Press.
Friedman, L. J. (2013). *The lives of Eric Fromm: Love's prophet*. New York, NY: Columbia University Press.
Fromm, E. (1960). *Fear of freedom*. London, England: Routledge.
Fromm, E. (1962). *Beyond the chains of illusion: My encounter with Marx & Freud*. New York, NY: Simon & Schuster.
Fromm, E. (1963). *The sane society*. London, England: Routledge.
Fromm, E. (1964). *The heart of man: Its genius for good and evil*. London, England: Routledge and Kegan Paul.
Fromm, E. (1973). *The anatomy of human destructiveness*. London, England: Jonathan Cape.
Fromm, E. (1978). *To have or to be?* London, England: Jonathan Cape.
Fromm, E. (2003). *Man for himself: An inquiry into the psychology of ethics*. London, England: Routledge.
Fromm, E. (2011). *Marx's concept of man*. New York, NY: Frederick Ungar Publishing.

Hoad, T. F. (Ed.). (1990). *The concise Oxford dictionary of word origins*. London, England: Guild Publishing.
Holloway, J. (2010). *Crack capitalism*. London, England: Pluto.
hooks, b. (2003). *Teaching community: A pedagogy of hope*. New York, NY: Routledge.
Horney, M. H. (1992). Fromm's concept of biophilia. *Journal of the American Academy of Psychoanalysis*, *20*(2), 233–240.
Lyon, M. M. (1998). The limitations of cultural constructionism in the study of emotion, In G. Bendelow & S. Williams (Eds.), *Emotions in social life: Critical theories and contemporary issues* (pp. 39–59). London, England: Routledge.
Maccoby, M. (1995). The two voices of Erich Fromm: Prophet and analyst. *Society,* July/August, 72–82.
Mann, S. J. (2001). Alternative perspectives on student learning: Alienation and engagement. *Studies in Higher Education*, *26*(1), 7–19.
Marx, K. (1946). *Capital: A critical analysis of capitalist production* (Vol. 1., S. Moore & E. Aveling, Trans.). London, England: Allen & Unwin.
Marx, K. (2011). Economical and philosophical manuscripts. In E. Fromm (Ed.), *Marx's concept of man* (T. Bottomore, Trans., pp. 85–196). New York, NY: Frederick Ungar Publishing.
McLaughlin, N. (1998). How to become a forgotten intellectual: Intellectual movements and the rise and fall of Erich Fromm. *Sociological Forum*, *13*(2), 215–246.
Morrs, J. R. (1996). *Growing critical: Alternatives to developmental psychology*, London, England: Routledge.
Ollman, B. (1976). *Alienation: Marx's conception of man in capitalist society*. Cambridge & Angleterre, England: CUP.
Perumal, J. (2008). Student resistance and teacher authority: The demands and dynamics of collaborative learning. *Journal of Curriculum Studies*, *40*(3), 381–398.
Roggero, G. (2011). *The production of living knowledge: The crisis of the university and the transformation of labor in Europe and North America*. Philadelphia, PA: Temple University Press.
Sutton, P. (2015). A paradoxical academic identity: Fate, utopia and critical hope. *Teaching in Higher Education*, *20*(1), 37–47.
Swift, G. (2010). *Waterland*. London & Basingstoke, England: Picador.
Weber, M. (1949). *The methodology of the social sciences* (E. A. Shills & H. A. Finch, Trans.). New York, NY: Free Press.
Williams, J. (2012). *Stoner: A novel*. London, England: Vintage.

Paul Sutton
Department of Education and Social Sciences
University of St Mark and St John
Plymouth, UK

NEIL MCLEAN AND LINDA PRICE

4. THE MECHANICS OF IDENTITY FORMATION

A Discursive Psychological Perspective on Academic Identity

INTRODUCTION

Research into academic identities is principally underpinned by sociological theory, stressing the relationship between individuals and the social institutions and structures with which they interact (McLean, 2012). This sociological research identifies how professional identities are negotiated within the constraints and affordances of these social structures and institutions. Central to this negotiation are lived experiences (Clegg, 2005; McAlpine & Lucas, 2011) and the institutions within which these take place. These institutions may be disciplines (Becher & Trowler, 2001; Ylijoki, 2000), departments (Fanghanel, 2007; Knight & Trowler, 2000), processes such as probation (Smith, 2010) or universities themselves (Clegg, 2008). Thus a key concept is the community of practice (Lave & Wenger, 1998) as the site of negotiating or forming a professional identity (Lave & Wenger, 1991). In the Foucauldian tradition, societal level discourses are also social structures within which, and in response to which, identities are formed (Moses & Knutsen, 2007). An example from the academic identities literature would be the impact of neo-liberal discourses on higher education (Deem & Brehony, 2005).

However, the macro-level focus on discourse as a cultural artefact leaves open the question of how people 'negotiate' their identities in everyday life. In the sociological tradition, this has been investigated at length by Goffman (1990). However in more recent years, empirical interest in the discursive realisation of identity has been developed within narrative and discursive psychological research that investigates the mechanics of how we negotiate identities as we interact with others. Discursive Psychological research investigates 'identity work' (Antaki & Widdicombe, 1998), which is the process of communicating such that we negotiate identity positions for ourselves relative to others. This research approach enables an exploration of the ways in which people present themselves, consciously and unconsciously, in order to create a positive identity position that they can occupy (Benwell & Stokoe, 2006). This psychological focus utilises discourse analysis to investigate what social goals speakers and writers achieve through their representations of themselves in their interactions with others (Edwards & Potter, 1992). This focus on discursive practice offers a complementary lens to the study of academic identities. Most recent studies of academic identities use interviewing and rely on self-reported accounts of decision-making and action from individuals in order to uncover their professional identities (Clegg & Stevenson, 2013). A discursive psychological perspective offers insight into 'what' respondents say, 'how' they say 'what' they say, and what this achieves in terms of identity positioning. This chapter showcases the additional value in adopting such a complementary lens.

DEFINING IDENTITY FROM A DISCURSIVE PERSPECTIVE

The sociological and psychological theories described in this chapter share a common interest in discourse. This focuses on the ways in which people's interactions shape their social lives. This emphasis on discourse is not the traditional approach to the concept of identity. Instead it reflects the so-called 'turn to discourse' evident across the social sciences since the 1970s and 1980s (Marková, 2003). The more traditional, 'essentialist' understanding of identity is that people have separate internal and external worlds. The internal, cognitive self was traditionally seen to be where a person's 'identity' resides. The beliefs, attitudes and intentions of this internal self are formed in thought and then expressed in language. A person's identity, in this paradigm, builds on the enlightenment sense of a rational Cartesian self, a *'cogito ergo sum'* ethos, where the individual is seen as a:

> … self-sufficient subject of action endowed with instrumental rationality. (Gill, 2000: 54)

The main 'discursive' critique of 'essentialist' notions of identity is that they underestimate the influence of the social on the individual (Harré, 1998).

Four Tenets of a Discursive Approach to Identity

Whether taking a sociological or psychological starting point, considering 'identity' though a discursive lens entails four broad observations. The first is that 'identity' is both an individual and a social phenomenon (Burke & Stets, 2009). The individual aspect reflects the exercise of personal agency, which is how an individual chooses to act when in a given social role, and indeed which social roles an individual chooses for him/herself. However, social roles are not free. They have properties, attributes and responsibilities that anyone acting within them must abide by or at least manage (Burke & Stets, 2009; Clegg, 2005). Also, some social roles, such as nationality, are not chosen, but are inherited or imposed (Howarth, 2002). In academic identities research, personal agency is therefore investigated within the contexts and constraints of influential social structures, such as disciplines, departments and institutional structures (Archer, 2008; Becher & Trowler, 1989; Clegg & McAuley, 2005; Fanghanel, 2007; Knight, 2002; Smith, 2010). Whether researching identity from a psychological or sociological perspective, the dual individual and social elements of identity are seen to be distinguishable but inseparable:

> The concept of identity serves as a pivot between the social and the individual. (Lave & Wenger, 1998: 13)

This interaction between individual and social elements of identity is because:

> Identity is built around social engagement and is constantly being renegotiated as individuals move through different forms of participation. However, the process of learning and identity construction is not simply the outcome of participation in the opportunities provided by existing structural arrangements, it is also shaped by the way individuals exercise their agency in the workplace. (Jawitz, 2009: 243)

Thus different academic identities researchers have stressed the situated nature of identity formation, often within communities of practice (Billett, 2001; Clegg, 2005; Knight & Trowler, 2000; Rainbird, Fuller, & Munro, 2004). As Jawitz argues, this provides individuals with the context within which to enact social roles. Communities of practice are therefore both enabling and restrictive, in that they require and reward certain kinds of behaviours (Henkel, 2000).

A second observation that a 'discursive' lens recognises is that professional identities are 'formed' through how an individual enacts their social role in their working context. Focussing more narrowly on teaching identities, influences on identity formation highlighted in Kahn (2009) include structural and cultural factors that foreground the importance of the context in which an academic learns and adapts to their teaching role. This encompasses the programme they are teaching on, their department and discipline, and their workload and teaching responsibilities (Archer, 2008; Becher & Trowler, 1989; Clegg & McAuley, 2005; Fanghanel, 2007; Knight, 2002; Smith, 2010). However, the individual's understanding of departmental expectations and how they negotiate their response to these with their colleagues and students will also be influential (Clegg, 2008; McAlpine & Weston, 2000; Remmik & Karm, 2009; Rice, Sorcinelli, & Austin, 2000). This reflection drives the 'progressive specification' of actions as appropriate or not, and desirable or not. In the critical realist tradition underpinning much of the academic identities literature, this deliberation offers an account for decision making and development (Archer, 2000, 2003, 2007).

A third 'discursive' observation on 'identity' is that each of us has multiple identity positions and that these can be seen to overlap with each other. So a person's identity as a disciplinary teacher will be part of their wider identity as a disciplinary academic. Academic identities are themselves subsumed within wider identity claims:

> … in so far as individuals conceptualise themselves as having an identity as an academic, this multiple and shifting term exists alongside other aspects of how people understand their personhood and ways of being in the world'. (Clegg, 2005: 329)

A linked and fourth observation about 'identity' is that the formation of academic identities also has a temporal element in two ways. The first is that the construction of identity through lived experience is on-going. This is because the negotiation of our multiple identity positions occurs in different circumstances and changes over time. Thus the interpretation of professional identity can be viewed as a form of 'argument' (Remmik, Karm, Haamer, & Lepp, 2011) that an individual uses to justify, explain, and provide meaning to their activity, situations, and values while representing the profession. Thus:

> Professional identity is an on-going process of interpretation and reinterpretation of experiences'. (2011: 189)

This theme of constant change is also common across studies of academic identity.

> Identity is understood not as a fixed property, but as part of the lived complexity of a person's project and their ways of being in those sites which are constituted as being part of the academic. (Clegg, 2005: 329)

While change is constant, it is also possible to identify coherence in identity claims over time. Just as Remmik et al. (2011) liken the negotiation of professional identity to an 'argument', so a similar analogy is that identities are 'narratives'. In line with narratives more generally, the psychologist Gergen (1994) outlines how this entails a coherent biographical element to identity. Within the academic identities literature, McAlpine and Amundsen (2011) refer to this as 'identity trajectory'. They argue that:

> The trajectory emerges through and is embodied in cumulative day-to-day experiences of varied and complex intentions, actions and interactions with others…that may include setbacks as well as unexpected detours and opportunities. The notion of an academic identity-trajectory underscores the extent to which individuals tend to link past-present-future experiences in some fashion, whether imagining forward or looking back on a journey that is not necessarily, or perhaps rarely, straightforward'. (2011: 129)

While these four broad observations hold for those interested in identity and discourse, there are important distinctions between sociological and psychological approaches. What a psychological lens adds is detailed focus on the actual mechanics of identity formation.

DISCURSIVE PSYCHOLOGY: HOW IDENTITY IS DISCURSIVELY FORMED

As shown, sociological and psychological conceptions of 'identity' share a number of features. Both focus on the duality of the concept as both individual and shared. However, where academic identities studies have tended to focus on the 'shared' element as the social structures within which agency is exercised (Fanghanel, 2007), discursive psychology focuses on language and discourse as the 'shared' communal resources through which identities are negotiated (Valsiner, 2002). Both traditions also focus on the overlapping nature of the multiple identities that individuals hold. However, where academic identity research has focused on participation in communities of practice (Lave & Wenger, 1998), discursive psychology is interested in the 'performances' that claim belonging to groups or communities (Wetherell & Edley, 1999). This emphasis on 'identity work' (Antaki & Widdicombe, 1998) can be defined as the ways in which self-presentation makes claims to identity positions.

Presentation of Self as the Holder of an Identity Position

This 'positive presentation of self' is the core difference between sociological and psychological conceptions of identity. Discursive Psychology investigates the realisation of the self, using culturally available linguistic and cultural resources, rather than how social institutions mediate and constrain individual agency (Benwell & Stokoe, 2006). In offering an account of this self-realisation, discursive psychological approaches are tied to the notion of the 'dialogical self' (Salgado & Gonçalves, 2007). This concept reflects a view that identity is achieved through talking and acting ourselves into being occupants of particular identity positions (Antaki & Widdicombe, 1998). In this perspective, thought is not an internal, secret cognitive process, but rather the process of speaking to ourselves (Wetherell, 2001). Since we speak to ourselves using the words we have inherited from others, our interactions and conversations with others shape our psychological development (Valsiner, 2002; Vygotsky, 1980). This interaction between external and internal interactions accounts for the 'formation' of a professional identity since 'identity' is understood to exist in interaction. For instance, many early career academics now complete reflective writing and coursework assignments as part of their development work. This writing is a dialogue about teaching and learning between a class teacher and an educational development course team. In this dialogue, the academic presents themselves as a particular kind of disciplinary teacher and the building of this routine presentation of self as a particular kind of teacher is what builds their teaching identity in this setting (Davies & Harre, 1990). In other settings, these academics may well present themselves as different kinds of disciplinary teacher.

Addressivity: Creating Ourselves as We Address Others

This is because dialogical relationships occur whenever there is communication. In human relations there is always an *other* whom we address (Mead, 1910). As a result:

> ... the person is always in a process of a new becoming, in a living act of addressing other people. (Salgado & Gonçalves, 2007: 611)

This psychological argument relates to the Bakhtinian (1981) concept of *simultaneity*, which holds that 'to be is to communicate'. In other words:

> ... each person is created in and through the communicational activity of addressivity. (Salgado & Gonçalves, 2007: 608)

To give a well-known example of 'addressivity' in action, in 2001, the energy company British Petroleum replaced its 'green shield' logo designed by AR Saunders in 1920 to the 'Helios sunburst' logo petal design, with the accompanying tag line of 'beyond petroleum'.[1]

Figure 4.1. BP shield   *Figure 4.2. Helios sunburst*

As a demonstration of the link between self-presentation and identity claims (Benwell & Stokoe, 2006), this famous, visual example demonstrates how changing addressivity attempted to shift identity positioning. By using the original 'green shield' BP logo, the company presented itself as noble, even chivalrous. The choice of symbol in the logo made claims to the attributes of this symbolic association. It was hoped that potential customers would believe the company to be strong, honourable and protective. Once this claim was undermined by scandals such as the Brent Spar and Nigerian delta incidents, the company wanted to change its identity and claim an ecologically sensitive one. The symbol of the 'sunburst' petal was chosen to suggest attributes of a caring, environmentally-minded enterprise, intimating that carbon-based fuels had apparently been replaced with renewable sources of energy. It is the communicative display of attributes associated with the different identity positions of 'noble' as opposed to 'environmentally aware' that seeks to create the 'identity' of the company. However, explicit positioning claims of this kind can be fraught. As BP has found, successful identity positioning requires that others with whom the company communicates accept the identity positioning claims. This 'negotiation' of an identity position with, and relative to, others needs care and credibility if claims are not to be rejected.

SUCCESSFUL IDENTITY POSITIONING: AUDIENCE AND NARRATIVE

A key device for the successful 'negotiation' of identity by individuals, as opposed to companies, relates to the temporal nature of identity. As mentioned, the role of time is two-fold. First, identity is not stable, but is flexible and in flux. From a critical realist perspective this reflects individual agency in responding to environmental cues and constraints (Archer, 2000). In Discursive Psychology, this flux relates to identity as a performed concept – as the on-going personal enactment of a social role through interaction with others, and with ourselves (Edwards & Potter, 1992). In order to successfully 'negotiate' identity positions with quite different audiences, this performance will change and accommodate with different circumstances, and in different company. Impression management is necessary here if a person's identity claims are to be accepted.

The second temporal element of identity is that over time, identities maintain some coherence. Within academic identities research, identity has been presented as an 'argument' (Remmik & Karm, 2009) or a 'trajectory' (McAlpine & Lucas, 2011) in which individuals link their past experiences to present positions and future aspirations through their stories of self. Discursive psychology understands narrative slightly differently. In this tradition, self-narrative is a form of self-presentation (Rosetti-Ferreira, Amorim, & Silva, 2007). How a story is told, and how protagonists are presented, is a choice (Wetherell, 2001). This choice achieves the social goal of a positive presentation of self as a holder of a particular identity position. As Rosenwald and Ochberg (1992) argue:

> How individuals recount their histories – what they emphasize and omit, their stance as protagonists or victims, the relationship the story establishes between teller and audience – all shape what individuals can claim of their own lives. Personal stories are not merely a way of telling someone (or oneself) about one's life; they are the means by which identities may be fashioned. (1992: 1)

This narrative analysis of the study of identity reflects the following view:

> When we talk, we have open to us multiple possibilities for characterizing ourselves and events ... Discourse is a designed activity. It involves work. (Yates, Taylor, & Wetherell, 2001: 17)

The self-reporting of interview participants is therefore not simply a neutral account of their teaching experiences. Participating in an interaction such as an interview is itself a site for identity negotiation. How participants recount their experiences is a presentation of their identity for the audience they are interacting with in that instance. And this presentation creates their 'identity' as a disciplinary teacher. This is best seen in the use of impression management techniques within the self-narratives that make up interview transcripts.

How Identity Positioning Is Used to Create Who We Are for Each Other

This psychological understanding of language use as forming identity positions has profound implications for the study of academic identity, particularly where the study's method relies on the self-reporting of research participants. This is because self-reporting cannot be separated from participants' presentations of self, which is the mechanism through which we all enact and negotiate our identities. The implication here is that all interactional data should be understood as naturally-occurring data, since all interaction will involve dialogical identity positioning through the process of 'addressitivity' (Davies & Harre, 1990). A potential concern about the use of naturally occurring data through which participants present themselves as academic teachers, is that how this presentation is done will be biased by their context (McLean & Bullard, 2000). This is of course right. Interactive contexts necessarily influence communicational content, delivery and response – and this is true for all qualitative data.

> If language, however, is constructive and constituting, performative as well as referential, then any simple notion of good data as neutral and transparent descriptions of states of mind or events in the world becomes complicated. (Wetherell, 2001: 18)

Considering self-presentation more generally, it is impossible to escape from the notion that it is inevitably purposive. In psychology, most 'theories of self' contain some sort of self-esteem motive underlying interaction (Gecas, 1989). This motive can be found, for example, in self-serving attributional bias (Epley & Dunning, 2000). Beyond the individual level, a self-esteem motive is also evident in intergroup bias (Smith, Seger, & Mackie, 2007). In Social Identity Theory (Tajfel, 2010), the preference for an individual's 'in-group' serves to increase and maintain high in-group status, which in turn offers a positive identity for members of such a group or community. In observing any form of communication, purposive presentation of self will be present within the interactional context. A famous example of this is the identification of 'ideal' and 'working' conceptions of teaching (Samuelowicz & Bain, 2001).

As an example of the ubiquity of purposive self-presentation from within the interview method, the quote below comes from an interview transcript from (Åkerlind, 2007: 30). The quote is a short self-narrative and in it there are a number of examples of impression management and contextual cues of the kind that do 'identity work' (Antaki & Widdicombe, 1998).

> The [institutional standardized student surveys] I filled out …you get a whole bunch of quantitative measures, right? You get it back, and it has little bar charts all over, an answer for each question. Which I got back and they were mostly pretty good. And that was great fun, in a way. But what they didn't say is, you could improve by doing this, or these 10 people thought you were crap because. All I got was, most of these people think you are doing all right. I was not able to use that information to change the way I teach at all. (Information sciences, male, Level A, interview 2)

Looking at this short excerpt, there are a number of ways in which this participant considers his audience as he presents himself as an academic teacher. One immediate contextual influence is reflected by the level of informality. This is the second interview and the interviewee is signalling affinity through colloquial language use, such as *'you were crap ... which was great fun'*. This signalling of affinity is also evident in the direct address (*'you / I'*) and the anecdotal use of evidence and analysis. It is highly unlikely that this academic would use this level of analysis and loose justification in a more formal or novel setting. The use of tag questions (*'right?'*), present tense for narrative (*'you get a whole bunch of quantitative measures'*) and non-specific quantifiers (*'whole bunch of'*) are all features of anecdotes or jokes which reflect the signalling of affinity being accomplished. In addition, the speaker positions himself for his audience in a number of ways. Firstly, the informality when discussing student feedback (often a challenging or contentious issue) signals confidence in himself as a teacher, since he doesn't need to take it too seriously. He uses indirectness and modesty (*'many of these people think you're doing all right'*) to guard against being seen as boasting about good scores (often termed *stake inoculation*). Also, his stated concern is that the feedback exercise wasn't useful for his development, which positions him as interested in his development and teaching. It seems reasonable to assume that this positioning has something to do with being in conversation with an educational researcher. If this lecturer was speaking to a member of his department with limited interest in teaching, his positioning and self-presentation might well be quite different.

Even in this fragment, it seems clear that the interactional context is influencing the communication. There are two powerful reasons why this is inevitable. The first, as discussed above in relation to essentialist and discursive understandings of identity, relates to whether it is possible to distinguish between a person's sovereign, internal cognitive world and the language that this individual uses. The turn to discourse across the social sciences, and the inheritance of the language that shapes our thoughts, reflects increasing evidence that it is futile to search for a 'pure' representation of a teacher's internal cognitive processes. Our thoughts are so closely intertwined with our social and thus communicative selves and the identities we form and use (Wetherell, 2001). The inevitable consequence of the notion that language influences, or indeed *is*, thought, is that context influences thought, since context is decisive in language use. Thus research into psychological concepts such as identity, conceptions, or beliefs for that matter, need to consider the context in which data has been gathered.

A second reason why context influences qualitative data is that pragmatically, interaction requires context for communication to be successful. Utterances are frequently analysed as working on three levels: *locution* (what is said), *illocution* (how this is said) and *perlocution* (what the utterance is intended to achieve) (Wardhaugh, 1998). It is through considering the combination of these channels that intended meaning is co-constructed by interactants, but all three channels are influenced by context. In the example above, the lexical choices made by the lecturer (*'crap ... whole bunch of ... great fun'*) are tailored to the interaction. The term *'crap'* could be offensive if used pointedly, however the speaker's use here reflects an established relationship with the researcher that offers permission to use this (albeit somewhat gentle) swear word. Similarly, while we do not have information on para-linguistic cues such as intonation patterns and gesture, the tone of the locution suggests that the illocutionary cues signalled friendly relations. The speaker may well have leaned forward, his palms open. His intonation may well have had pronounced pitch movement, rising and falling to demonstrate interest and connection. This would be in keeping with the anecdotal tone of the fragment. In a more formal context where use of the word 'crap' would be offensive, an entirely different posture and gesture might have accompanied the word. Finally, the listener divining the purpose of the utterance enables comprehension. This is because communication is indexical, that is meaning depends on the context of its use (Heritage, 1984). In the fragment analysed here, the use of the word 'crap' signals openness and honesty and offers respect to the listener. Had the lecturer intended offence, this would have been made clear and the interview would have ended shortly after its use as the researcher would have understood that swearing was being used to create an adversarial relationship and to end the communication. The combination of these three channels enables the appropriate use of language, but appropriacy implies that it serves a given purpose. In other words, that it relates effectively to the interactional context. This illustrates how identity is discursively constituted and why understanding discourse from this perspective is important.

CONCLUSION

Discursive psychology offers a complementary and important paradigm for researching academic identity. It offers a method for researching academic identity as it is realised, rather than the circumstances in which it is realised. The mechanics of identity formation lie in 'identity positioning' and the ways in which our communication with others perform 'work' that creates positive presentations of ourselves for others (and us) to relate to. This observation has implications for interview-based research. Interviews are not neutral spaces in which participants share their experiences in a disinterested and dispassionate fashion. Rather, interviews are interactions in which identities are created by how the researcher and participants choose to present themselves to one another. These interactions will be a negotiation during which both sides will 'position' themselves and thus broker a basis for reciprocal exchange. The example given above illustrates how impression management and positioning work mechanistically.

An implication of this complementary lens on identity formation is the confirmation that interview data is not neutral (Clegg & Stevenson, 2013). Rather, interview data should be seen as a naturally occurring example of identity negotiation in a particular setting. A second implication is that this process of identity positioning is available to be investigated in other kinds of interactions about teaching and learning. For example, the reflective and coursework writing completed on teacher development programmes is illustrative of identity negotiation between early career academics and those they learn with. Lectures and seminars are examples of interactions within which teaching staff and students develop and negotiate identities as disciplinary insiders. Research that investigates interaction in these settings would offer better insights into how best to structure such communicative exchanges to promote the development of identities as members of the academy, whether as professionals or as students.

NOTE

[1] Images retrieved from: https://www.google.co.uk/search?q=bp+logo&client=firefox-a&rls=org.mozilla:enUS:official&channel=np&tbm=isch&tbo=u&source=univ&sa=X&ei=Mfn9U52hKsi00QX9hYDICA&sqi=2&ved=0CCAQsAQ&biw=980&bih=874

REFERENCES

Åkerlind, G. S. (2007). Constraints on academics' potential for developing as a teacher. *Studies in higher education, 32*(1), 21–37.
Antaki, C., & Widdicombe, S. (1998). Identity as an achievement and as a tool. In C. Antaki & S. Widdicombe (Eds.), *Identities in talk*. London, England & Thousand Oaks, CA: Sage.
Archer, L. (2008). The new neoliberal subjects? Young/er academics' constructions of professional identity. *Journal of Education Policy, 23*(3), 265–285.
Archer, M. S. (2000). *Being human: The problem of agency*. Cambridge, England: Cambridge University Press.
Archer, M. S. (2003). *Structure, agency and the internal conversation*. Cambridge, England: Cambridge University Press.
Archer, M. S. (2007). *Making our way through the world: Human reflexivity and social mobility*. Cambridge, England: Cambridge University Press.
Becher, T., & Trowler, P. (1989). *Academic tribes and territories: Intellectual inquiry and the cultures of disciplines*. Milton Keynes, England: Oxford Brookes University.
Becher, T., & Trowler, P. R. (Eds.). (2001). *Academic tribes and territories: Intellectual enquiry and the cultures of disciplines* (2nd ed.). Buckingham, England: Society for Research into Higher Education & Open University Press.
Benwell, B., & Stokoe, E. (2006). *Discourse and identity*. Edinburgh, England: Edinburgh University Press.
Billett, S. (2001). Learning through work: Workplace affordances and individual engagement. *Journal of Workplace Learning, 13*(5), 209–214.
Burke, P. J., & Stets, J. E. (2009). *Identity theory*. Oxford, NY: Oxford University Press.
Clegg, S. (2005). Theorising the mundane: The significance of agency. *International Studies in the Sociology of Education, 15*(2), 149–164.
Clegg, S. (2008). Academic identities under threat? *British Educational Research Journal, 34*(3), 329–345.
Clegg, S., & McAuley, J. (2005). Conceptualising middle management in higher education: A multifaceted discourse. *Journal of Higher Education Policy and Management, 27*(1), 19–34.
Clegg, S., & Stevenson, J. (2013). The interview reconsidered: Context, genre, reflexivity and interpretation in sociological approaches to interviews in higher education research. *Higher Education Research and Development, 32*(1), 5–16.
Davies, B., & Harre, R. (1990). Positioning: The discursive production of selves. *Journal for the Theory of Social Behaviour, 20*(1), 43–63.
Deem, R., & Brehony, K. J. (2005). Management as ideology: The case of 'new managerialism' in higher education. *Oxford Review of Education, 31*(2), 217–235.
Edwards, D., & Potter, J. (1992). *Discursive psychology* (Vol. 8). London, England & Thousand Oaks, CA: Sage.

Epley, N., & Dunning, D. (2000). Feeling "holier than thou": Are self-serving assessments produced by errors in self-or social prediction? *Journal of Personality and Social Psychology, 79*(6), 861–875.

Fanghanel, J. (2007). Investigating university lecturers' pedagogical constructs in the working context. *The Higher Education Academy, 1*, 1–15.

Gecas, V. (1989). The social psychology of self-efficacy. *Annual Review Of Sociology, 15*, 291–316.

Gergen, K. J. (1994). Exploring the postmodern: Perils or potentials? *American psychologist, 49*(5), 412.

Gill, R. (2000). Discourse analysis. In M. W. Bauer & G. Gaskell (Eds.), *Qualitative researching with text, sound and image* (pp. 172–190). London, England & Thousand Oaks, CA: Sage.

Goffman, E. (1990). *The presentation of self in everyday life*. London, England: Penguin.

Harré, R. (1998). *The singular self: An introduction to the psychology of personhood*. London, England & Thousand Oaks, CA: Sage.

Henkel, M. (2000). *Academic identities and policy change in higher education* (Higher Education Policy Series). London, England & Philadelphia, PA: J. Kingsley.

Heritage, J. (1984). *Garfinkel and ethnomethodology*. Cambridge, NY: Polity Press.

Howarth, C. (2002). So, you're from Brixton? The struggle for recognition and esteem in a stigmatized community. *Ethnicities, 2*(2), 237–260.

Jawitz, J. (2009). Learning in the academic workplace: The harmonization of the collective and the individual habitus. *Studies in Higher Education, 34*(6), 242–251.

Kahn, P. (2009). Contexts for teaching and the exercise of agency in early career academics: Perspectives from realist social theory. *International Journal for Academic Development, 14*(3), 197–207.

Knight, P. T. (2002). Learning from schools. *Higher Education, 44*(2), 283–298.

Knight, P. T., & Trowler, P. R. (2000). Department-level cultures and the improvement of learning and teaching. *Studies in Higher Education, 25*(1), 69–83.

Lave, J., & Wenger, E. (1991). *Situated learning: Legitimate peripheral participation*. Cambridge, England: Cambridge University Press.

Lave, J., & Wenger, E. (1998). *Communities of practice: Learning, meaning, and identity*. Cambridge, England: Cambridge University Press.

Marková, I. (2003). Constitution of the self: Intersubjectivity and dialogicality. *Culture & Psychology, 9*(3), 249–259.

McAlpine, L., & Amundsen, C. (Eds.). (2011). *Doctoral education: research-based strategies for doctoral students, supervisors and administrators*. Dordrecht, The Netherlands & New York, NY: Springer.

McAlpine, L., & Lucas, L. (2011). Different places, different specialisms: Similar questions of doctoral identities under construction. *Teaching in Higher Education, 16*(6), 695–706.

McAlpine, L., & Weston, C. (2000). Reflection: Issues related to improving professors' teaching and students' learning. *Instructional Science, 28*(5), 363–385.

McLean, M., & Bullard, J. E. (2000). Becoming a university teacher: Evidence from teaching portfolios (how academics learn to teach). *Teacher Development, 4*(1), 79–101.

McLean, N. (2012). Researching academic identity: Using discursive psychology as an approach. *International Journal for Academic Development, 17*(2), 97–108.

Mead, G. H. (1910). Social consciousness and the consciousness of meaning. *Psychological Bulletin, 7*(12), 397–405.

Moses, J. W., & Knutsen, T. L. (2007). *Ways of knowing: Competing methodologies in social and political research*. Basingstoke, NY: Palgrave Macmillan.

Rainbird, H., Fuller, A., & Munro, A. (2004). *Workplace learning in context*. London, England: Routledge.

Remmik, M., & Karm, M. (2009). Impact of training on the teaching skills of university lecturers: Challenges and opportunities. *Haridus, 11*(12), 20–26.

Remmik, M., Karm, M., Haamer, A., & Lepp, L. (2011). Early-career academics' learning in academic communities. *International Journal for Academic Development, 16*(3), 187–199.

Rice, R., Sorcinelli, M., & Austin, A. (2000). *Heeding new voices: Academic careers for a new generation*. Washington, WA: American Association for Higher Education (Working paper).

Rosenwald, G. C., & Ochberg, R. L. (1992). *Storied lives: The cultural politics of self-understanding*. New Haven, CT: Yale University Press.

Rosetti-Ferreira, C., Amorim, K., & Silva, A. (2007). Network of meanings: A theoretical-methodological perspective for the investigation of human developmental process. In J. Valsiner & A. Rosa (Eds.), *The Cambridge handbook of sociocultural psychology* (pp. 277–292). Cambridge, England: Cambridge University Press.

Salgado, J., & Gonçalves, M. (2007). The dialogical self: Social, personal, and (un)conscious. In J. Salgado & M. Gonçalves (Eds.), *Cambridge handbook of socio-cultural psychology* (pp. 608–621). Cambridge, England: Cambridge University Press.

Samuelowicz, K., & Bain, J. D. (2001). Revisiting academics' beliefs about teaching and learning. *Higher Education, 41*(3), 299–325.

Smith, E. R., Seger, C. R., & Mackie, D. M. (2007). Can emotions be truly group level? Evidence regarding four conceptual criteria. *Journal of Personality and Social Psychology, 93*(3), 431–446.

Smith, J. (2010). Forging identities: The experiences of probationary lecturers in the UK. *Studies in Higher Education, 35*(5), 577–591.

Tajfel, H. (Ed.). (2010). *Social identity and intergroup relations* (Vol. 7). Cambridge, England: Cambridge University Press.

Valsiner, J. (2002). Forms of dialogical relations and semiotic autoregulation within the self. *Theory & Psychology, 12*(2), 251–265.

Vygotsky, L. S. (1980). *Mind in society: The development of higher psychological processes*. Cambridge, MA: Harvard University Press.

Wardhaugh, R. (1998). *An introduction to sociolinguistics*. Oxford, NY: Blackwell.

Wetherell, M. (2001). Themes in discourse research: The case of Diana. In S. J. Yates, M. Wetherell, & S. Taylor (Eds.), *Discourse research and practice: A reader* (pp. 14–28). London, England: Sage.

Wetherell, M., & Edley, N. (1999). Negotiating hegemonic masculinity: Imaginary positions and psycho-discursive practices. *Feminism & Psychology, 9*(3), 335–356.

Yates, S. J., Taylor, S., & Wetherell, M. (2001). *Discourse theory and practice: A reader*. London, England: Sage.

Ylijoki, O.-H. (2000). Disciplinary cultures and the moral order of studying: A case-study of four Finnish university departments. *Higher Education, 39*(3), 339–362.

Neil McLean
London School of Economics and Political Science
UK

Linda Price
Open University, UK

PART II

ON RESEARCHING ACADEMIC IDENTITIES

SANDRA ACKER AND MICHELLE WEBBER

5. UNEASY ACADEMIC SUBJECTIVITIES IN THE CONTEMPORARY ONTARIO UNIVERSITY

INTRODUCTION

For the past few years, we have been conducting a project exploring the relationship between what we call accountability governance in higher education, specifically in the Canadian province of Ontario, and the (re)formation of academic subjectivities. Our starting point was the burgeoning critical literature about the corporatization of universities and its many consequences, including increased surveillance of workers and emphasis on accountability and performativity. We use the term 'accountability governance' to encompass the set of ideologies and practices linked with the promotion of discourses of quality, accountability, performance, economy, efficiency and enterprise in post-secondary education.

Our theoretical framework has roots in the work of Michel Foucault (1977) on governmentality processes. Foucault provides us with a language with which to understand regulatory systems as surveillance mechanisms that normalize conformity and self-regulation. Additionally, we draw on a feminist perspective that alerts us to organizational micropolitics related to gender, race, class and other social divisions (Morley, 1999, 2005).

This chapter asks how highly satisfied academics can simultaneously be critical of the changing context in which their work is situated. Questions about job satisfaction asked of twenty-four academics produced a generally positive picture, in line with claims that Canada is an exception to some of the international trends. Yet other aspects of our data, more in keeping with those developments, indicate that participants are generally uneasy about the 'university as a business' and its pressures toward performativity. Before presenting our analysis, we review some of the relevant literature on change in academic work and describe our study.

THE RISE OF ACCOUNTABILITY GOVERNANCE

General Trends

Accountability governance as a global phenomenon (Stensaker & Harvey, 2011) has become prominent in the past thirty years, as budget cuts and their accompaniments—hiring freezes and intensified workloads—have come to characterize universities in many jurisdictions. Reductions in state funding seem to produce managerialist practices, including restructuring, searches for efficiencies and greater scrutiny of all institutional activities. While such systems and mechanisms can be analyzed at the macro-level, they also carry strong implications for the sense of self of individual academics who are 'subject' to these disciplinary technologies (Foucault, 1977; Lynch, 2006). Too much impression management or performativity—the need to ensure that the performance is noted (Ball, 2003)—may produce mistrust, alienation, cynicism and/or superficial conformity (Findlow, 2008; Lorenz, 2012; Teelken, 2012). Feminist writers, in particular, have explored the effects of new managerialism, corporatization and accountability on academic subjectivities, especially those of women (Gill, 2014; Grant & Elizabeth, 2015; Leathwood & Hey, 2009; Morley, 2005; Thomas & Davies, 2002). Arguably, women's history of exclusion in academe and socialization into conformity may leave them more severely affected by the corpus of performative requirements (Gill, 2014; Leathwood & Read, 2013; Wyn et al., 2000).

Much of the literature on accountability governance in post-secondary education comes from the UK, Australia and New Zealand, as the systems for academic accountability in those countries are highly formalized, mandated by central government and carry a risk of punitive consequences such as reductions in program or research funding (Fitzgerald, White & Gunter, 2012; Lucas, 2006). European countries have also been developing ways to make academic work more tightly regulated (Enders, de Boer & Leišytė, 2009; Ylijoki, 2013), as have countries in the 'periphery' like Mexico and Turkey (Uzuner-Smith & Englander, 2015). In part, these schemes work by harnessing emotions: pleasure in accomplishments, anxiety about achievement, shame if work is deemed inadequate (Grant & Elizabeth, 2015; Leathwood & Hey, 2009; Leathwood & Read, 2013; Morley, 2005; Wilson & Holligan, 2013).

Canada

Canadian higher education is often thought to deviate from global trends in accountability governance. Metcalfe (2010) argues that in recent years Canada has not been exceptional after all, as universities with reduced government funding increase their use of private funds (including tuition), partnerships with industry and various entrepreneurial activities. Other scholars see Canadian universities as developing unwelcome tendencies towards accountability governance and corporatization (e.g. Bruneau & Savage, 2002; Polster, 2010).

At the same time, there is a competing discourse that identifies Canada as 'less bad' than elsewhere (Shanahan & Jones, 2007). Canadian universities still have primarily enrolment-driven funding, control over hiring, curriculum and admissions, and a strong tenure system (Axelrod, 2008, p. 101; Shanahan & Jones, 2007). Canadian university faculty are mostly unionized (Dobbie & Robinson, 2008), in theory providing a base for resistance to interference with academic autonomy (Jones, 2013). Canadian academics seem to be relatively well paid and generally satisfied with their jobs (Weinrib et al., 2013).

Two points are especially important here. First, changes in Canadian post-secondary education in the direction of accountability and audit have been incremental (Newson & Polster, 2008) and have come of age later than in comparable countries: 'the accountability movement in higher education emerged internationally in the late 1970s, in the US in the 1980s and in Canada in the early 1990s' (Shanahan, 2009: 6). Second, the way in which education, including post-secondary education, is governed and financed in Canada puts a brake on potential excesses of imposed accountability. The federal government does not have a direct role in regulating higher education (although its indirect influence can be substantial), and it has no ministry of education. Thus, we do not see nation-wide accountability systems or evaluations of academic performance; rather, each individual province puts its own initiatives into place.

The province in which our research takes place, Ontario, has gradually moved to exert greater control over post-secondary institutions. An advisory and research-commissioning body called the Higher Education Quality Council of Ontario (HEQCO) was set up in 2007. In 2010 a provincial Quality Council and a Quality Assurance Framework were established to systematize program reviews. Since 2012, the Ontario ministry has negotiated individual agreements with each institution called Strategic Mandate Agreements, identifying priority areas. The government intends that these agreements and associated strategic funding will encourage 'differentiation' in the system, i.e. specialization rather than duplication (Government of Ontario, 2013). Metrics that involve research performance have been mentioned in policy documents, though are not at this time enforced at an individual level. More immediately threatening may be the 'program prioritization processes' instituted by some universities, though not prescribed by the province, whereby programs, sometimes including both administrative and academic units, are ranked against each other (Ontario Confederation of University Faculty Associations, 2014). These schemes are based on a model imported from the United States and may be intended by universities to help them deal with financial shortages through program mergers or closures.

THE STUDY

Semi-structured, qualitative, face-to-face interviews were conducted between 2011 and 2014 with twenty-four full-time tenured or tenure-track[1] faculty members[2] in the fields of education, geography, political science and sociology. Interviews generally lasted about 90 minutes and were audiotaped and transcribed.

We developed a means of purposive sampling. Possible participants were initially identified by searches of department web sites. A list of potential interviewees was drawn up that distributed them across categories of subject field, university type and rank, with efforts made to equalize numbers of women and men and include ethnic minorities where possible. Individuals were then contacted a few at a time over email with an attached contact letter explaining the study in detail. If someone did not reply or was unwilling or unable to be interviewed, we replaced them in our list with someone else, keeping the overall aim of balance among categories as our priority.

Analysis proceeded by first reading and re-reading transcripts in order to identify provisional key themes; then to make these long transcripts more manageable and following the example of McAlpine, Amundsen and Turner (2013), writing cameo-type summaries of each interview, from two to six single-spaced pages, isolating discussion of the key themes (for example, 'performance', which would be in evidence not only in response to direct questions but throughout other parts of the discussion as well). Cameos (with full transcripts available for reference as necessary) were then divided into groups according to rank (assistant, associate and full professor) and summaries made of the key themes for each group, with illustrative quotations, before combining sections of the summaries as needed in writing up particular papers.

Participants were drawn from ten universities in the province of Ontario across the spectrum of medical/doctoral, comprehensive and primarily undergraduate university types, and were equally divided among four subject fields, six each in education, geography, political science and sociology. In multi-disciplinary fields such as education and geography we looked for participants who could be classified as social scientists (e.g., a health geographer rather than a climate scientist). To compare perspectives across career points, we selected seven assistant professors, eight associate professors and nine full professors. There are approximately equal numbers of women (thirteen) and men (eleven). Twenty of the participants are white and four from ethnic minorities.

In the following sections we look at aspects of the data concerning satisfaction, corporatization and performance, paying attention to career point and gender variations.

THE SATISFACTIONS OF THE ACADEMIC CAREER

A 2007–2008 survey of Canadian academics (The 'Changing Academic Profession' study [CAP]), conducted in concert with a number of other nations, concluded not only that full-time Canadian academics had high levels of job satisfaction but that they were more satisfied 'than their peers in other countries, such as the United States, United Kingdom, or Australia' (Jones, 2013; see also Weinrib et al., 2013). The results of our study, while using very different methods, much smaller and limited to four social science fields, are generally compatible with the larger-scale quantitative research. But for our group we can get a more in-depth idea of what they are 'satisfied' about. We asked participants (all names are pseudonyms) what the satisfactions were for them in academic life, followed by a question about the 'downsides'. Responses were somewhat different in the three rank groupings.

Counter-intuitively, and unlike the CAP results, the pre-tenure assistant professors were the most enthusiastic (see Acker, Haque & Webber, in press, for more detail about this group). Almost all talked about 'love' and 'flexibility'. For example:

> I love teaching ... I have to enter into my little bubble but it gives me such a high ... I just love it. (Ellie)

> I love the research. I love the research. (Kyle)

> It's great the flexibility that you have in your day to day life and your work schedule and being able to stay home in your jammies and write, and your ten-second commute from your bed to your desk by way of your coffee machine. (Zoe)

> It's a great job, like in terms of life style, to have flexibility, to be able to, like, go on a class trip with my son, I feel so fortunate. (Tricia)

Associate professors were generally more guarded, although there were also many positive sentiments. 'Love' was less evident, however, than in the assistant professor group and only a few mentioned flexibility. Flexibility seemed to be replaced by 'autonomy', perhaps more obvious once past the tenure review:

> I am able to teach in my area of interest ... I have virtually complete autonomy to define what courses I want to teach, how I want to teach them. (Brenda)

> You can conduct the research that you want to conduct as long as it's rigorous and ethical and informed by theory. (Caitlyn)

Full professors, while still clearly tilting towards satisfactions of the career outweighing the dissatisfactions, were less effusive, less likely to use the words 'love' or 'flexibility' although autonomy is still mentioned. A partial explanation might be provided by Ethan's quip: 'probably the 50 year old faculty member generally doesn't find things quite as fun as a 30 year old faculty member who's just starting out does'. Henry and Aiden spoke of the pleasure of having their work recognized while Stella and Rosanna, along with Henry and Aiden, talked about the satisfactions associated with teaching and mentoring, consistent with their speaking from late in the career.

'Downsides' were relatively few at all three career points. Some participants, such as these two associate professors, could not see *any* downsides: 'I can't think of anything actually' (Ivan); 'I don't think I have one' (Bethany). A few of the younger women assistant professors mentioned the need to devote endless hours to work and the difficulty of balancing home and work, especially for women in their reproductive years. While one of the women associate professors echoed this point, two others said that they enjoyed the way sectors of their lives overlapped—what Gill (2014: 16) calls the 'merge'. Some of the full professors, especially women, looked back on difficulties they encountered through sexism and discrimination when building a career, while several women and men alluded to a cost to personal relationships.

Given the results above, readers from other countries may conclude that Canada provides a relatively unthreatening and peaceful site for the development of an academic career. There is some truth in this vision, at least for individuals who are tenured or on track to become so. Nor were the participants in our study unduly worried by provincial policy initiatives; in fact, they were often unfamiliar with quality discourses, even when quality assessment offices were being opened in their own institutions (Acker & Webber, 2014b). Yet all is not well in Canadian academe, as our next sections show. Participants were deeply critical of the corporatization of universities and of the ways in which their performance was being monitored.

THE UNIVERSITY AS A BUSINESS

We asked: 'Some authors have argued that universities are now being run more like businesses than institutions of education. Do you agree, at all, with this argument or not?' Most participants agreed: 'Oh yeah' (Marcy); 'I agree with it, unfortunately' (Teresa); 'I see it unfolding before my eyes' (Sam). Those who disagreed believed that business principles were not applied successfully enough for that designation or drew distinctions between academic purposes and a business focus on profits. Edward stated that it depended on the institution 'and the personalities of the senior administrators' while Robert cautiously agreed with our statement: 'I guess, so, in our own strange way, in an academic way'.

Many of the participants questioned how budget decisions were being made. The idea that academics should fund-raise was particularly antipathetic to full professors, perhaps because they could recall a different era (see Enders, de Boer & Leišytė, 2009). These professors were unhappy with the shift in the purposes of education: 'it's a long time since anyone said we're here to educate people to the best of their potential' (Trevor). Associate and assistant professors raised a series of concerns: branding and marketing; colleagues competing for merit ratings; a secondary labour market with poor treatment of contingent faculty; new programs developed simply to make money; and student consumerism. They gave examples of departments or programs such as women's studies struggling to demonstrate their worth in narrow terms such as making money, and they worried that decisions would be made on business grounds rather than educational ones.

While one assistant professor (Katie) mentioned the hiring of more managers than faculty, managerialism and top-down directives within the university were usually a target of associate and full professors. The increasing number of administrators[3] and their different priorities were noted: 'there is a whole layer of administration that seems to be increasingly detached from faculty' (Ivan); 'administration seems to be sort of expanding, mushrooming all over the place' (Ethan). Sam was especially worried by top-down decision-making and a lack of transparency: 'It's so managerial, so hierarchical ... we get told things that were not discussed at all and because this is the best for the university and so on'. Others disliked the feeling that administrators were always requiring something from them. Edward stated 'there's just a lot more paperwork involved in anything, I mean when I started I was, in most respects, just trusted more than now; I don't feel as though faculty are trusted as much'. Older full professors seemed particularly hostile to senior administrators. For example:

> I try to stay away from senior administrators. They just give me the willies. They're the 'suits'. I don't know how to talk to them. I don't trust them. Even if they are decent people, they have different agendas. (Stella)

THE PERILS OF PERFORMANCE

Participants had no difficulty talking about what 'performance' meant to them, in detail and at length. They explained that performance is evaluated for research, teaching and service (administration), most often with an implied or explicit percentage distribution known colloquially as '40-40-20'. Four areas of performance evaluation brought extended commentary: the push to publish in certain ways; the emphasis placed on obtaining external research grants; the assessment of teaching through student course evaluations; and the packaging of these pressures in the form of annual performance reviews.

Publishing Properly

When asked what performance meant to her, Stella, a full professor, replied:

> It means publish, publish, publish. And as I keep telling my younger colleagues, don't believe all the crap, it's publish. So it's publish. It's how much you publish, more and more. And a bit, I guess, where you publish, if you are publishing in top journals. I don't think anyone has the time to actually read what you publish, so I think there are some very fine scholars who don't publish very much, who are really disadvantaged because the emphasis is really on quantity.

Participants were critical of narrow criteria for judging publications (e.g. placement in 'top tier refereed journals'), overemphasis on quantity and measurement, overly systematized requirements and reporting formats, and relative discounting of co-authorship, edited volumes and books placed with lesser-known publishers. Unusually, Tricia, an assistant professor, used the word 'performativity' to allude to the importance of work not only being done, but being recognized in order to count (Butterwick & Dawson, 2005): 'It's like [to be] seen to be performing, so the kind of work that I do behind the scenes, the intellectual work, is not captured'.

Securing Research Grants

A second area that attracted widespread angst was the emphasis on obtaining external research grants as an indicator of superior performance. Senior faculty realized that this emphasis was new—'now everyone is expected to do research, to publish, to get grants. That's more and more the case' (Aiden)—and often felt that this skewing of academic priorities was wrong. Following the money could mean compromising one's own interests (Enders, de Boer & Leišytė, 2009), and the chances of success for grant proposals were relatively small for Social Sciences and Humanities Research Council (SSHRC) grants.[4] Assistant professors were concerned about the impact of these pressures on their developing careers, especially when there was so much else to do: 'the teaching hasn't gone away' (Poppy).

Increased pressure to obtain grants was mentioned by many associate professors as well: 'the dean is really pushing research' (Ivan); 'there's been a lot of talk around how many people are getting Tri-Council [including SSHRC] grants' (Bethany). Full professor Ethan explained that during his career, grant-writing had shifted from an intellectual pleasure to a bureaucratized process. Along the same lines, associate professor Teresa commented that 'it seems like grant applications are killing so many things that are exciting about academic research'.

Evaluating Teaching

Exclusive or near-exclusive reliance on student course evaluations as an indicator of teaching competence was seen as a key issue and a flawed practice (Iqbal, 2013). Several participants, especially junior ones whose teaching must pass muster to achieve tenure, talked about the 'student as consumer' ethos. Zoe, for example, noted that universities are providing more and more services to students and because the students are paying, they begin to think that 'one of these goods is an "A" in my class'. Katie commented that regardless of one's competence as a teacher, 'if a kid gets a bad grade, they give you a bad evaluation'. It was difficult for pre-tenure faculty to take risks, as Kyle explained:

> I'm pitching a new course this term and you know a new course being what it is, there's all sorts of false starts and all the rest of it. I don't know how they're feeling about it, I'm assuming I'm going to get a low teaching evaluation or lower compared to my other classes and I know I will have to account for that when I go up for tenure.

Students were thought to sometimes react negatively to personal qualities of the instructor, such as accent, race or gender. Teresa said: 'Some faculty of colour, especially female faculty of colour … often find that there is not much respect for their authority'. Marcy connected the lack of respect to course evaluations: 'I have, often, very gendered comments, inappropriate, commenting on my appearance, my clothing, questioning my femininity … attacking my sense of self'. On-line out-of-class evaluations were seen as particularly problematic:

> Since last year [University name] started a new system of evaluation where students do this on-line, and so you have a student who doesn't come to your class, who came to the first class and the last class to see what's going to be on the exam, and then they evaluate you on how you are as a communicator…
> … *The university has done that, given more power to the students than faculty.* [our italics] (Sam)

Reviewing Performance

The tenure review process looms large for junior faculty (Acker, Webber, & Smyth, 2012; Webber & Acker, 2014). Not achieving tenure means losing one's job, and in a sense, one's future. So Katie remarked: 'my entire career is at stake right now'. She added a comment about conformity: 'rocking the boat as an assistant professor is truly not a good idea'. Like participants in our earlier research (Webber & Acker, 2014), Ryan wished for more precise standards: 'How many publications do I need to get, just give me a number'.

But unease around evaluation went beyond points of tenure or promotion. Adding annual performance reviews to the mix appeared to create a sense of being under constant surveillance. Annual reviews, which go by various names (performance review, activity reports, 'merit'), were mentioned by most of the participants. They required that considerable detail and documentation about all of one's accomplishments in a given year be pulled together and submitted, often accompanied by student course evaluations. Details of the assessment process varied, usually including some involvement of a departmental committee, the head of department and the dean. In some universities, the outcome had salary implications. In others, there were no salary improvements, just an assessment, normally taking the form of some type of score or grade, sometimes determined in competition with one's colleagues. Feedback beyond a grade varied from 'nothing', to a one-page form letter, to sitting down with the dean discussing performance and goals for the future. Pre-tenure faculty were more likely than their colleagues to receive feedback and advice.

The reductionism of the annual review process seemed to be particularly disturbing to women, to associate professors, and to faculty of colour. Two scholars of colour were the most critical among the men, both developing the point that it was important first to meet the conventional standards and then go further to 'move across boundaries' or mentor students, even if 'there's no reward for that, almost zero'. The only other complaint from some of the men was the waste of time involved: 'to put these documents together every year takes time, and then certainly for the people who are evaluating all of these files, year in and year out, you know it eats up a great amount of time that people could be putting to better use' (Connor).

Men at all career points were likely to state that they, personally, did not have problems with the various assessments. A typical comment was full professor Edward's:

> I don't have any complaints, myself, about how [annual assessments] have been done, maybe because I tend to do pretty well.

Contrast his response with that of Lillian, a woman full professor:

> I get discouraged with this process of having to think about this annual report every single day, every single year; the putting in of it takes a week of my time; I hate it and I don't know how to actually represent what I do.

Here she echoed Tricia's comment on performativity, quoted above, about the invisibility of work behind the scenes. Lillian elaborated, explaining that 'if a student comes and talks to me in my office ... I never talk to them for less than a couple of hours', while her colleagues might give them fifteen minutes. '[That's how] I choose to do it, but there's no way of reporting that on my annual report, [and] while the other person is writing their next paper, I'm not because I'm still sitting with the student'.

Three women associate professors, Teresa, Brenda and Marcy, showed concern about the lack of feedback in the process. Teresa talked about reports being submitted electronically 'so there's a sense of everything disappearing in a black hole ... there's no feedback whatsoever', while Brenda said 'I've never actually had any feedback ... it's just shovelling more paperwork into a void'. Marcy explained that prior to tenure, the annual report was accompanied by a meeting with the dean, 'But since I've gotten it [tenure], I don't have any feedback ... [just] a form letter, it's not really all that personalized and it's not meaningful at all'.

Opaqueness of the criteria was also a problem. Lillian's university had a complex point system: 'it's made to look like it's objective but in fact, it's totally subjective and some people, especially those working from critical frameworks, like feminists and so on, you could do cartwheels off the CN Tower,[5] you would not get any more than average'. When associate professor Bethany received a rating lower than the one she expected, she wondered what it was that she did not know:

> I started to reflect on that moment ... because for ... years I had no problem and then all of a sudden something happened and where I'm still confused is I don't know how to get those rules of the game. I don't know where the bar is because no one will tell you where the bar is.

We were surprised to see the annual review so prominent in the discussion of performance. Lillian, Teresa, Brenda, Marcy and Bethany work at five different institutions, so this issue is widespread. While universities have, at their best, developed procedures to assist junior faculty through the difficulties of effective teaching, appropriate publishing and even grant acquisition, there seems to be a sudden cessation of effort when people cross the line into a tenured position, while expectations for performance, if anything, continue to rise. The gender difference that we report is understandable in the light of extensive research on the struggles women have had to become an accepted part of the academy, as we noted earlier. With a few exceptions, the women in the study were less overtly confident about their performance and more concerned about performativity and feedback than the men at the same rank (see also Acker & Webber, 2014a). Morley (2005) considers this phenomenon to be in line with 'cultural pressures on women in general to strive for perfection ... like diets and exercise regimes' (p. 425). There was a similar tendency for ethnic minority faculty to express reservations about the annual review (Tierney & Bensimon, 1996). Our few examples are reminiscent of the concept of 'cultural taxation' for minority scholars (Hirshfield & Joseph, 2012)—in this case an extra layer of work as they first need to meet expectations and then do more to meet their commitments to students, community and social justice.

CONCLUSION

While there were variations in how our participants described their job satisfaction, it was clear that overall they enjoyed their work. Yet a different set of questions produced a barrage of complaints. The corporatization of the university (bottom-line decision making, pressures to raise funds, proliferation of administrators) and over-emphasis on performance/performativity together with questionable evaluative criteria combined to produce a sense of what we are labelling *unease*.

To a certain extent, these findings appear contradictory. How can academics be so positive about jobs in a context about which they have become so critical? We think they have simply learned to compartmentalize. Fredman and Doughney (2012) note other studies with similar results, suggesting that academics find ways around the worst aspects of managerialism (p. 45). Yet their own study, in Australia, finds low satisfaction related to perceptions of management culture and policy directions (p. 55). Australia's tightly controlled system for evaluating research performance may have reduced autonomy beyond what most academics can tolerate (Woelert & Yates, 2015).

In general, we agree with Jones (2013) that 'the narrative of crisis that seems to be present in most of the international literature on higher education does not accurately capture the Canadian situation' (p. 78). There are nuances to this narrative. Even when tenure, promotion or annual reviews are a source of stress, academics in Canada who are tenured or on the tenure track have very little fear of job loss and continued expectations of autonomy. This reward comes at the expense of an army of contingent faculty who are increasingly taking up the slack of teaching under conditions inferior to those of regular faculty (Jones, 2013). As we write, faculty on contract at one of Ontario's small northern universities—some of whom have been repeatedly hired for up to ten years—have been told that their contracts will not be renewed.

For 'regular' faculty, a culture of continuous evaluation, while not directly threatening to jobs, apart from the rare tenure review failure (see Acker, Webber, & Smyth, 2012), is a challenge to the cherished academic value of autonomy. Moreover, it reinforces the practice of intensive concentration on one's own research and teaching, a kind of 'eyes-down' effect. Requiring repeated demonstrations of performance in annual reviews without much associated feedback or tangible reward does seem fairly pointless on the face of it. But behind the force of what Foucault (1977) called a 'normalizing judgment' (p. 177) is a disciplinary system based on rewards and punishment that encourages homogeneity (p. 184) and self-surveillance. Bourdieu (1990, p. 112) might call it symbolic violence, a situation where control over definitions of reality (symbolic power) is used to perpetuate the dominance of powerful groups while accepted or 'misrecognized' as an inevitable state of affairs by those less powerful.

We suspect (and certainly hope) that even processes such as the ongoing program prioritization reviews are unlikely to produce redundancies or early retirements like those seen in the UK or Australia (Tuchman, 2013). Technically, financial exigencies can result in program closure and firing of tenured faculty, but there would be a great deal of resistance by faculty unions to such a move. A key point here is that none of the initiatives so far taken by the province reward or punish individuals or departments for good or poor research performance, although it is possible that this situation will change. But the lack of federal governance of higher education means there is no real counterpart to Britain's RAE/REF, New Zealand's PBRF or Australia's ERA. For the time being, provincial quality reviews operate at the level of institutions or departments, not individuals.

Instead of national research exercises there is the drip, drip of peer reviews for papers, grants and conferences, and within the university, judgments around tenure, promotion and 'merit'. Performance is rewarded or punished on an *individual* basis and largely in *internal* processes. These processes are not new – for example, the University of Toronto's 'merit' system was introduced in 1973 – although they may be taking on a new level of intensity as the universities become more immersed in accountability governance. Following years of socialization into an academic habitus (Mendoza et al., 2012), and increasing expectations to be available for work anywhere and anytime (Ylijoki, 2013), academics find what Hey (2004) calls 'perverse pleasures' in driving themselves to ever greater levels of productivity that threaten to swallow up any other life (Gornall & Salisbury, 2012). High levels of satisfaction probably do mean that people come to terms with the drawbacks of the process. We should not be surprised when there are contradictions in social life, but we can also surmise that the aspects of satisfaction attainable for full-time faculty in the Canadian academic workplace are, for now, strong enough to keep at bay the forces of despair.

NOTES

[1] Being hired onto the so-called 'tenure track' means that the individual, usually designated an 'assistant professor', will have their work reviewed in an elaborate process after about 5 years (as well as

earlier interim reviews in less depth) and if satisfactory, will obtain a permanent position, usually accompanied by or followed by a promotion to 'associate professor'. Later in the career, a further promotion to 'full professor' may occur but it is not mandatory to apply, as it is for tenure. We note that hiring is increasingly occurring on a contingent, 'off-track' basis, where there is no guarantee of job security (Acker, Haque, & Webber, in press).

[2] i.e., academic staff. 'Professor' is also used as a generic term.
[3] The references to 'administrators' or 'administrative' would encompass what in the UK would be termed managers/managerial, and may include academic and/or non-academic positions.
[4] Success rates for the SSHRC 'insight grant' competitions were 27% in 2012–2013 and 21.1% in 2013–2014. See http://www.sshrc-crsh.gc.ca/results-resultats/stats-statistiques/index-eng.aspx
[5] A tall landmark building in Toronto.

REFERENCES

Acker, S., & Webber, M. (2014a). Academia as the (com)promised land for women? In L. Gornall, C. Cook, L. Daunton, J. Salisbury, & B. Thomas (Eds.), *Academic working lives* (pp. 199–206). London, England: Bloomsbury.

Acker, S., & Webber, M. (2014b, July 9). *The uneasy academics: Performing and conforming in the contemporary Ontario university*. Paper presented at the Academic Identities Conference, Durham University.

Acker, S., Haque, E., & Webber, M. (in press). The two faces of flexibility—careers and jobs in contemporary academe. In G. Wisker, L. Marshall, S. Greener, & J. Canning (Eds.), *Flexible futures*. Brighton, England: University of Brighton Press.

Acker, S., Webber, M., & Smyth, E. (2012). Tenure troubles and equity matters in Canadian academe. *British Journal of Sociology of Education, 33*(5), 743–761.

Axelrod, P. (2008). Public policy in Ontario higher education: From Frost to Harris. In A. Chan & D. Fisher (Eds.), *The exchange university: Corporatization of academic culture* (pp. 90–114). Vancouver, BC: University of British Columbia Press.

Ball, S. J. (2003). The teacher's soul and the terrors of performativity. *Journal of Education Policy, 18*(2), 215–228.

Bourdieu, P. (1990). *In other words: Essays towards a reflexive sociology*. Stanford, CA: Stanford University Press.

Bruneau, W., & Savage, D. (2002). *Counting out the scholars: The case against performance indicators in higher education*. Toronto, ON: Lorimer.

Butterwick, S., & Dawson, J. (2005). Undone business: Examining the production of academic labour. *Women's Studies International Forum, 28*, 51–65.

Dobbie, D., & Robinson, I. (2008). Reorganizing higher education in the United States and Canada: The erosion of tenure and the unionization of contingent faculty. *Labour Studies Journal, 33*(2), 117–140.

Enders, J., de Boer, H., & Leišytė, L. (2009). New public management and the academic profession: The rationalisation of academic work revisited. In J. Enders & E. de Weert (Eds.), *The changing face of academic life* (pp. 36–57). London, England: Palgrave Macmillan.

Findlow, S. (2008). Accountability and innovation in higher education: A disabling tension? *Studies in Higher Education, 33*(3), 313–329.

Fitzgerald, T., White, J., & Gunter, H. M. (2012). *Hard labour? Academic work and the changing landscape of higher education*. Bingley, England: Emerald.

Foucault, M. (1977). *Discipline and punish: The birth of the prison*. New York, NY: Vintage Books.

Fredman, N., & Doughney, J. (2012). Academic dissatisfaction, managerial change and neo-liberalism. *Higher Education, 64*, 41–58.

Gill, R. (2014). Academics, cultural workers and critical labour studies. *Journal of Cultural Economy, 7*(1), 12–30.

Gornall, L., & Salisbury, J. (2012). Compulsive working, 'hyperprofessionality' and the unseen pleasures of academic work. *Higher Education Quarterly, 66*(2), 135–154.

Government of Ontario, Ministry of Training, Colleges and Universities. (2013, November). *Ontario's differentiation policy framework for post-secondary education*. Retrieved from http://www.tcu.gov.on.ca/pepg/publications/PolicyFramework_PostSec.pdf

Grant, B. M., & Elizabeth, V. (2015). Unpredictable feelings: Academic women under research audit. *British Educational Research Journal, 41*(2), 287–302.

Hey, V. (2004). Perverse pleasures—Identity work and the paradoxes of greedy institutions. *Journal of International Women's Studies, 5*(3), 33–43.

Hirshfield, L., & Joseph, T. (2012). We need a woman, we need a black woman: Gender, race, and identity taxation in the academy. *Gender and Education, 24*(2), 213–227.

Iqbal, I. (2013). Academics' resistance to summative peer review of teaching: Questionable rewards and the importance of student evaluations. *Teaching in Higher Education, 18*(5), 557–569.

Jones, G. A. (2013). The horizontal and vertical fragmentation of academic work and the challenge for academic governance and leadership. *Asia Pacific Educational Review, 14*, 75–83.

Leathwood, C., & Hey, V. (2009). Gender/ed discourses and emotional sub-texts: Theorising emotion in UK higher education. *Teaching in Higher Education, 14*(4), 429–440.

Leathwood, C., & Read, B. (2013). Research policy and academic performativity: Compliance, contestation and complicity. *Studies in Higher Education, 38*(8), 1162–1174.

Lorenz, C. (2012). If you're so smart, why are you under surveillance? Universities, neoliberalism, and new public management. *Critical Inquiry, 38*(3), 599–629.

Lucas, L. (2006). *The research game in academic life*. Maidenhead, England & New York, NY: Open University Press.

Lynch, K. (2006). Neo-liberalism and marketization: The implications for higher education. *European Educational Research Journal, 5*(1), 1–17.

McAlpine, L., Amundsen, C., & Turner, G. (2013). Constructing post-PhD careers: Negotiating opportunities and personal goals. *International Journal for Researcher Development, 4*(1), 39–54.

Mendoza, P., Kuntz, A., & Berger, J. (2012). Bourdieu and academic capitalism: Faculty "habitus" in materials science and engineering. *Journal of Higher Education, 83*(4), 558–581.

Metcalfe, A. (2010). Revising academic capitalism in Canada: No longer the exception. *Journal of Higher Education, 81*(4), 489–514.

Morley, L. (1999). *Organising feminisms: The micropolitics of the academy*. New York, NY: St Martin's Press.

Morley, L. (2005). Opportunity or exploitation? Women and quality assurance in higher education. *Gender and Education, 17*(4), 411–429.

Newson, J., & Polster, C. (2008). Reclaiming our centre: Toward a robust defence of academic autonomy. In A. Chan & D. Fisher (Eds.), *The exchange university: Corporatization of academic culture* (pp. 125–146). Vancouver, BC: University of British Columbia Press.

Ontario Confederation of University Faculty Associations. (2014, December). *Program prioritization reports released at York, Laurier*. Retrieved from http://ocufa.on.ca/blog-posts/faculty/program-prioritization-reports-released-at-york-laurier

Polster, C. (2010). Are we losing our minds? Unreason in Canadian universities today. In J. Newson & C. Polster (Eds.), *Academic callings* (pp. 11–18). Toronto, ON: Canadian Scholars' Press.

Shanahan, T. (2009, January). An overview of the impetus to accountability, its expressions and implications. *Proceedings of the Ontario Confederation of University Faculty Associations, Accounting or Accountability in higher education* (pp. 3–15). Toronto, ON. Retrieved from http://ocufa.on.ca/wordpress/assets/ConferenceProceedingsJan082009.pdf

Shanahan, T., & Jones, G. A. (2007). Shifting roles and approaches: Government coordination of post-secondary education in Canada. *Higher Education Research and Development, 26*(1), 31–43.

Stensaker, B., & Harvey, L. (Eds.). (2011). *Accountability in higher education: Global perspectives on trust and power*. New York, NY: Routledge.

Teelken, C. (2012). Compliance or pragmatism: How do academics deal with managerialism in higher education? A comparative study in three countries. *Studies in Higher Education, 37*(3), 271–290.

Thomas, R., & Davies, A. (2002). Gender and new public management: Reconstituting academic subjectivities. *Gender, Work and Organization, 9*(4), 372–397.

Tierney, W., & Bensimon, E. (1996). *Promotion and tenure: Community and socialization in academe*. Albany, NY: State University of New York Press.

Tuchman, G. (2013, May 7). Oz and us. *Inside Higher Education*. Retrieved from https://www.insidehighered.com/views/2013/05/07/essay-state-budget-cuts-academe-australia-and-us

Uzuner-Smith, S., & Englander, K. (2015). Exposing ideology within university policies: A critical discourse analysis of faculty hiring, promotion and remuneration practices. *Journal of Education Policy, 30*(1), 62–85.

Webber, M., & Acker, S. (March, 2014). *'I'm thinking about tenure from day one': Surveillance, subjectivity and the tenure review process in Ontario universities*. Paper presented at the Comparative and International Education Society Conference, Toronto, ON.

Weinrib, J., Jones, G., Metcalfe, A. S., Fisher, D., Gingras, Y., Rubenson, K., & Snee, I. (2013). Canadian university faculty perceptions of job satisfaction: 'The future is not what it used to be'. In P. Bentley, H. Coates, I. Dobson, L. Goedegebuure, & V. L. Meek (Eds.), *Job satisfaction around the academic world*. Dordrecht, The Netherlands: Springer.

Wilson, M., & Holligan, C. (2013). Performativity, work-related emotions and collective research identities in UK university education departments: An exploratory study. *Cambridge Journal of Education, 43*(2), 223–241.

Woelert, P., & Yates, L. (2015). Too little and too much trust: Performance measurement in Australian higher education. *Critical Studies in Education, 56*(2), 175–189.

Wyn, J., Acker, S., & Richards, E. (2000). Making a difference: Women in management in Australian and Canadian faculties of education. *Gender and Education, 12*(4), 435–447.

Ylijoki, O. H. (2013). Boundary-work between work and life in the high-speed university. *Studies in Higher Education, 38*(2), 242–255.

Sandra Acker
Department of Social Justice Education
Ontario Institute for Studies in Education
University of Toronto, Canada

Michelle Webber
Department of Sociology
Brock University, Canada

TAI PESETA, GIEDRE KLIGYTE, JAN MCLEAN
AND JAN SMITH

6. ON THE CONDUCT OF CONCERN

Exploring How University Teachers Recognise, Engage in, and Perform 'Identity' Practices within Academic Workgroups

INTRODUCTION

In contrast to decades of research attention on individual cognitive based explanations of university teacher thinking and change (Haggis, 2009), the meso-level focus on practice is now receiving greater attention among higher education researchers – influenced in large part by the growing interest in socio-cultural theories of practice (Trowler, 2005; 2008; Roxå & Mårtensson, 2009). Yet the meso-level is a layer of the university that is especially difficult to uncover. Roxå and Mårtensson (2013) argue that this is because of its multiplicity, permeability and fluidity, for instance: is it to be found at the department or discipline level, or within activities that coalesce around specific academic tasks related to research, teaching, curriculum and innovation? Since academic work is itself both messy and political, the literature offers no clear organisational boundaries and it is for these reasons that Roxå and Mårtensson (2013) argue that the meso-level needs to be constructed analytically and understood in terms of both stability and change within local, practice-based contexts. Much existing research about the influences that shape academics' teaching identities interrogates the structuring capacities of disciplines (Kreber, 2009) and departments (Knight & Trowler, 2000). Yet these two entities carry the problem that disciplinarity has been complicated by the interdisciplinarity of mode 2 knowledge (Nowotny, Scott, & Gibbons, 2001) – that is knowledge generated and applied in-situ – and that academic department formation and transformation is as much about the logic of risk management as it is about providing a home for cognate intellectual interests, paradigms and traditions. The emerging emphasis on what Trowler (2008) terms a *workgroup* – 'the point of social interaction by small groups such as those in the classroom, in university departments, in the curriculum planning team, or in a hundred other task-based teams within the higher education system' (p. 20) is, however, capturing the imagination of researchers interested in both how academics negotiate the local terrain of learning, teaching and curriculum renewal and change, and how the efforts of large-scale institution-wide educational change programs become understood, internalised, and in some cases, subject to refusal.

With the workgroup as fertile ground for interrogating university teacher identity formation and transformation, many questions appear fresh on the horizon. One set of curiosities relates to the knowledge and know-how that informs teaching practices, and how these flow through and are taken up in the workgroup. While many beginning university teachers tend to teach in the way they were themselves taught or as a reaction against those experiences, the workgroup may well be seen as a site for conversation – where neophyte understandings of teaching, learning and curriculum are tested, reframed, affirmed or challenged by others. It is through discourses of regulation, control, concern and exclusion that academics learn about the ideas, practices, and identities that count as legitimate. These processes become more visible when scholarly and institutional knowledge and know-how circulates anew within the workgroup, testing established identities and practices. One source of new knowledge and know-how is the formal award course known as the graduate/postgraduate certificate in university teaching (hereafter GCert). Research indicates that university teachers exit these courses armed with an increased repertoire of teaching strategies together with a more complex way of approaching teaching and conceptualising student learning (Ho, Watkins, & Kelly, 2001; Gibbs & Coffey, 2004). While little is known about how the teachers' new knowledge and know-how gained via these programs flows through the academic workgroups they labour in, even less is known about how these workgroups operate when a number of university teachers come to share new scholarly knowledge and know-how.

In this chapter, we draw on semi-structured interviews with academics from an interdisciplinary field of social sciences who have completed a GCert[1] and who work together in a research-intensive university. We suggest that their labour together as teachers comprises an academic workgroup. We first provide a rationale for our focus on GCerts as a vehicle for our study; second, we offer a contextual description of the workgroup as well as a brief account of the participants involved in the study;[2] third, we draw on interview data to explore the kinds of teacher identities that are made available (or summoned) through the agendas, structures, and assemblages of activity and interaction that these academics engage in. We are especially interested in how scholarly and institutional knowledge and know-how from the GCert becomes mobilised; that is, how it is put to use by our interviewees as a mechanism for them to (mis)recognise the identity struggles of others, and perform appropriate university teacher identities themselves. Our analysis draws primarily on Bendix Petersen's (2008) notion of the 'conduct of concern' – a reading of Foucault's notion of governmentality:

> Exploring the conduct of concern as a readily available discursive practice is a way of analysing the 'microphysics' of power (Foucault, 1980) at play within academic culture; a way of asking how academic cultures are continued or discontinued, and how it comes to be that certain subjects and positionings are recognised as appropriate or inappropriate. It is an entry into trying to understand 'who makes it' and who doesn't; what subjects need to do, think,

say and be in order to be recognised, by themselves and others, as relevant and competent in an academic context. (p. 397)

For Bendix Petersen (2008), like us, it is the discursive regulation of self and other that is the focus of attention, rather than the truth or accuracy of individual experiences per se. In other words, 'the conduct of concern is a kind of governmental style, shaping, sculpting or regulating the discursive practices of others; as a kind of positioning and subject position' (p. 396). And in relation to the peculiarities of academic work, Bendix Petersen (2008) writes 'when we find academic colleagues' actions, utterances and enterprises disturbing or wrong, we publicly express *concern* for them. We might even express *serious* concern' (p. 396). In this chapter, we flesh out precisely how this 'concern' is conducted about university teaching among the academics in our workgroup as a mechanism for recognising, performing and renewing their own identities.

RESEARCHING THE RELATIONS BETWEEN GCERTS AND ACADEMIC WORKGROUPS

The GCert option is available to academics keen to improve their teaching, assessment and curriculum practices. Despite criticism of its length (typically between 1–2 years), timing (for new academics, to be completed before the probation and/or confirmation period), and relevance (Onsman, 2011), it remains a mainstay of academic and educational development in many Anglophone universities. While there is a desire for in-depth, challenging, and reflective engagement with the powerful knowledge that has informed the foundations of higher education teaching and learning as a field of study (Kandlbinder & Peseta, 2009), the question of the GCert's direct impact on actual students' learning remains for some, unanswered.

While GCerts appear to have had positive impacts in significant areas (on teachers' conceptions of teaching and student learning; teacher confidence; developing a greater repertoire of student-focused teaching strategies), Chalmers and Gardiner (2015) accept that 'there is limited research which shows the impact of teacher training on organisational policy, culture, practices and support... the consequence of the focus and purpose of the training program being targeted at the teachers and students' (p. 60). Because our study is an attempt to learn how groups of academics deploy knowledge and know-how from the GCert to enact a teaching identity, we focus on local academic cultures, practices and histories, and how these instantiate loose boundaries of propriety for developing and transforming as a teacher. Trowler and Cooper (2002) call these 'teaching and learning regimes' (TLRs) – workgroup level understandings about how things are done (including values and assumptions established over time about students, curriculum, knowledge, the discipline and the relations between them). TLRs do not, however, imply consensus. Trowler (2009) argues that although they are shot through with 'power, conflict, and diversity' (p. 186), it is precisely this layer of relations, activities and interactions, that require further and sensitive interrogation if institutional ambitions for learning and teaching enhancement are to be realised.

Our attention is on one specific workgroup in the social sciences. Four of its members have achieved a GCert and our curiosity traces two particular themes from interviews with them. First, we draw on the idea of 'the conduct of concern' as a site that generates friction for the development of teacher identities. We explore how these academics express 'concern' as a political strategy for accomplishing themselves as teachers who are distinct from others. Second, we trace how knowledge and know-how learned via the GCert is deployed as a form of identity (mis)recognition in the workgroup.

CHARACTERISING THE WORKGROUP

Organizationally, the workgroup sits within a faculty of arts and social sciences with specific links to law and social sciences for its teaching programs. Undergraduate student numbers are strong with projected future growth, presenting a challenge to the Faculty who now need to offer the program for two cohorts each year. Staffing comprises seven academic staff: two professors and five lecturers/senior lecturers (L/SL). Three of the five L/SLs provided data for our project, as did the Deputy Head of School (Learning & Teaching, L&T), who considers this team as amongst the School's most innovative teachers. The teaching team has a mainly productive work ethos, rotating the teaching of large core subjects among them.

Our interviewees are Rose, Helen, Ian, and Margo (all pseudonyms). Rose is a lecturer with a long history at the University beginning with her doctoral studies in the early 2000s. She earned a full-time academic appointment by the mid-2000s and completed the GCert in 2011. Helen arrived at the University in 2010. She began the GCert at her previous university and completed in 2013 at the University in question. She was recently promoted to senior lecturer. Ian was also recently promoted to SL. While he has more than 10 years of itinerant university teaching experience, he transitioned to a full-time teaching and research position only in the last three years after considerable experience in a research-only post. He completed the GCert in 2014. Margo has led the School's L&T portfolio since 2012 having arrived at the university in 2011. While she is not strictly located in the workgroup, Margo is considered by the other interviewees to lead strategy and enhancement in ways that shape and affect their experiences and practices as teachers. She completed a GCert at a university overseas.

Constructing the 'Subject/Object/Relations' of Concern

In her article teasing out the ways academics participate in the conduct of concern as a strategy for delineating legitimacy and boundary maintenance, Bendix Petersen (2008) proposes a number of related storylines. The first storyline she calls 'coming to the rescue'. It works on the idea that 'a particular researcher, a group of researchers, or a school of thought seem to need some help of some kind' (p. 397) and that the person expressing concern is best placed to offer the solution. In her study, concern is directed at getting misguided researchers on the 'right track'; in ours, we are interested in interrogating how this storyline plays out for academics' teaching roles. The second storyline Bendix Petersen (2008) offers is a concern that some academics have become 'worryingly trendy'. This is about '… being positioned as subscribing to a fashionable trend within academia [and] within this discursive framework, [is] concerning because it invokes images of being a casualty of mass whim and for undertaking the academic enterprise for the wrong reasons' (p. 400). The third summons the ideal and default subject position that academics must be rational and autonomous. To be otherwise suggests that:

> … something has taken possession of this colleague's or this group of colleagues' sensible and critical judgement. They are insensate victims of some sort; they have somehow forgotten or betrayed the idea/l of 'the good', 'the true', and 'the right'. What they have failed to do, the storyline seems to imply, is to embody the notion of the autonomous, rational academic subject. (p. 401)

Across all four interviews, we explore the way these storylines can be read into these teachers' accounts of themselves, their positioning of others, and how they mobilise the knowledge and know-how that the GCert has made available to them to establish, renew and perform particular sorts of university teacher identities. First, Margo:

> … it's not a matter of individual academics determining what they want to teach and how they want to teach it with no regulation or oversight but actually, all courses feeding into a program which feeds into attaining a [particular University] level of graduate capabilities, and a recognition of the individual academic as a course authority, playing a role in a bigger machine if you like. I think for some that's quite a challenging realisation, especially given the very strong culture of academic freedom that seems to have been in place. So I think there's an element of resistance to that, but equally all the people that I work with are very smart and very committed and it's about finding the right way to communicate the changes that are happening, to not say to people, I don't care if you've always done it like that, you're doing it wrong. But to say to people, look this is the changing environment; this is the reason why it's really important that we do adhere to this practice, or this particular protocol, which has actually always been in place. It's now just that we are held to a higher standard, or there's more accountability, or a need for more transparency. So a lot of it is about guiding practice in a particular way and finding the right words to communicate that to teaching staff. (*Margo, Deputy Head of L&T*)

Margo's leadership responsibilities indicate that she is especially prone to discourses of change, flexibility and inevitability. She sees herself as someone who is an astute 'reader' of change. Margo hopes to persuade her colleagues to get on the 'right track', with her. She recognises that the time of unfettered academic autonomy is no longer, and that new forms of institutional subjectivity trump rather than erase individual academic judgement. She leads change through a collective appeal to 'reason' believing that academics as smart and rational subjects will come to realise that the 'system' now contains a different sort of logic from which contradictory pressures flow. Margo appears to understand that the machinery of university bureaucracy relies on protocols, accountability, and transparency (particularly prevalent in the overseas context she came from), which she sees as an inevitable consequence of the marketization of education. It is not clear, however, whether she personally equates these functions with holding academics to some higher moral standard. She relies on her communicative skill to put these additional bureaucratic demands into some 'reasonable' context, and by doing so, Margo invites teaching staff into a discourse of 'responsibilisation' where she is looking to lead others in her own image. Like many leaders, she embodies a form of the 'coming to the rescue' narrative.

The 'big picture' reading and the larger narrative do not appear in Ian's account of himself. His concerns are practical: for students – will they have the proper skills?; for the teachers – how can we make the content real and applied?; and the discipline – will it have a workforce and practitioners adequate to what the future demands?

> I trained in psychology and I was teaching into a Masters program where it was quite practically focused teaching students professional skills. Because I did the Masters program degree myself, my experiences of being taught was that it was just too focused on content and not on translating that into something real and practical, so I was really keen to try to give students something that was a bit more applied. (*Ian, SL*)

In the effort to ameliorate the dangers and inadequacies of his own student learning experience, Ian's pedagogical concerns seem real and sensible. Like Margo, he believes in the power of rational argument when it comes to convincing others, and perceives no resistance in advancing his ideas. Left alone to conduct themselves, Ian offers a view of the academic subject acting rationally – the second of Bendix Petersen's storylines.

> I think that academics, in the end, are convinced by good, reasoned argument about why we do things, and arguments that focus on student experience and on good pedagogy. […] These are – I don't think they're very controversial types of issues. I really haven't had any push back at all from others. (*Ian*)

Rose, on the other hand is blunt about the ways teaching and curriculum are organised in the workgroup. Like Ian, she expresses concern about whether students will leave the university with the wrong, or no skills but unlike him, Rose worries that the discipline has been inappropriately loosened from its proper social science moorings. She also positions her views about curriculum change in relation to her lack of influence in the academic hierarchy.

> I have grand visions of completely revamping our curricula to move towards a problem solving, problem oriented design because I still think we have heaps of problems, and our graduates have none of the skills we actually want them to have [laughs]. Rather than just doing these 12week lectures where no one comes, we should be taking real life [cases], putting them [students] into small groups, getting them to solve these problems and teaching the content that they need to solve the problems along the way. At the moment, we divide up our courses based on traditional ways of teaching – we teach theory in third year, we teach methods in the first, second and third. It's all segmented and really what they need to be a real [specialist in the sub-discipline] is social science. I have actually tried to have that conversation and I do believe that because I'm at the bottom of the pecking order as a lecturer, those conversations have gone nowhere [laughs]. They're not popular because people think they're going to be too much work. (*Rose, Lecturer*)

Rose appears to be alone in diagnosing the particularities of the problem (the workgroup is too bound to traditional modes of organising teaching; knowledge of the discipline is inherently messy which should be reflected in the teaching) and alone in wanting to shoulder the work load of curriculum change. Working part-time, Rose appears to be somewhat disconnected from the conversations that maintain the workgroup cohesion. This may also be due to Rose's long tenure at the University (considerably longer than Helen and Ian): 'I was here by myself to start with so I just made all the decisions. Then by the time we had new staff coming in, the program was building'. It is also likely that Rose carries institutional memories not shared by others, and she attributes her lack of influence over learning and teaching matters in the workgroup to her status as a lecturer. While the transcripts make clear that Ian and Helen have a robust and trusted working relationship, (for them, conversations are the result of co-teaching and co-designing courses) despite being a pioneer, Rose is largely absent from either of their accounts of how the workgroup operates. With Rose, it is her reading of what 'students need' that ought to drive curriculum change. The laughter might indicate a belief that Rose's colleagues cannot see, or are dismissive of her concerns. In other words, Rose chooses the education of students, while her colleagues choose other things. With Margo, there is something of the 'rescue' storyline evident, however the dynamics shape up in ways that carry less institutional authority and appear to alienate Rose from her workgroup colleagues.

Helen's pedagogical views are attuned with the rest of the workgroup members, including Margo, and she is comfortable with her positioning in the group.

> … like everyone's luckily all on the same page about teaching and we all think it's important and want to make sure that we do everything right, or as best we can…. I wouldn't say there's necessarily a pedagogical approach that we've explicitly articulated amongst ourselves but we all meet at the end of every semester and we'll talk about how courses went and we'll discuss the core courses which any one of us could teach at any time, and speak about how

things might be done differently or what worked and didn't work. So we share that knowledge and share ideas informally. (*Helen, SL*)

For her, the expression of 'concern' comes to the fore not so much in terms of teaching practices or concern about students, but when there is a potential new entrant to the workgroup.

> Honestly, every time we get someone new we're always paranoid that it's going to be someone that maybe won't want to talk to us or won't want to see the things the way we do.... It would be for example, and maybe this is not so much around teaching, but it has an impact on teaching, if someone's really research focused, often they're not that interested in teaching, and so they'll do what they have to... but they won't do any more than that. I mean obviously we're all interested in research but, touch wood, it doesn't seem like anyone's interested to the point of neglecting teaching, or, I don't know. Maybe that doesn't happen in other groups, I know – but I do know that other areas, people will be very precious about things they do want to teach or don't want to teach and when they want to teach or how. (*Helen*)

Focused on the prospect that the workgroup might be disrupted, Helen makes clear that there are established rhythms, routines and dispositions that have been worked out between them, and that hold the group together. Helen expresses the expectation that workgroup members regularly do more than they are allocated, and more than they have to. In Helen's portrayal, the message is clear: this is a workgroup looking for colleagues that align with the way teaching is done. In Bendix Petersen's (2008) terms, the rational academic is invited to operate in concert with the logic enacted by the workgroup rather than that of individual advancement. While the enactment of 'concern' in the workgroup draws identity boundaries in all manner of ways – explicit, subtle, and indirect among them – the equilibrium seems fragile. There is every likelihood that it could be disrupted by a new workgroup member who prioritises research, or whose view of teaching is out of kilter with its existing members and what they are seeking to accomplish.

Knowledge and Know-How: The Struggle for Identity Recognition in the Workgroup

Two aspects of this theme interest us: the first is *knowledge* (a new vocabulary or framework for making sense of teaching), and the second is *know-how* (confidence to innovate, undertake teaching and learning inquiry, and engagement with institutional agendas). While new knowledge and know-how feature prominently in the research about what academics learn through participating in GCerts (Butcher & Stoncel, 2012; Stewart, 2014), our curiosity takes a slightly different shape. We explore how these academics position their knowledge and know-how in ways that bring them recognition – especially in ways that link these practices to the pleasures of being good teachers. Typical in the literature about GCerts and other educational development programs is that there is an increase in the repertoire of teaching strategies, and a confidence to try them out in practice. For instance Rose takes the traditional lecture and turns around its associated didacticism:

> I learned a whole heap of actual strategies. So if you're doing a lecture and you've got 600 first year students in a tiered lecture theatre, what can you still do to make that an active learning environment? You don't have to start with something really boring. You can have the lights out and you can start with a newspaper article talking about [...] to wake them up. You can do pop quizzes. You can do things under their seat where they get a prize. You can do periods of solo reflection or turn to the person next to you. All those things – that's in the lecture theatre. (*Rose*)

In doing so, she establishes herself as someone who is a capable and lively teacher despite the containment of the lecture space. Rose's commitment to providing students with an active learning environment signals that she is willing to take her inspiration from anywhere – and in this way, she accomplishes herself as someone with the knowledge and know-how of seeing the discipline through the students' eyes. There is also a quantitative aspect to Rose's account of her lecture strategies – it is the sheer number of different activities at her disposal, and a delight perhaps, that no one lecture might ever be the same. And, there is undoubtedly pride in being able to exercise the full range of her repertoire. The diversity of techniques Rose can deploy in a lecture is how she recognises herself as distinct from others.

For Helen, the GCert and the opportunities that have flowed from it, have positioned her as the local expert:

> I mean it's [GCert] not always teaching you how to teach per se but it's giving you, I guess, different ways of thinking in terms of approaching your teaching and approaching course design and students and learning styles and all that sort of stuff will pop up. It also, like, I don't know, everyone thinks I'm now the learning and teaching guru. I don't know how that happened... I'm like the expert and I get to do these things... ok, well I suppose that's a benefit as well. (*Helen*)

While she seems bemused and slightly ambivalent about this new prestige being bestowed upon her, she accepts its rewards too – a promotion to Senior Lecturer as well as funding to lead blended learning initiatives. Helen's guru status is confirmed by her colleague Ian whose own teacher development owes a great deal to the nature of her influence: 'compared to other conversations I've had with other academics, she did have a more – a deeper appreciation for assessment and teaching and the philosophies underlying it'. For Ian, co-teaching with Helen before he had completed the GCert himself, had heightened his desire to learn what she knew – perhaps the ultimate expression of recognition:

...when I would talk with her, she would talk about the materials that she'd got from doing the GCert and the fact that she learnt about rubrics and how to put rubrics together and how to construct assessments and alignment and all those kinds of things. So that was an influence, a positive influence. (*Ian*)

As one might expect, Margo's knowledge, know-how, and leadership is subject to regular assessment. Because she too has the equivalent of a GCert, Margo shares the vocabulary of learning and teaching scholarship, and can draw on its conceptual resources to frame and re-frame responses to learning and teaching challenges. This is very often a point of difference and distinction among senior leaders who may be seen to be driving an educational change program from an impoverished view of scholarship and evidence (Ramsden, 1998). And it helps too that Margo's style is regarded favourably by the workgroup, and that she exhibits a commitment to testing out the teaching ideas she commends to others. Margo is recognised as both a teacher, and a leader and communicator of learning and teaching change:

She gives us a very good 40-minute discussion in our school meetings about what's happening at faculty level, school level, expectations at course level, areas where you can opt in and out of projects. She's really great, we always know what's going on. (*Rose*)

She knows what we're doing and is quite supportive of what we do... I think she's tried out quite a few things in her teaching practice, trying to be innovative. Yeah, so she's very proactive, not just doing the admin she has to do but actually trying to implement changes, strengthen policy, all that stuff. She is way across everything so she's the best person. (*Helen*)

Academics in the workgroup depict the desired teacher subjectivity as someone who displays genuine pedagogical interests, demonstrates flexibility, openness and a willingness to explore. Innovation and risk-taking are legitimised, recognised by Margo as the hallmark of this workgroup.

They're a very effective group. They're very functional in terms of their group dynamic. They're very willing to innovate, or to explore innovation. I wonder whether that perhaps comes from a confidence in their own pedagogical ability...I see in [this] group a real willingness to go out on a limb, try something new, but also the ability to say, you know what, after 2 years that didn't work. We tried it, we thought it might work, it didn't work, and that's okay. I think that confidence comes from grounding in an understanding that good pedagogy is driven by creativity and a willingness to take risks. (*Margo*)

Workgroup members welcome and expect from each other an appetite for continuous improvement; for designing teaching and curriculum in ways that enhance the student experience; for rotating teaching leadership responsibilities enabling opportunities for promotion; for supporting Margo's strategic School-based efforts at assessment renewal; and for engaging with the University's current priorities on technological innovation. This is where knowledge encounters know-how in the workgroup. Rose, however, questions the underlying motivation for much of the innovation the workgroup prides itself on, including the recognition it receives from others:

> If you can change your course to make it cheaper, then well done! That's great. But really, that's all. You're never going to get recognition for being a good teacher. It was not going to get you a promotion. It's not going to get you a pat on the back. Nobody will notice [laughs]. (*Rose*)

Rose's experiences do not accord much with Margo's portrayal of learning and teaching in the workgroup or the School – which tends toward an imperative of improvement connected with facilitating quality student learning. Rose highlights the tensions between the efficiency so valued in the University, and the genuine pedagogical benefits for the students. Her dissidence, however, does not seem to affect the general workings of the group. It is glossed over, and good relations prevail. It is not so much that conflict in the workgroup is avoided, it is rather, sublimated to the general collegial disposition and commitment to teaching.

As a learning and teaching leader, Margo hopes for a new breed of academic; someone unattached to old ways, who recognises the need for efficiency, and who concedes their academic freedoms for the benefit of students. The GCert holders appear to fit the bill:

> I perceive a difference between staff that have the GCert versus staff that have come a different route to develop their teaching expertise. I see generally they are quicker, more willing to grasp the big picture issues. Also, a different engagement with the students – I think actually a much healthier engagement with the student. I mean I see very committed teachers that see all students as individuals, but then consider that this means every course needs tailoring for that individual student rather than recognising that personalised learning isn't about treating every student as an individual and tracking an individual path for them, but about actually about making the student the centre of the learning experience and putting the onus on the student. (*Margo*)

UNIVERSITY TEACHER IDENTITIES IN CONTEXT: OPENINGS FOR NEW CONVERSATIONS

An aim of so many GCerts is that university teachers develop an appreciation that students are at the heart of the learning endeavour, and that it is student learning rather than teaching performance that galvanises a workgroup into action. In many cases, appropriate university teacher identities come to be synonymous with the capacity to facilitate student learning, no matter the circumstance, difficulty or consequences for academics. And this is mainly what GCerts have set out to achieve – in its curricula and institutional strategy. In the contemporary university, it is near impossible to escape what Ramsden (1992: 5) has so eloquently expressed, that, 'good teaching makes student learning possible'. This conflation has emerged as the legitimate and recognised identity for university teachers everywhere.

These interviews suggest that knowledge and know-how learned via GCert participation does indeed circulate through the workgroup, and unsurprisingly, with different effects. Each of the four academics draws on its knowledge and know-how (and their active construction of it) to make arguments about improving teaching and learning. As L&T leader, Margo's concerns set the tone for the problems that require attention and the available courses of action. She works to translate the unending horizon of higher education change for her colleagues, and by and large, she is supported in that venture. This is a powerful form of boundary setting yet the enactment of concern does not appear to be part of Margo's understanding of her leadership. In Helen and Ian's case, the knowledge and know-how that informs their teaching practices and frames how they see problems is shared and collegial in part because they teach together – actively co-producing meaning with each other. In Roxå and Mårtensson's (2009) terms, there is trust and they are significant to each other. In many ways, the workgroup has become the testing ground for their new teaching know-how, and in working together, they lean on each other to navigate the terrain, to marshal resources and to shape the rules of engagement. Yet for Rose, although we are privy to the display of her internal confidence, we also see a struggle for recognition that manifests in routine disempowerment. Ultimately, there are clearly some confident teacher identities emerging – ones that may subjugate individual desire for cohesion and program effectiveness.

Our study is an attempt to contribute to existing research conversations about the impact and effects of university teaching development programs, and to expand the conceptual lenses that are put to use in that effort. While our focus on workgroups is perhaps an unusual one, with Bendix Petersen (2008), we argue that attending to the micro-physics of power – or concern and recognition as styles of governmentality – offers a set of compelling insights about the mechanisms that animate stability and change in local academic cultures.

NOTES

[1] This study is part of a larger project: *The flow of new knowledge practices: an inquiry into teaching, learning and curriculum dynamics in academic workgroups* involving 8 universities across Australia, England and South Africa. It is led by Tai Peseta at the University of Sydney.
[2] Consistent with the project's ethics approval, the interviewees' names have been changed.

REFERENCES

Bendix Petersen, E. (2008). The conduct of concern: Exclusionary discursive practices and subject positions in academia. *Educational Philosophy and Theory, 40*(3), 394–406.
Butcher, J., & Stoncel, D. (2012). The impact of a postgraduate certificate in teaching in higher education on university lecturers appointed for their professional expertise at a teaching-led university: 'It's made me braver'. *International Journal for Academic Development, 17*(2), 149–162.

Chalmers, D., & Gardiner, D. (2015). The measurement and impact of university teacher development programs. *Educar, 51*(1), 53–80.
Gibbs, G., & Coffey, M. (2004). The impact of training of university teachers on their teaching skills, their approach to teaching and the approach to learning of their students. *Active Learning in Higher Education, 5*(1), 87–100.
Haggis, T. (2009). What have we been thinking of? A critical overview of 40 years of student learning research in higher education. *Studies in Higher Education, 34*(4), 377–390.
Ho, A., Watkins, D., & Kelly, M. (2001). The conceptual change approach to improving teaching and learning: An evaluation of a Hong Kong staff development program. *Higher Education, 42,* 143–169.
Kandlbinder, P., & Peseta, T. (2009). Key concepts in postgraduate certificates in higher education teaching and learning in Australasia and the United Kingdom. *International Journal for Academic Development, 14*(1), 19–31.
Knight, P. T., & Trowler, P. R. (2000). Department-level cultures and the improvement of learning and teaching. *Studies in Higher Education, 25*(1), 69–83.
Kreber, C. (Ed.). (2009). *The university and its disciplines: Teaching and learning within and beyond disciplinary boundaries.* New York, NY: Routledge.
Nowotny, H., Scott, P., & Gibbons, M. (2001). *Re-thinking science: Knowledge and the public in an age of uncertainty.* Cambridge, England: Polity Press.
Onsman, A. (2011). Proving the pudding: Optimising the structure of academic development. *Journal of Higher Education and Policy Management, 33*(5), 485–496.
Ramsden, P. (1992). *Learning to teach in higher education.* New York, NY & England: Routledge.
Ramsden, P. (1998). *Learning to lead in higher education.* London, England & New York, NY: Routledge.
Roxå, T., & Mårtensson, K. (2009). Significant conversations and significant networks – Exploring the backstage of the teaching arena. *Studies in Higher Education, 34*(5), 547–559.
Roxå, T., & Mårtensson, K. (2013). How effects from teaching-training of academic teachers propagate in the meso level and beyond. In E. Simon & G. Pleschová (Eds.), *Teacher development in higher education: Existing programs, program impact and future trends* (pp. 213–233). New York, NY: Routledge.
Stewart, M. (2014). Making sense of a teaching programme for university academics: Exploring the longer-term effects. *Teaching and Teacher Education, 38,* 89–98.
Trowler, P. (2008). *Cultures and change in higher education: Theories and practice.* Gordonsville, VA: Palgrave MacMillan.
Trowler, P. (2009). Beyond epistemological essentialism: Academic tribes in the twenty-first century. In C. Kreber (Ed.), *The university and its disciplines: Teaching and learning within and beyond disciplinary boundaries* (pp. 181–195). New York, NY: Routledge.
Trowler, P. R. (2005). A sociology of teaching, learning and enhancement: Improving practices in higher education. *Revisita de Sociologica, 76,* 13–32.
Trowler, P., & Cooper, A. (2002). Teaching and learning regimes: Implicit theories and recurrent practices in the enhancement of teaching and learning through educational development programs. *Higher Education Research and Development, 21*(3), 221–240.

Tai Peseta
Institute for Teaching and Learning
University of Sydney, Australia

Giedre Kligyte
Learning and Teaching Unit
University of New South Wales, Australia

Jan McLean
Learning and Teaching Unit
University of New South Wales, Australia

Jan Smith
School of Education
Durham University, UK

DOROTHY SPILLER AND PIP BRUCE FERGUSON

7. FINDING A TŪRANGAWAEWAE

A Place to Stand as a Tertiary Educator

INTRODUCTION

To the uninitiated, the story of an academic career may appear relatively straightforward; individuals succeed in a particular discipline at undergraduate and postgraduate level, complete a doctorate in a specialised aspect of that discipline and then take up a position at a tertiary institution that usually requires some combination of teaching, research and administration. This linear narrative has probably always been illusory and disguised the complex challenges of the academic profession. This complexity is even more apparent today, when obtaining a permanent academic position is increasingly difficult, and academics are beset by multiple narratives about the purposes of higher education. Some of these stories are in the public and institutional domains, other narrative fragments are told and retold in staffrooms and over coffee, while others are private hopes and uncertainties. Many stories and story fragments are deeply buried in the collective memory and barely articulated, but retain a powerful grip on teacher thinking and behaviours.

While it is impossible to separate the different strands of an academic's work, we are particularly interested in the power that public and private stories have over academics in their role as tertiary educators. It is our belief, based on work as teaching developers and our research that academics need to examine their cognitive and emotional understanding of their teacher identity as an integral part of their professional development. The weight of multiple narratives and story fragments is so powerful and full of contradictions that individuals need a space to explore and begin to claim a voice for themselves as tertiary educators. This does not mean that they will escape the turbulent tides of the contemporary tertiary environment, but they can navigate these tides more effectively. We draw respectfully on the Māori concept of tūrangawaewae which conveys the idea of having a place to stand with a sense of belonging and conviction. It is our belief that in our role as teaching developers, we have an obligation to help academics to find that firm space to stand as tertiary educators. In this chapter, we focus on the role that the personal portfolio in our Postgraduate Certificate in Tertiary Teaching can have in sharpening this tertiary educator understanding. We share a small research study that was designed to investigate whether the development of the personal portfolio helped academics to strengthen their identity as tertiary educators. In this research account, two words are especially important: emotion and story. Emotion is important because it is a key component of teacher identity and stories because of the interest in how the personal portfolio enables exploration of multiple narratives and the crafting of a personal story of educator identity.

Literature

Two main strands in the literature informed this research: the importance of emotional knowledge in the complicated tapestry of knowledge that equips teachers to engage with their work and the presence of multiple narratives which influence the way teachers understand themselves and their role.

While there has been a growing literature about the significance of emotion in teachers' lives, tertiary teacher education does not often acknowledge explicitly that managing the affective dimension is a core component of teacher understanding. As Zembylas (2007) suggests, making sense of this tumultuous terrain should be a core component of PCK (Pedagogical Content Knowledge). Zembylas (2007) terms the complex amalgam of knowledge systems that a teacher needs 'knowledge ecology' (p. 356) which consists of multiple strands of essential knowledge including discipline and curriculum knowledge, knowledge of learners and self, emotional knowledge and core values. In the emotionally charged space in which teachers and learners meet, a key element in this knowledge needs to be 'emotional ecology' (Zembylas, 2007: 356). This is a term from organisational theory used to refer to the emotional milieu in which learning interactions occur. Zembylas reminds us of the multi-textured nature of these interactions and (drawing on the work of Bronfenbrenner, 1989) conceptualises this complex fabric of interrelationships as an 'ecological system' with a number of sub-systems (2007). These are the 'microsystem' (the immediate context), the 'mesosystem' (the connections between microsystems), the 'ecosystem' (forces that are not experienced directly by the teacher but still impact on them) and the 'chromosystem', time-specific patterns and influences. Our conceptualisation of the multi-layered context in which teachers have to find their way is close to that proffered by Zembylas, but in keeping with our narrative model, we conceptualise these sub-systems as intersecting narratives.

The influence of multiple narratives on teacher thinking and behaviours is well-documented in the work of Clandinin and Connelly (1996). For these authors the question is '[h]ow is teacher knowledge shaped by the professional knowledge context in which teachers work?' (1996: 24). They coined the term 'professional knowledge landscapes' which they position at 'the interface of practice and theory in teachers' lives' (1996: 24) and distinguish between 'secret stories' the stories that teachers play out within their classrooms and 'sacred stories' which are 'funnelled into' the system from a range of sources outside of the classroom. The part of the narrative landscape that Day and Leitch (2001) focus on in their study of the role of emotion in teachers' lives is personal autobiography and the way in which personal histories can help teachers to understand their professional identity; this approach corresponds closely to the interests of our research inquiry.

Moon and Fowler (2008) provide a useful typology of narrative genres that we draw on in trying to highlight specific features of teachers' individual stories and the narratives in their 'professional knowledge landscapes' (Clandinin & Connelly, 1996). Moon and Fowler (2008) distinguish between personal stories, 'known' stories, non-fiction, but 'not personally known stories' and 'fiction and fantasy'. The idea of 'known' and 'not personally known stories' is especially pertinent; Moon and Fowler (2008) describe these respectively as 'the stories told informally or formally among people who share experiences such as within a profession' and the stories 'that are at a distance from an individual, but that are taken to be "true" or authentic accounts within a real experience or context' (p. 234). The idea of influential narratives that are not 'personally known' corresponds to some degree to Boje's 'organisational stories' (2001). Boje's concept of 'antenarratives', multiple interwoven fragments that do not have the coherence of ordered narratives, is a helpful corrective to analytical distinctions between types of stories. We suggest, that in the higher education context, 'not personally known' stories are infused with 'fiction and fantasy' (Moon & Fowler, 2008) because they have been overlaid by telling and retelling sometimes acquiring the power of mythology.

A framework built on these different understandings of teacher landscapes has been constructed as a tool for investigating the individual teaching and learning narratives that academics explored in their personal portfolios. In order to group the ways in which the process of personal portfolio writing impacted on the tertiary teacher identity of these academics, we try to identify recurrent storylines and associated metaphors in their narratives, reflections and interviews. In paying attention to metaphor we draw on the study of Martin and Lueckenhausen (2005) who analyse metaphor to capture affective as well as cognitive changes in university teachers. Building on the work of Lakoff and Johnson (1983, 1999) among others, Martin and Lueckenhausen argue for the rich mix of cognition, emotion and practical lived experience that metaphor can capture. These authors see metaphor as something which 'cross maps our overall abstract experience of the world to solid structures that underpin our concrete experience' (2005: 391).

Method

Participants in this study were drawn from a group of teachers who completed their portfolios as part of the Postgraduate Certificate in Tertiary Teaching at the University of Waikato New Zealand in 2013. After obtaining ethical approval, we contacted this cohort and invited them to participate in the research. Six teachers out of a total of 12 agreed to be involved, four from the university sector and two from the polytechnic context. Interviews were conducted in person or via Skype, audio-recorded and subsequently transcribed. In addition to the interviews, the researchers analysed the personal portfolios and the participants' reflections on the experience of compiling them. As we worked from the hypothesis that storytelling, story-making, story interpretation and the reconstruction of one's story as an academic teacher is a way of affirming identity, we analysed these three data sources by identifying and analysing recurrent storylines and associated metaphors that were used by the participants. In focussing on metaphors our premise is that metaphors are a key tool that people use in recounting their experience. Equally significantly, we believe that metaphors often capture subterranean emotions. Analysis of metaphors is in keeping with our belief that emotion is important to the development of teacher identity. We use the term metaphor in a broad sense as communicated by particular language choices.

The Story Terrain

Our analysis of the three document sources uncovered multiple narratives (or 'antenarratives') in participants' portfolios. The articulation of both complementary and contradictory storylines appeared to facilitate sense-making and enhance wellbeing in relation to their role as tertiary educators. The stories can be grouped into personal stories (Moon & Fowler, 2008) or 'personal autobiography' (Day & Leitch, 2001), 'known stories' that are 'stories told informally or formally among people who share experiences such as in a workplace' (Moon & Fowler, 2008: 234) and stories 'that are not personally known…but taken to be true' (Moon & Fowler, 2008: 234). Moon and Fowler (2008) distinguish between non-fiction and fictional stories, but we suggest that in the higher education context, non-fiction and fiction (including mythology) are often deeply intertwined.

While individual narratives inevitably were very varied, a common story line was the recognition of *connections between aspects of past personal history and current tertiary educator identity*. In some cases these reflections identified a congruence between past experience and current educator identity, while, for others, past history helped to explain contradictions and inconsistencies in current teaching attitudes and behaviours. For example, the portfolio helped one participant to connect inherited values and his current teacher identity:

> In teaching I have found a profession that mixes two of my most prized inheritances – my father's love of knowledge and my mother's deep sense of compassion. (Finance lecturer, Polytechninc, Personal Portfolio)

By contrast, for a university Sport and Leisure Studies Lecturer, a humiliating childhood classroom experience was a barrier to implementing newer understandings, noting in her portfolio:

> I can still remember my feelings of hurt and humiliation at the hands of my form 2 teacher….When I could not (or would not) answer a question that my teacher had directed at me, she responded with "you are nothing but a cabbage" to which everyone in the class laughed. Many students in my paper

may feel the same way [as I did] and so I need to remember this. However, there are probably just as many who want to be asked questions because this is the way they learn. Despite this awareness I have not had the confidence to single out students in class... That childhood experience affected me deeply.... and changing will take time.

Jostling alongside these personal narratives, participants reported on a range of 'known stories' (Moon & Fowler, 2008: 234). There are multiple strands of both formal and informal stories. One repeated narrative is the powerful influence of remembered stories of how they themselves were taught. For the finance tutor, following the models of those who taught him contradicted his instincts:

As there was no apparent help available to me I drew on previous teaching experiences to develop my own style. The really good and the really bad influenced how I taught on the first day of teaching. I still had a nagging memory that the education system was not designed for me, and very few of the teachers I had were effective. If I wanted to make a difference to fledgling careers I would need to develop my own style. The real issue was how; I did not know the answer. I did not know how to get it. (Personal Portfolio)

The Leisure Studies lecturer observes:

I automatically fell into a transmission style of lecturing... I find it interesting that I automatically included aspects in my teaching that I reflected on as being bad teaching. A common theme here is that when I lack confidence in my teaching, I automatically revert to my safe place. (Personal Portfolio)

A Biology tutor at the university suggests that it was unusually good luck to observe a teacher whose approach felt comfortable with her personally and which has informed her own practice positively:

I was extremely lucky that one of the people I had observed and now teach with was X. Not only is she a trained teacher, she has an obvious passion for teaching and cares about her students. I suspect if I had been working closely with someone else, I might have ended down a different path and perhaps not care about teaching in the same way. (Personal Portfolio)

Another repeated 'known' story is the information gleaned about *how things are done* in the discipline or in the institution, and these precepts are often reinforced by participants' own learning experiences and by fuzzier notions about how things are done in academia which are not personally known and may be a combination of fact and fiction. A notable theme is the idea of academic expertise and the corollary that it is unacceptable to display ignorance. The Biology tutor comments:

I didn't like the feeling of not knowing. I thought admitting I did not know something would make the students have less respect for me, when in fact the honesty is more important. Yet again I fell into the trap that the teacher is the expert, the student is the novice, and knowing more makes me a better teacher.

I desperately needed someone to help me, but didn't feel I could ask, as that would mean I didn't know. (Personal Portfolio)

The personal portfolio gave this tutor space to reflect back on the contradictions between what she knew from direct experience and the power of inherited narratives about how things are:

What strikes me as strange is that I also remember saying during undergrad that because someone was a professor it doesn't mean they could teach. It seems as though I had forgotten my undergraduate experience.

These comments were not restricted to those from a university background, and the Polytechnic Finance lecturer notes the difficulty of acknowledging ignorance in his discipline:

In the world of Finance and Accounting it is frowned upon to say 'I don't know-teach me'. (Personal Portfolio)

Similarly, the Leisure Studies lecturer felt that it would be unacceptable to reveal her uncertainties:

There is a lack of support for new teachers as well as a stigma attached to seeking help. (Personal Portfolio)

The Biology tutor suggests that rigid norms about teaching behaviours and an undervaluing of teaching are particularly evident in the Sciences:

On the whole Science lecturers view teaching as something they 'have' to do, it is of less value than research and in many cases they do not like to think of themselves as teachers, preferring to focus instead on being members of their discipline who sometimes teach. (Personal portfolio)

The participants observed, as they recalled these inherited stories with the almost magical powers of folklore, that what they heard or were told had an impact on specific behaviours. For example, the Sport and Leisure Studies Lecturer, got some clear messages about teaching as a product:

I had the powerpoint slides from the previous lecturer and people kept saying to make it easier on myself and just use them. (Personal portfolio)

In her first year of teaching, a university Social Work lecturer invited feedback from her students and the responses led her to make a number of changes. While she did not talk explicitly about teaching narratives that had influenced her, student feedback and her own comments suggest that she was influenced by *implicit narratives* about how things are done at university. For example, one student had given her the feedback that there was 'too much pressure to read, too much information to process'. Another student commented that she was 'acting like a nasty school principle' [student's spelling] and 'treating students like children' (personal reflections). Interestingly, after this lecturer reduced the content and adjusted her expectations she recorded that she was able to 'relax more', implicitly suggesting borrowed notions of teacher control and a requirement that students absorb large amounts of material.

While the common theme is that of operating according to unscrutinised outmoded narratives, an interesting slant can be seen in the story recounted by the Leisure Studies lecturer. Her portfolio gave her the space to report on how she put together a teaching philosophy for her appointment interview:

> Thinking back to when I wrote that teaching philosophy, there was no ownership of it on my part… I also perceived that the words I had written were those that my potential new employer would want to hear. Essentially I produced what I thought someone in authority wanted, not something that I necessarily resonated with. (Personal Portfolio)

Her comments indicate that new narratives can easily become as paralysing, contradictory and unhelpful as the old ones unless they are experienced, lived and owned by the teachers themselves. Each academic in a particular context and time has to scrutinise the different narratives, whether old or new, and make and keep remaking their own understanding of these narratives.

As part of the Postgraduate Certificate process, we invite our participants to draw on another metanarrative to investigate the personal and inherited stories that they bring to their teaching spaces. These are the narratives that are built on higher education research and pedagogical theories. The data sources indicate that reference to these ideas helps academics to make sense of, interpret and manage the multiple stories that influence their practice and the process of developing an identity as a tertiary educator:

> And it's that reinforcement of 'Oh, someone says to do what you are doing' and I realise that I'm doing something worthwhile. I'm doing a good job. That's really rewarding. (Biology Tutor, interview)

> In a way confidence that what I do has got some grounds to it, that I'm not just making it up. There's some theory and frameworks that I'm finally using in teaching and learning, that backs what I'm trying to do with students. I'm forever reflecting on what I do… I'm checking against what I learned. (Management School University Lecturer, interview)

The Social Work lecturer deliberately began to engage herself in formal learning opportunities to learn about higher education teaching and learning. However, she reports that she was only able to integrate these formal teaching and learning narratives into her practice after a while:

> By the end of the first year, the learning from [course] was starting to make sense and I was integrating a lot of the workshop learning into my practice as a teacher. (Reflections)

Her story suggests that exposure to research 'narratives' about teaching does not always mean that teachers are ready or able to match these ideas to their practice.

RECURRENT METAPHORS

A common metaphor that participants used to capture their feelings about writing the personal portfolio was the notion of *travelling* and its associated emotional complexity. In the light of the multiple narratives that can hinder movement and change, the analogy between the portfolio process and a journey can be seen as essentially optimistic, because it denotes movement. It is interesting how a midwifery educator at a Polytechnic intertwines the personal and professional self-knowledge that she gained through writing the portfolio:

> There have been many moments as I travel this pathway to discovery when I have been challenged by who I am as a student, as a teacher and even as a mother. This journey has offered me both layers of discomfort and elation. (Reflections)

She also uses the term 'baggage' which she says she was able to 'address' and 'pack away' suggesting that, having been on the portfolio journey, she will be less encumbered subsequently in her teaching by what she brings from her past. While the Biology tutor does not use the word journey, her idea of travelling through the portfolio experience is expressed in her phrase that the writing 'was a shift in realisation' (interview).

Language intimating *space* complements the journey theme, suggesting movement into a different space which can feel inviting or challenging and may evoke feelings of spaciousness and freedom to explore. A comment from the midwifery educator evokes feelings of relief through the vigorous metaphor of 'leg room' and a sense of being offered a rare space in the accompanying phrase 'long awaited'. The repetition of 'I' indicates an appreciation of a unique personal space to connect past, present and future journeying:

> Allowed me some long awaited legroom to explore who I am and what I know, where I have been and where I am going. (Reflections)

The space idea becomes indulgent delight in the words of the Social Work lecturer:

> The personal portfolio was like a little luxury, it was like sitting and letting someone massage you.

The idea of space also takes on a different nuance in the comments of the university social work lecturer in the notion of being given permission:

> The personal portfolio has allowed me to affirm myself as a teacher. (Reflections)

She also expresses a sense of personal liberation in another comment:

I feel I can be more open and real in the personal portfolio. (Reflections)

By contrast, the Biology tutor uses language that demonstrates how she initially felt uncomfortable in the different space in which she found herself:

It makes me fearful though, well maybe fearful is the wrong word. Apprehensive? Uncomfortable maybe. I don't like being the centre of a piece of work. I like to be dispassionate in writing and the personal portfolio feels awkward to me.

For a number of participants, the journey into the portfolio space surfaced questions, feelings and assertions about their *worth* both personally and professionally. This language indicates a fear about not measuring up to some imagined standard (another part of academic folklore) as well as the absence of spaces to explore these emotions openly and honestly. For example, the midwifery tutor speaks of 'the vulnerability of being measured' and 'a fear… that I am being elevated to a role that I am not worthy of' (Reflections*).* Likewise, the Social Work lecturer, said that she worried about the quality of what she was doing and felt a 'bit of a fraud' (Reflections). The comments of the Biology tutor in relation to compiling the personal portfolio provide an interesting insight into the way in which assessment measures can affect our sense of self:

There is a little part of me that worries that I will fail at this. It's a non-intellectual idea because if I really think about it I know I won't, but I suspect it's a hangover from undergraduate days when I worried so much about failing assessments. The idea of failing seemed the worst thing in the world to me. (Reflections)

A further significant repeated metaphor was the notion of *remembering* or healing through recollection. For example, the Social Work lecturer noted:

I've had a very broad and wide range of experiences in my career and by doing the portfolio, I had to look at them again, examine all those things. (Reflections)

Her comment captures a recurrent theme of revisiting experiences through the portfolio and attaining a new sense of wholeness as a result. This feeling is well captured in the idea of a jigsaw used by the Finance lecturer.

Absolutely, it helped me to discover who I am… it made me reflect on everything in my life… when you start putting the jigsaw together and you lay it out in this thing called a personal portfolio, in front of you, you can relate to it, it helps you to see who you are. (Interview)

In many cases, the remembering process left participants with a better sense of themselves and more comfortable about their teaching role. This is expressed in the repeated uses of the word 'confidence' and affirmations about the value of self – such as this statement from the midwifery educator:

In truth I have been forced to appreciate and value myself.

The Social Work lecturer felt that revisiting teaching through the portfolio was healing:

I feel that writing about some teaching miscues has also somehow defused their intensity and the comments have lost their sting, rather [they] are fitting into the larger picture of my journey as a teacher. I feel recommitted to being a teacher. (Reflections)

Similarly, the Finance lecturer said:

Confidence thing for me – that I can be an academic… there's a whole different realm to being an academic –I really felt nervous about that and hence I wasn't engaging with anyone. I guess doing the portfolio made me pull it into line and see what academia was all about it. (Interview)

Remembering also sometimes means facing up to inconsistencies. For example, the Biology tutor notes:

A realisation that I wasn't the teacher that I thought I was, but that wasn't a bad thing… a shift in realisation… It really makes you think about who you are as a teacher, not who you think you are as a teacher. The way I thought I taught as a teacher wasn't what I was actually doing. (Interview)

These recognitions did not necessarily lead to resolution, but generally to a more peaceful view of the self and the landscape. For the Sport and Leisure Studies lecturer, the portfolio process brought her to a changed space in which she could name herself as an educator. She also acknowledged that it is not about closure, but a step in a long-term process:

I never considered myself as an educator… So in doing the portfolio and the PGCert… I've come to recognise that I am a tertiary educator and maybe understanding what an educator is… And I think that will continue to change.

For the Management lecturer, the remembering process was an opportunity to reconsider his teaching and learning choices and the rationale behind them:

It helped me to think about what I have been doing…why do I do it – why do I do it?

CONCLUSION

Our study confirmed the hypothesis stated in different ways by Clandinin and Connelly (1996), Zembylas (2007) and Moon and Fowler (2008) that teachers have to navigate their way through multiple 'landscapes', 'systems' and 'stories'. The data sources suggest that these complex narratives and their intersection can have a powerful hold on academic teachers, sometimes causing serious discomfort in their academic space, contradicting their insights or crippling their capacity to move forward. For our teachers, the most powerful storylines that they articulated were inheritances from their personal history, their experience of how others teach in the post-compulsory sector, and the tapestry of interwoven narratives (or 'ante-narratives') about how things are done here, which varies according to context. It is important to note that these different story fragments which may range from theoretically grounded aspirations to corridor mutterings are often contradictory and their relationship to each other may be unexamined. The metaphors of travel, space, value and remembering indicate that the process of writing a personal portfolio can provide space to unpack the many stories that shape academic identity and articulate their influence. The degree to which teachers feel trapped in a particular landscape differs according to multiple influences such as career stage, process of induction into academia, colleagues' values, engagement with formal professional development, past learning histories and academic disciplines. As the sample is small, it is difficult to make generalisations about the most significant struggles, but the powerful emotional hold exerted by narratives of how things are done is a consistent theme.

It would be naïve to claim that surety about one's own teacher 'story' identity is achieved through the writing of the personal portfolio. The terrain of the landscape is too complex, dynamic and fluid for repose. However, the metaphors of travelling, space, worth and remembering suggest that the personal portfolio process can enhance well-being and confidence and strengthen the commitment to core values and practices. The metaphors people use suggest stocktaking, growth and enhanced feelings of control through looking at what shapes them as teachers. But as most participants noted, the process of exploration needs to be ongoing. The personal portfolio gives participants the space and the freedom to begin to craft their own story in the midst of multiple, often contradictory, narratives.

REFERENCES

Boje, D. M. (2001). *Narrative methods for organisational and communication research.* London, England: Sage.

Brofenbrenner, U. (1989). Ecological systems theory. In R. Vasta (Ed.), *Six theories of child development: Revised foundations and current issues* (pp. 187–205). Greenwich, CT: Jai Press.

Clandinin, D. J., & Connelly, F. M. (1996). Teachers' professional knowledge landscapes: Teacher stories – Stories of teachers, School stories – Stories of schools. *Educational Researcher, 25*(3), 24–30.

Day, C., & Leitch, R. (2001). Teachers' and teacher educators' lives: The role of emotion. *Teaching and Teacher Education, 17,* 403–415.

Lakoff, G., & Johnson, M. (1983). *Metaphors we live by.* Chicago, IL: University of Chicago Press.

Lakoff, G., & Johnson, M. (1999). *Philosophy in the flesh: The embodied mind and its challenge to Western thought.* New York, NY: Basic Books.

Martin, E., & Lueckenhausen, G. (2005). How university teaching changes teachers: Affective as well as cognitive challenges. *Higher Education, 49*(3), 389–412.

Moon, J., & Fowler, J. (2008). There is a story to be told...: A framework for the conception of story in higher education and professional development. *Nurse Education Today, 28*, 232–239.

Zembylas, M. (2007). Emotional ecology: The intersection of emotional knowledge and pedagogical content knowledge in teaching. *Teaching and Teacher Education, 23*, 35–367.

Dorothy Spiller
University of Waikato, New Zealand

Pip Bruce Ferguson
Dublin City University
Republic of Ireland

PART III

ON WRITING ACADEMIC IDENTITIES

SIMON WARREN

8. WRITING OF THE HEART

Auto-Ethnographic Writing as Subversive Story Telling – A Song of Pain and Liberation[1]

1 – A(N) (UN) KIND [OF] INTRODUCTION

13th February 2012

…as with every day last week, and all through the conference and study school, I get up, I wash and dress. I have breakfast — something resembling breakfast. I put on the mask and perform the competent academic and adult. Inside, though, I am dissolving. Each moment it is harder to maintain this fiction of calmness, of 'togetherness'…I am caught between anxiety and normality. Normality is increasingly unreal. Anxiety is increasingly normal. The idea of facing all my colleagues tomorrow at the staff meeting…God, I don't know…I MUST. I MUST…just get through this week…GET THROUGH THIS WEEK.

A 2012 survey on occupational stress carried out by the University and College Union found that staff in British universities are more stressed now than in 2008, and experience considerably higher average levels of stress relating to the demands made on them at work than the British working population as a whole.[2]

I have moved here from a 'me' story to an 'us' story;
from a personal biographical account to a scholastic account. The first is an extract from my personal diary
the night before I finally succumbed to….clinical depression. The second is a report of a survey in the British Guardian newspaper.
They both speak of the same phenomena,
but in different ways.
The energy produced
by placing these two different texts next to each other –
the first pathic, the second gnostic[3] –
is the kind of energy that is produced by a 'layered account'
as found in much autoethnographic work.[4]
And this approach to speaking of academic life and practice is the content of
this text.

J. Smith et al. (Eds.), *Identity Work in the Contemporary University*, 105–116.
© 2016 Sense Publishers. All rights reserved.

The writing is about my experience of a particular context –
of the impossibly competing demands between teaching, research
and administration.
Increasing student numbers
with fewer resources
whilst also increasing research productivity
and 'grant capture'
in a culture of measurement and surveillance.[5]
   This is a context where the very institutions we work in and for create what
                    Barabara Jago has called 'academic depression',
and what Art Bochner refers to as

'...*institutional depression*, a pattern of anxiety, hopelessness, demoralization, isolation, and disharmony that circulates through university life.",

the way we succumb to performative institutional culture, especially the ways we are conditioned to split our academic and personal lives,
to privilege the former and suppress the latter.[6]
                                 Academic depression, as discussed here,
           is then both a disenchantment with the romance of a scholarly life
                                        and psychological trauma.
BUT - How do we write…how do we write
of 'academic depression' without emptying the experience of its visceral reality?
In this text I draw on a number of personal,
intellectual,
and cultural resources
to tell a story about how I am trying to write of academic depression, of writing a:

       MY/YOU/US STORY of life in the modern university.

In particular I speak to the capacity of autoethnographic writing to be transformative,
to remoralise us in a context of demoralisation;
                                       and of the pause [……..]
                    the pause that such writing and reading can create,
                                                within which
                different ways of being an academic can emerge.
But there is a craft to this
and I speak also to this craft-work.
I speak to a kind of playful writing,
of autoethnographic writing as a sampling and remixing of introspection, memory, anecdote and scholarly work
to create an evocative text.

2 – CONFRONTING THE SPECTACLE

This text represents something I want to term 'authentic'. That is,
my experience of academic depression, I feel,
says something not just about me personally
but about a wider experience of academic life in neo-liberal times.
In reading the many texts of academic capitalism
or new public management
sometimes I feel as if I cannot see the human experience, the panic attacks,
the joy at being published,
the dark night of the day.
While eloquent in their analysis I cannot FEEL myself in them.[7]
        I am involved in a project of redefining my academic purpose.
   And in writing I want to enter into dialogue with others, and because of the
                  mode of engagement – autoethnography –
           I am signaling which kinds of folk I want to talk with,
                what kinds of conversation I want to have.
                   There is an ethical dimension to this.
                  Autoethnography is an ethical choosing,
                         a political position.
BUT – but, at the same time, my efforts,
my existential choosing,
is caught up in what Guy Debord referred to as the SPECTACLE.
That is,
the substance of my authentic and choiceful activity is also taken up in the knowledge factory of the modern university,
emptied of meaningful content,
transformed into a commodity,
and utilized in the pursuit of institutional ambition.[8] Imagine the modern world of global higher education as being like a fashion show.
What is important is the glamour,
the style,
the posturing.
What we are not invited to see is the ecological damage of a culture that persuades us that we MUST
keep going out to buy more and newer clothes
so that we end up with wardrobes bursting with unused items
while the majority of the world's population struggle to secure the basics.
        We are not invited to think about the child labour that will underpin the
                cheapness of the latest fashions we purchase.
                              In other words,
                    image and illusion come to dominate.
                We don't experience the world directly,

Debord argued,
instead
we increasingly meet the world through images of the world.[9]

3 – ACADEMIC LIFE AS SADOMASOCHISM

And so,
my article will be denuded of meaning,
it will be taken up by the production of writing plans,
it will be linked to performance indicators and professional development meetings,
it will become a commodity that is accumulated by the university,
and will eventually be reflected back to me as an item on my CV,
as part of an institutional submission
to a research assessment exercise –
as something emptied of its choicefulness,
of its ethical claim,
of its authenticity.[10]

And this is perhaps why so many of us feel demoralised.
And so this is why it is important to write in ways that remoralise,
that can open up the possibility of imagining what an authentic academic might be –
to give moral purpose to what we do.[11]

4 – AND SO THE DÉRIVE

The 'managed' academic CV is one that increasingly must be cohesive,
must be linear.
BUT –but –
cohesiveness and linearity is a product of retrospection –
an afterthought.
Yet, we are asked to write plans AS IF intellectual thought was linear,
tidy,
bullet points.

This is a world that cannot entertain the idea of "dérive",
of wandering, of meandering through intellectual landscapes.
Imagine drawing a straight line on a map and attempting to follow that path regardless of what obstacles might be in the way;
of having to negotiate those obstacles as best we can;
of having to encounter people;
and to encounter the space without GPS or smartphone or Google Maps.[12]

Or psychogeography where you might be given a set of simple instructions
(2nd left, 1st right, 2nd left, repeat)

and use this to navigate an urban space
and to observe what you see and experience –
experience it directly without the concepts provided by a map.
Or, choosing a familiar space
(work building, journey to work, etc.)
you are asked to travel in silence.
The silence immediately forces
a pause,
a reflection,
where we might start to notice certain aspects of the 'familiar' environment in different ways,
where we might find ourselves drawn to certain objects, feelings, anticipations
As well as this mode of academic practice being contrary to the managed CV
it is also how I am imagining the writing I am talking about.
It is much more akin to psychogeography –
a methodology that enables me to walk through my experience of academic depression in a structured way
but which makes possible new observations[13].

5 – THE AIM OF AN AIMLESS WALK

A dérive is a methodology that poses this question –
what if there is no point B?

It is a methodology that invites the researcher
(me)
to begin in a particular place
– now –
looking back at my experience of academic depression
– and to traverse this recovered experience with no specific destination in mind.
The dérive…
Is Disruptive –
like the walk following an arbitrary straight line
it is a methodology that is disruptive of traditional social scientific practice.
It disregards the arbitrary distinction between public and private –
so my person
and personal feelings
are viewed as important,
it plays with creative and scientific writing,
It is
An embodied methodology:

it places emphasis on capturing the emotive experience without rushing to abstraction....
it tries to speak of the bodily response
and not to give undue weight to the cognitive.
It places the pathic as equal to the gnostic...

part of the aim of an aimless walk
is to identify the way everyday life,
the mundane,
is ordered or structured.
But this requires something like the phenomenological reduction,
the bracketing of our normal understandings,
and the cultivation of a open attitude.
Similarly,
the wandering through cycles of introspection and analysis can,
it is hoped,
produce a kind of disorientation.
And disoriented
we identify what we find ourselves attracted to
(what incidents, emotions, ideas induce us towards them) and what discourages us
(what feels uncomfortable, distasteful).

In Other Words

What Is It That Presents Itself To Our Consciousness

And What Sense Can We Make Of It?

6 – ETHICS

And so the dérive is also an ethical intervention to encourage a deep reflection on the nature of academic life as we live it.
A political intervention.

7 – A LAYERED ACCOUNT

One way of doing this in the craft of writing
is the use of the Layered Account
used to produce disruptive and evocative texts.
This can involve the varied use of memoir or diary,
as well as academic analysis
in order to reconnect the private and academic self –
as in my opening quotes.
It is Ruth Behar's combination of 'a novelistic and scholarly voice';

or Carolyn Ellis' invitation
to write in a way that moves back and forth between personal introspection and academic reflection,
methods that are simultaneously social and psychological[14].
    This is similar to the Situationist method of détournement.
      Détournement is 'culture jamming' or 'culture hacking'.
This is where everyday objects,
normally those associated with
power
and capitalism
and patriarchy
are subverted,
are hacked and reproduced –
where items from personal life are conjoined with scholarly writing
to disrupt our consciousness
and reveal not only the child labour behind the glamorous clothes,
but what this means to us,
what this feels like.

8 – THE NAKED ACADEMIC?

It is a process of sampling and remixing everyday objects,
of using familiar items
and putting them together in ways that disrupt perceptions, that create new, possibly subversive stories.
    The hope is to invoke such disruptions for me
      but also for the reader.
  To subvert the tidiness of academic writing that can abstract us from lived experience
  That asserts academic life and academic practice as embodied and embedded
    in social-political space
That produces a pause
or intensified awareness of the object of study
so questioning my sense of being
and opening up space to reimagine academic life

And In Reimagining Academic Life

Seek to Live It Differently

NOTES

[1] Here I am paraphrasing the title of a paper by Patricia Ewick and Susan Silbey 'Subversive Stories and Hegemonic Tales: Towards Sociology of Narrative' where they argue for the production of 'subversive

stories, narratives that challenge the dominant understandings of our times, and in particular to make explicit the relationship between lives-as-lived and social structure' (Ewick & Silbey, 1995). In this regard I am locating my own narrativisation as potentially a subversive act. My decision to write this piece in verse builds on this initial commitment. This poem could be categorized, following Monica Prendergast (Prendergast, Leggo, & Sameshima, 2009), as a form of "VOX THEORIA - Literature-voiced poems" (xxii), since it speaks of inquiry itself, the rationale for my particular autoethnographic approach. In the 'Introduction' to the 2009 volume Ivan Brady discusses the way poetic inquiry gets up close and personal, inverts the telescope to magnify what is going on with life as lived (by us?) It is a mode that disrupts the distancing technologies of academic research. He makes the point that since research is a process of languaging, is dependent on language, it is already involved in poetics, in the use of metaphor for instance (xii) (see also Brady, 2004). Further more, the poetic can be conceived as a bridge, or method for linking life as lived to sociological writing, to make explicit the created, constructed, fabricated, 'produced' fact of sociological text (Richardson, 1993). Poetry, or spoken-word is used in an attempt to be authentic to the motivations for my research, for my social scientific writing.

[2] While much media and scholarly attention has been focused on the stress and wellbeing of students in higher education, there is an increasing recognition of the impact of the intensification of academic labour on the lives and health of academics. Here I refer to a report by the University and College Union, the largest trade union and professional association for academics in UK higher education (Kinman & Wray, 2013). Therefore, the results would appear to be fairly representative of the situation facing British academics. The survey results clearly point to a perception of increasing work intensification and a decline in work-life balance. One aspect that emerges from the report is the rise in occupational stress as higher education institutions struggle to cope with increasing competition and performance management. It could be said that the reforms faced by higher education over the past 20 years are making people sick. This resonates with previous academic research in both the UK (Tytherleigh, Webb, Cooper, & Ricketts, 2005) and Australia (Gillespie, Walsh, Winefield, Dua, & Stough, 2001).

[3] Max van Manen, in a number of papers, refers to the 'pathic' and the 'gnostic' aspects of knowing (van Manen, 2007; van Manen & Li, 2001). Whereas the 'gnostic' relates to knowledge as we would normally understand it – that is in terms of the cognitive, 'pathic' knowing is related to ideas of empathy or sympathy, to the affective and kinesthetic aspects of knowing. He discusses this most poignantly in his examination of the practice of nursing and the combination of 'pathic' and 'gnostic' knowing required in order to be competent. This stress upon the 'pathic' is important in terms of the importance I give to affective in both a commitment to a passionate ethnography and role of the senses in academic practice as a form of dérive.

[4] The particular 'craft' of autoethnographic writing indexed here will be addressed more fully later.

[5] I return to these themes again more fully when addressing the notion of the 'managed CV'.

[6] I am indebted to both Barbara Jago and Art Bochner both in terms of personal support (Barbara) and political/scholarly license (both). Early in my attempts to give scholarly meaning to my experience of depression and its place in academic life I came across their work. They were 'beginnings' as Edward Said (1975) might put it, instances that have provoked me to continue this particular project. Both have exposed themselves, something that is not encouraged in academia where the masculine objective expert is King. They have placed the first-person account centre stage, and in doing so travelled with the sociological imagination, have connected the personal to the public, connected the way private experiences of trauma are related to the neo-liberal restructuring of academic practice (Bochner, 1997; Jago, 2002).

[7] I am inspired by much excellent scholarship that carefully details the way higher education is being remade in the image of neo-liberalism, as an adjunct of certain kinds of economic activity. In the North American context Sheila Slaughter, Larry Leslie, and Gary Rhoades have shown how academic practice has been pushed into the service of producing private rather than public goods, of being an aspect of a market economy (Rhoades & Slaughter, 1997; Slaughter & Leslie, 1999). Other scholars have demonstrated how this is a global phenomena, and furthermore, that the specific features of globalized higher education competition are overdetermined by the image of economically and

socially prestigious institutions (Marginson, 2000; 2004; Marginson & Considine, 2000; Marginson & Rhoades, 2002). This mirrors the analysis by such scholars as Pierre Bourdieu and others (Bourdieu, 1988; Naidoo, 2004; 2008). But what I feel is missing, for me, in these works is the felt experience. This is not a criticism of these scholars. Not at all. But I do raise a concerned hand and seek to point out that we can only go so far narrating this story of neo-liberal capture through the disembodied language of orthodox academic writing. Politically, we need to accept the invitation offered by Critical Race Theory that the production of 'counter-narratives' is essential in destabilising 'hegemonic tales' (Delgado, 1989; 1990; Rollock, 2012).

[8] I am clearly making direct reference to Guy Debord's 'The Society of the Spectacle' (Debord, 1994). This text emerged out of the revolutionary climate of Paris leading up to and just beyond 1968. It was one of the key texts of the Situationist International (SI), combining anti-authoritarian Marxism with the radical artistic movements of Dada and Surrealism. I draw on some of the key terminology of the SI both analogously and substantively. As analogies terms such as 'spectacle', 'dérive', and 'détournement' enable me broaden my descriptive and analytical imagery, and employ terms that have the potential to be disruptive because the reader or listener, perhaps encountering something unfamiliar, will have to pay attention and consider the meaning of what I say. In that sense they work as heuristic devices. But I also use them substantively, momentarily aligning myself with the ambition, if not the actual content, of the SI. Of central importance for the project contained in this text is the desire to assert that academic writing is artifice, is an act of creation and construction. Referring back to the case I make for writing in verse, this SI terminology also questions the presumption that normal academic writing is 'natural' and close to 'natural speech', whereas art is not.

[9] In reading Debord's 'The Society of the Spectacle' I am struck by how much it resonates with contemporary higher education. One phrase rings loud in my mind: "In a world which really is topsy-turvy, the true is a moment of the false." Using a different descriptive language Mats Alvesson discusses how modern globalised higher education is increasingly devoid of substance and is overtaken by an obsession with image, brand, and impression management. For Alvesson, the modern university is caught up in a competitive struggle for relative status. The actual substance of academic labour – what we teach, what we research, our contributions to knowledge, are of less importance than the marginal improvement in our standing in relation to other higher education institutions. The behaviour of university managers is dominated by grandiose claims and boosting the institution's image (Alvesson, 2013). In other words, SPECTACLE. And in this climate the university becomes increasingly careless of the humans who work within it and provide it with the material with which to make such claims (Lynch, 2006).

[10] These are all features of what I call the 'managed CV'. In using this term I am itemizing how 'new public management' and the auditing culture of education work as kinds of 'illusion tricks', to borrow a phrase from Mats Alvesson. These are processes whereby we are invited to think of our academic labour in terms of 'outputs', and to massage and manipulate these outputs in order to create an 'impression' that feeds the status competition of our employing institutions. Linked to this is the rise of particular kinds of management practice that seek to align our individual academic practices to institutional strategy (Decramer & Smolders, 2013; Deem, 1998; Deem, Hillyard, & Reed, 2007).

[11] I am speaking directly to Arthur Frank's championing of the 'standpoint of the storyteller' as an antidote to the disembodied, socially and politically dislocated 'hegemonic tales'. Frank argues for the standpoint of the storyteller, that story infers relationship with a listener, that storytelling invites other stories, other listenings, not just analysis from nowhere. Standpoint is the opposite of speaking from nowhere. It privileges a location (in theory, in methodology, in politics). It is an ethical stance. But it is not fixed, immovable. It demands a responsibility.

[12] Like the technologies that are ubiquitous and appear benign, performance management and strategic alignment disguise power and the powerful. It took the Wikileaks scandal to bring the attention of most people to the way large corporations routinely appropriated our personal data, and colluded with national security services. In this part of the text I invite the reader to imagine, not just a world without these technologies, instead to rely on their own judgment and ethical choosing, but to imagine different academic worlds where we didn't so willingly give ourselves to the spying eyes of the audit culture.

[13] The dérive, in its original formulation, was both a method of analysis and a manifesto for social transformation. Dérive, or the associated practice of psychogeography, can be methods for inquiring into the way academic practice is being re-made under the pressure of research assessment exercises, global league tables, and performance management. It is a methodology, in both a metaphorical sense and substantively, for inquiring into the neo-liberal university. It is an investigation into the ways new routines of teaching, researching, and socializing in the university re-form the social relations of academic practice. Metaphorically it works here to step out of the comfort of 'known' methodology and see where the language of the SI and psychogeography takes me in how I think and write. In that sense it has a similar function to the poetic approach. As metaphor it is also a way of speaking of 'career' in a different way, of reframing academic practice beyond and against the confines of the current situation. Substantively, it also provides a methodology, a way of doing inquiry that is only 'aimless' in that it is not designed to fit with strategic alignment, is not done with global league tables or audit points in mind (Bonnett, 2009 for more on psychogeography as political inquiry; Bridger, 2010; Jenks & Neves, 2000).

[14] There is, I hope, a clear line of travel emerging here that links 'subversive stories' with the 'poetic' approach to 'dérive' and now to 'autoethnography'. The heuristic of the 'layered account' I borrow from Carol Rambo Ronai (Ronai, 1998; 1999). In particular I take this image of layers on a journey through Tami Spry's distinction between 'being there' and 'being here' (Spry, 2001), between the 'thereness' of the narrative and poetic and introspective and the 'hereness' of the analytic, so mirroring other calls for a careful oscillation between the literary and the academic voice (Behar, 2009; Ellis, 1991;1999). It is in this oscillation that I make use of 'found objects' – diary, email, scholarly text, policy briefing, etc. It is here that the artifice of fabricating (or creating) a truth account happens, its validity arising from the degree to which my story connects and also becomes your story, becomes a collective story.

REFERENCES

Alvesson, M. (2013). *The triumph of emptiness: Consumption, higher education, and work organization.* Oxford, England: Oxford University Press.

Behar, R. (2009). Believing in anthropology as literature. In A. Waterston & M. D. Vesperi (Eds.), *Anthropology off the shelf anthropologists on writing.* Oxford, England: Blackwell Publishing.

Bochner, A. P. (1997). It's about time: Narrative and the divided self. *Qualitative Inquiry, 3*(4), 418–438.

Bonnett, A. (2009). The dilemmas of radical nostalgia in British psychogeography. *Theory, Culture and Society, 26*(1), 45–70.

Bourdieu, P. (1988). *Homo academicus* (P. Collier, Trans.). Stanford, CA: Stanford University Press.

Brady, I. (2004). In defense of the sensual: Meaning construction in ethnography and poetics. *Qualitative Inquiry, 10*(4), 622–644.

Bridger, A. J. (2010). Walking as a "radicalized" critical psychological method? A review of academic, artistic and activist contributions to the study of social environments. *Social and Personality Psychology Compass, 4*(2), 131–139.

Debord, G. (1994). *Societys of the spectacle.* New York, NY: Zone Books.

Decramer, A., Smolders, C., & Vanderstraeten, A. (2013). Employee performance management culture and system features in higher education: Relationship with employee performance management satisfaction. *The International Journal of Human Resource Management, 24*(2), 352–371.

Deem, R. (1998). "New managerialism" and higher education: The management of performances and cultures in universities in the United Kingdom. *International Studies in Sociology of Education, 8*(1), 47–70.

Deem, R., Hillyard, S., & Reed, M. (2007). *Knowledge, higher education, and the new managerialism: The changing management of UK universities.* Oxford, NY: Oxford University Press.

Delgado, R. (1989). Storytelling for oppositionists and others: A plea for narrative. *Michigan Law Review, 87*(8), 2411–2441.

Delgado, R. (1990). When a story is just a story: Does voice really matter? *Virginia Law Review, 76*(1), 95–111.

Ellis, C. (1991). Sociological introspection and emotional experience. *Symbolic Interaction*, *14*(1), 23–50.
Ellis, C. (1999). Heartful autoethnography. *Qualitative Health Research*, *9*(5), 669–683.
Ewick, P., & Silbey, S. S. (1995). Subversive stories and hegemonic tales: Toward a sociology of narrative. *Law & Society Review*, *29*(2), 197–226.
Gillespie, N. A., Walsh, M., Winefield, A. H., Dua, J., & Stough, C. (2001). Occupational stress in universities: Staff perceptions of the causes, consequences and moderators of stress. *Work & Stress*, *15*(1), 53–72.
Jago, B. J. (2002). Chronicling an academic depression. *Journal of Contemporary Ethnography*, *31*(6), 729–757.
Jenks, C., & Neves, T. (2000). A walk on the wild side: Urban ethnography meets the flâneur. *Journal for Cultural Research*, *4*(1), 1–17.
Kinman, G., & Wray, S. (2013). *Higher stress: A survey of stress and well-being among staff in higher education* (pp. 1–52). London, England: University and College Union.
Lynch, K. (2006). Neo-liberalism and marketisation: The implications for higher education. *European Educational Research Journal*, *5*(1), 1–17.
Marginson, S. (2000). Rethinking academic work in the global era. *Journal of Higher Education Policy and Management*, *22*(1), 23–35.
Marginson, S. (2004). Competition and markets in higher education: A "glonacal" analysis. *Policy Futures in Education*, *2*(2), 175.
Marginson, S., & Considine, M. (2000). *The enterprise university: Power, governance and reinvention in Australia*. Cambridge, England: Cambridge University Press.
Marginson, S., & Rhoades, G. (2002). Beyond national states, markets, and systems of higher education: A glonacal agency heuristic. *Higher Education*, *43*(3), 281–309.
Naidoo, R. (2004). Fields and institutional strategy: Bourdieu on the relationship between higher education, inequality and society. *British Journal of Sociology of Education*, *25*(4), 457–471.
Naidoo, R. (2008). Higher education: A powerhouse for development in a neo-liberal age? In D. Epstein, R. Boden, R. Deem, F. Rizvi, & S. Wright (Eds.), *World yearbook of higher education 2008* (pp. 248–265). London, England: Routledge.
Prendergast, M., Leggo, C., & Sameshima, P. (2009). *Poetic inquiry*. Rotterdam, The Netherlands; Boston, MA: Sense Publishers.
Rhoades, G., & Slaughter, S. (1997). Academic capitalism, managed professionals, and supply-side higher education. *Social Text*, *51*(51), 9–38.
Richardson, L. (1993). Poetics, dramatics, and transgressive validity: The case of the skipped line. *The Sociological Quarterly*, *34*(4), 695–710.
Rollock, N. (2012). The invisibility of race: Intersectional reflections on the liminal space of alterity. *Special Issue: Critical Race Theory in England, Race Ethnicity & Education*, *15*(1), 65–84.
Ronai, C. R. (1998). Sketching with Derrida: An ethnography of a researcher/erotic dancer. *Qualitative Inquiry*, *4*(3), 405–420.
Ronai, C. R. (1999). The next night sous rature: Wrestling with Derrida's mimesis. *Qualitative Inquiry*, *5*(1), 114–129.
Said, E. (1975). *Beginnings: Intention and method*. New York, NY: Basic Books.
Slaughter, S., & Leslie, L. L. (1999). *Academic capitalism: Politics, policies, and the entrepreneurial university*. Baltimore, MD: John Hopkins University Press.
Spry, T. (2001). Performing autoethnography: An embodied methodological praxis. *Qualitative Inquiry*, *7*(6), 706–732.
Tytherleigh, M. Y., Webb, C., Cooper, C. L., & Ricketts, C. (2005). Occupational stress in UK higher education institutions: A comparative study of all staff categories. *Higher Education Research and Development*, *24*(1), 41–61.
van Manen, M. (2007). Phenomenology of practice. *Phenomenology & Practice*, *1*(1), 11–30.
van Manen, M., & Li, S. (2001). The pathic principle of pedagogical language. *Teaching and Teacher Education*, *18*(2), 215–224.

Simon Warren
Centre for Excellence in Learning and Teaching
National University of Ireland, Galway
Republic of Ireland

JAMES BURFORD

9. DOCTORAL INDUCTION DAY

An Ethnographic Fiction on Doctoral Emotions

HOW TO ATTEND TO THE 'AFFECTIVE LANDSCAPES' OF DOCTORAL EDUCATION?

Exhaustion / stress / overload / insomnia / anxiety / shame / aggression / hurt / fraudulence / fear / stealing time / out of control / drowning / breaking point. (Gill, 2010: 228–229)

The words above are a patchwork of text I selected from Gill's (2010) book chapter on the 'hidden injuries' of the neoliberal university. Do these feelings characterise contemporary academic work and life? Across critical higher education (HE) research it would seem the answer to this question is an increasingly emphatic 'yes'. A consensus has begun to emerge that 'something has changed' regarding the conditions, and emotions of academic labour (Burrows, 2012: 355; Elizabeth & Grant, 2013; Saltmarsh & Randell-Moon, 2014). Some have gone further, suggesting that academic work has reached a point of "affective, somatic crisis" (Burrows, 2012: 355). Changes to the emotional experience of academic work are situated within broader reforms to the HE sector. Over recent decades academics have negotiated higher workloads, fraying job security, and the spread of accountability and audit cultures, among other changes.

While the worrying state of academic wellbeing has received critical attention, what of doctoral students? Considerations of the emotions of contemporary doctoral study remain rather thin on the ground. This is despite the fact that doctoral education has also become a more intense and diversified practice. Doctoral students encounter increasing pressure to publish their work and build marketable 'profiles', while also completing their PhDs within more strictly enforced timeframes. This has coincided with cuts to entitlements for doctoral students in many countries and reports of shrinking possibilities for secure academic employment. Given the profound nature of these changes I suggest there is a growing need for research about the impact of HE reform on doctoral education's 'affective landscapes' (Nöbauer, 2012), that is, a broad view of the patterning of emotion and affect.

The key concern that motivates this chapter is to expand the toolkit of methods available for researchers to examine doctoral affect. My concern with finding new ways of 'doing' writing has arisen in response to my doubts as to whether received modes of representing HE research adequately evoke the thickness of emotion and embodiment. I am not alone in following this line of thought. Carr and colleagues (2013) and Warren (this volume) have argued that researchers need to find new modes of representation that can constitute HE as a 'full-bodied, affective, and interactive experience' (n.p.). Increasingly, researchers have begun to infuse their work on academic emotions with vignettes (Gill, 2010), personal narratives (Saltmarsh & Randell-Moon, 2014) autoethnographic writing (Pelias, 2004) and poetry (Burford, 2014; Elizabeth & Grant, 2013). This chapter extends these movements by experimenting with one particular evocative writing methodology (Richardson, 1994): ethnographic fiction.

ETHNOGRAPHIC FICTION

Ethnographic fiction has an established history in education research. Its writers use stories to invite their readers 'to become immersed into the immediacy and vividness of others' life situations, and to inhabit viscerally their world' (Gray, 2004: 44–45). The method draws on many of the techniques used in creative fiction, such as using scenes to show rather than tell; building interest through character development; and using plot to create dramatic tension (Sparkes, 2002). In contrast to creative fiction, however, ethnographic fiction requires proximity; the researcher needs to have 'been there' (Sparkes, 2002: 2) gathering data from the research field. As a form of research, ethnographic fiction does not offer 'reliability' in the traditional sense; instead, the goal is 'verisimilitude' (Sparkes, 1997: 36). Looking at HE research in particular, there are several ethnographic fictions that have made important contributions to understanding university life. For example, Tierney's (1993) fiction on the intersection of organizational change and sexual orientation, and Andrew Sparkes' (2007) piece on the struggles of academic work amidst audit culture. Both used ethnographic fiction to 'surface' and evoke a number of everyday features of living and working in the university.

This story has emerged from reflections I noted down in 2012 during my own compulsory doctoral induction. I had felt reluctant to take part in the event, and delayed participating until the end of my first doctoral year. One day I was talking to a friend about how frustrated I felt about being compelled to attend. My friend offered some helpful advice. Would it be possible, he asked, for me to do something with my frustration? Could I attend the event in the 'role' of an ethnographer, rather than reluctant doctoral student? The possibility that I could arrive in character appealed to me immensely! If I was compelled to attend the induction, I figured, at least might I go more on my own terms, redirecting my gaze onto the induction itself. I determined to go as a 'researcher', taking down notes about what I observed, and how I felt before, during and after the induction. In the months following, I began to play with these observations, eventually turning them into the fictional account I present in this chapter.

Through its telling, *Doctoral Induction Day* seeks to patch together a 'scene' of doctoral education. Readers may wish to contemplate what the story might teach us about HE reform, the enactment of doctoral identity, and the patterning of doctoral emotions in the present.

DOCTORAL INDUCTION DAY

'Just get up.' Tom spoke flatly, tugging open the curtains. He'd been awake for an hour already, and seemed bored by the wake-up ritual he'd begun performing daily.

'No. I'm tired. I need just five minutes' Lew pleaded as he pulled a pillow smelling faintly of his uncle away from his face.

'You have to be at the airport by seven and you know what fascists Air-Square are, if you're late they wont let you on, and since I don't know the roads yet it will take me longer to drive, and…'

'OK, OK' Lew sat up, swinging his legs down with dramatic effect to meet the collection of washed clothes that still blanketed the floor several months after their move back to his uncle's house. He felt nausea churning in his stomach.

'Oh, and there's a mess in the toilet' Tom reported factually.

Lew nodded and made his way to their bathroom. Though still waking up, his thoughts turned to the instructions he'd leave for his uncle and brother for the next few days while he was away in the city. Whenever he went out for longer than a few hours he'd write a note of instructions and sellotape it to the kitchen table. He'd probably check in a couple of times with his younger brother Edwin. He'd be checking in on Aunty Suze.

Aunty Suze was an alcoholic. Well, now she was sober, but only because she was sick and they'd taken her car keys. No one was sure what was wrong exactly. But for the last five months she'd sat on the couch, watching re-runs of Border Patrol and Ellen.

When she got out of hospital last time, Edwin had called,

'It's not looking good' he said, 'I'd say at this rate she's only got one year left'.

Lew decided to head home. He really shouldn't have been driving. He sped through small towns singing Mahalia Jackson's version of 'Summertime':

Sometime I feeeel
Like a motherless child
Just alone
Long way,
From my home

Lew let out a whimper when he saw Aunty, shrunken and pale. She couldn't even get out of bed to greet him. Her sheets were stained and her nails were dirty.

He dropped everything and moved in. He quit his job (he'd wanted to anyway) packed his suitcase, put Romeo the cat in a cage and went home. Sometime later Tom joined him. Lew suspended his PhD for three months and became the main caregiver for Aunty Suze, nursing her six days a week. The lady from Nurse Maude would drop in too, but she was just for showers every second day, and if Aunty Suze didn't want a shower, she wouldn't force her. Most of the time she'd be in for a cup of tea then off again.

On Sundays Lew would drive into the hills, park up and read a book or an article. He was trying to keep his PhD ticking over, but it was a challenge. Aunty Suze would be OK some days, and he'd get at least a couple of hours in. But other days she was a tyrant. Yesterday she'd refused to eat, or take her pills, burying them in the dirt of a dried out pot plant. He threatened to take her back to hospital into the care of the nurses she'd nicknamed Mussolini and Hitler.

'What's the difference?', she'd replied.

Tom was waiting in the car when Lew finally got out the door. They drove silently down the streets, still broken and marked by cones since the earthquakes several years back. They had to take a circuitous route down the road by the beach and past the pier to get to New Brighton's main drag. The sky was sombre, and the pier itself loomed like a concrete scrum braced against southern winds.

* * *

Lew had planned to sleep on the flight, because it was still early but ended up reading instead. He was going to the city to attend the doctoral induction, and sit the compulsory English language test. The email reminders from the school manager Rachel had been polite and encouraging at first, later brusque and vaguely threatening. If he didn't complete the tasks before the end of the provisional year his candidature could not be confirmed. Flying to the city was expensive, and inconvenient at the best of times, but he bristled even more now that Aunty was sick. He was pretty sure his brother wouldn't convince her to take her pills, that would mean arriving home to more soiled bed sheets, and trying to get her strength up again.

Sitting in the doctoral lounge Lew felt anxious, both about the requirement to meet new people, and about what might (or might not) be happening at home. He felt guilty leaving his family with Aunty. After all, his brother was only sixteen, and everyone knew she listened to Lew. Guilt and hunger clawed at his stomach. He looked around for coffee but saw only carafes of water.

The induction proper began with introductions in small groups. Lew sat facing two mid-thirties women, one blonde and one brunette, who were both stylishly dressed; and next to a thin and handsome man who appeared to be in his late twenties. The thin man began,

'Well, I guess I can start, my name is Garoon, I am studying geology, and what I want to know today is who decides which person gets a scholarship? I don't have a scholarship yet and I am paying for my studies myself. I am not a rich person and it is quite expensive, you know? Everyone needs money, right?'

Garoon's question is met with embarrassed nods by the other three, who it transpires, have each secured scholarships. The question flashes like a car crash in front of Lew. The As on his transcript, always shimmery and somewhat hard to grasp now felt more distant than ever.

'I didn't do well in one of my courses for my Masters', Garoon continued, 'but it was the most difficult course in the faculty. I feel I am being punished for that. And who decides whether the research is important or not?'

Amanda writes down Garoon's question, adding that they can ask the facilitator later. She seems keen to contain Garoon, given that his introduction alone has taken up three quarters of the time they had to complete the task. Maria introduces herself next, and Amanda beside her. They are both students in psychology and work in the same lab looking at pain thresholds. Maria is wearing a navy dress and has a neck full of pearls. She folds her legs, leans forward and indicates that she wants to know if doctoral students can work overseas, as her husband is an engineer and can't find a decent job in the city. Amanda is also well dressed, with high boots and a high ponytail. Her rural vibe contrasts with Maria's urban chic. She is interested in exchange programmes. He isn't sure but Lew thinks he hears Amanda refer to her partner using the pronoun 'she'. He wants to find some way to clarify and connect, but their ten minutes is almost up.

Lew goes last, describing his own PhD topic. His face is flushed as he talks about his Masters experience, he fumbles at the hook of connecting this to his current topic and is interrupted by the facilitator, Kim, who introduces a guest, the Dean of postgraduate studies.

The Dean is plainly dressed. The brown-on-brown outfit they have selected shrinks their already small frame even further. They have not prepared advice, and will instead respond to students' questions. Lew zones out as one seemingly obvious question after another is put forward. The Dean speaks mindfully, like a diplomat, tries to balance friendly 'I've been there too' with their role as handmaiden of the university.

'By original we mean you can't just repeat someone else's study, you have to change some aspect to it. Perhaps you use a different method for your experiments, for example. You also cannot use material from your Masters research. It must be *original research.* In reality most PhDs are simply moving the literature forward, incrementally, they are not going to make a big impact. Some do, but most gather dust. PhD students need to come to terms with this.'

'Hardly inspiring is it?' Lew whispers at Maria who appears similarly disaffected, and has begun to draw pictures of playschool-style houses on a notepad in front of her.

'If you hate writing think about how you will manage a whole PhD. It really isn't for everyone. And unfortunately a number of students aren't prepared for the realities when they begin, that is why we have days like this. And as many of you know, a number of students who begin their studies don't complete them, and personally I don't think that is a bad thing. It *is* better than it used to be, but non-completion is a reality of the degree.'

'I don't have the attrition rates on me, but, ah let me rephrase this, what I wish to say is, we *are* glad you're here, the university wants as many postgraduates as possible. But if you do have troubles early think carefully about whether this is for you. There are many different paths you could take in life, the PhD is only one.'

As Lew hears these comments he immediately redirects them onto the bodies of other students in the room. He is sure he is doctoral material. He has already written off other options anyway.

'Some students find receiving feedback very difficult', The Dean continued, 'you need to develop a thick skin, toughen up a bit. This is just the way the academy works. We all get harsh feedback, even established academics, so you mustn't take it personally. There are also eight free sessions of counseling available per year. The university has budgeted for these, so you might as well use them.'

Lew has already used five of his eight free sessions and *hates* the idea of thick skin. 'Harden up' is The Dean's message. He gets it. It is the message he has heard in schools his whole life:

'Man-up'

'Don't be a pussy'

Chick-chick-chick-chicken'

He appreciates The Dean's intent, but he wonders if they ever dreamed it otherwise…

'We do what you might call surveillance. The PhD is not a walled garden anymore. We don't leave students out there in the wilderness like the old days. There are now a set of guidelines, and responsibilities for doctoral students and supervisors. Ultimately this is a good thing. You might say we are being cruel to be kind.'

The Dean's mouth forms a rare smile as they utter that final sentence. Lew sees them in a new light, mousey dean by day, kinkster by night. The thought of surveillance gives Lew the creeps, but he enjoys the image of the walled garden. He thinks of white and purple orchids, moss-covered rocks, and ponds of writhing koi carp.

The session has run over time. Kim announces that the final question will be Garoon's. He begins speaking about his failure to get a scholarship at length, including individual grades, and the performance of his lecturer in GEOL419. Lew shifts the weight of his body to the right, away from him. Aware that Garoon is a talker, Kim the facilitator interrupts and directs the question to The Dean. They pause for a long moment, before answering,

'Thanks for your question. The University allocates each faculty a number of positions each year, they have their own selection processes, but in general you must meet two criteria. Firstly, you must have a high GPA, ah grade point average, and secondly your proposed research must be recognized as significant. It sounds like you did not have a sufficiently high GPA and will be unlikely to receive a scholarship from this university. This is unfortunate for you, but we only have a set number of scholarships that the university can afford, and many more students. Therefore we give scholarships only to the highest achieving students. We can't discuss the difficulties of any particular course, we just allow the grades to speak, in the end. That is the fairest way of doing it… for everyone."

Garoon begins to respond, obviously stung by the Dean's response, but is interrupted by Kim, who announces it is lunchtime.

Lew lingers in his seat, watching Maria and Amanda and hoping they will want to chat about the last session. Instead they gather their bags and head out for lunch off-campus. Lew gets up after them, queues for one of the sandwiches provided, and heads over to the computer in the left-hand corner of the room. He notices a number of students have formed a semi-circle around Garoon who expands on his story. Lew spends lunchtime online. He emails his uncle reminding him to go to the community law centre and investigate getting power of attorney for Aunty. Halfway through lunch a message arrives from Rachel, the manager of his faculty, who he still hasn't met one year in to his PhD:

To: lewis.archer@gmail.com; bcb@city.ac.nz; hrs@city.ac.nz
Subject: Urgent – progress report/doctoral goals

Dear Lewis,

I am emailing again because you have not yet replied to my last message about your provisional doctoral goals. All City University doctoral students must complete the ten goals in order to be confirmed as full doctoral candidates within the first year of their enrolment. You have not yet submitted your annual progress report, which outlines whether or not you have met the goals. I need this urgently so I can report on your progress to graduate studies and the scholarships office. Please advise when you will submit the annual progress report. I have cc'd your supervisors into this email.

Thank you in advance.

Kind regards.
Rachel

Lew reads the email twice. His hands feel cold and his face is flushed red. He feels caught out. Of course he has made progress in the first year of his PhD – but he has only met just over half the goals he is supposed to have completed by next month. After today another one will be ticked off. He notices that his original view of these goals as jumping through unnecessary hoops, is unsettled by another feeling. He doesn't want to keep being told off. Rachel doesn't seem like the kind of manager who is going to let things slide anyway.

To: r.conner@city.ac.nz
Subject: RE: Urgent – progress report/doctoral goals

Hi Rachel,

I am sorry I didn't reply sooner. I was on suspension and have just come back to study, so I haven't been checking my emails as regularly. I am happy to send through the progress report to you – I am almost there! I am at the doctoral induction today, and hope to complete the English test tomorrow. That just leaves me with submitting my ethics forms, and the comprehensive piece of writing. I will organize a presentation next time I come up to the city.

Apologies for my delay – and for making things difficult for you.

Best wishes,
Lew

Lew feels motivated to finish today and get on with the other goals. At least it'd keep Rachel out of his inbox. He also feels a sense of achievement that he now has no unread emails, this feeling borders on a sense of superiority over the other doctoral students who sit chatting about their topics.

His thoughts return to Uncle and Aunty. Aunty had two degrees, arts and science, and always advised Lew against doing a PhD. Uncle had none and was proud of Lew. But every time he talked about going to Lew's masters graduation he emphasized the hotel Lew had organized for them in the city,

'They had a cooked brekkie, bacon, hashbrowns, fried tomatoes, fried mushrooms. But they had poached eggs, and no fried bread!'

I said, 'you can't have a fry-up without fried eggs, or fried bread. I spoke to the waitress girl, and she got a bloke out from the kitchen. I had to teach him how to cook fried bread!'

Kim reenters the room. She and her colleague had left for lunch. She asks students to mark themselves against the roll again. Lew obliges with a flourishing tick that the small box given fails to contain. The next session is the fundamentals of doctoral study: time-management, writing and examination. The session starts with the facilitators asking questions to establish the backgrounds of the students present. Lew learns he is the only geographer at the induction and feels relieved. He is not one to keep in touch afterwards.

The beginning of the session keeps Lew's interest. The facilitators talk about the history of the doctoral degree, but he zones out completely for the discussion which follows. It is focused on time-management, one topic that always seems so high-schooly. He stares out the window at the students scurrying between wet concrete buildings. One woman appears to slip over on the tiles, and is helped up by another. Almost immediately after they depart in different directions.

Lew is warmed up to the section on writing. The facilitators ask the students to position themselves as 'reluctant' or 'confident' writers. Lew identifies with both, but knows the correct answer for someone like him is 'confident'. The session is well facilitated, guided at the beginning, then opening out to a discussion.

'So what makes good writing?' Kim asks.

A short, middle-aged man's wrist shoots up, he answers, 'Good writing is clear, to the point, not unnecessarily verbose.'

'Good.' Kim responds, writing words on the board. 'Any other thoughts? What kind of writing do you like to read?'

This question prompts quiet discussions to emerge across the seminar room. A pale, red haired woman responds,

'Obviously it should be objective and in formal academic style. My pet peeve is really wordy writing. I think often academics are just hiding behind big words and theories and stuff because they don't know what they are talking about. It actually takes much more intelligence to make it simpler.'

Laughter breaks out, which encourages Red to continue.

'I have been a tutor for undergrad classes, and when you mark their essays it is always the ones who write succinctly that actually know what they are talking about. I think too often people use their thesauruses. Academic writing should be straightforward. Anybody should be able to read it if you do it carefully. You also have to watch that they don't let their bias come into their writing.' Lew is bored by these arguments. They come up every single time. His confidence waivers, but he puts up his hand to respond.

'Yes' Kim gestures toward him.

'I think good writing comes in lots of different styles and … genres. Personally, I like writing that is challenging, that requires different kinds of reading. Sometimes complex writing is a part of the work of the text'. The words come out slippery and he is aware that he is precisely the kind of academic-to-be Red doesn't approve of.

'I enjoy reading queer theory, for example, *because* it is challenging, it often pushes me, and makes me think. I enjoy the playfulness of it and I don't think it's lazy. I think it can be choiceful actually, and tactical. I would find it problematic for us to label 'good' writing as clear and straightforward and 'bad' writing as complex. And, yeah, what I like to read, or write may not be the same as you…'

Lew realizes his contribution has been a stretch. He has possibly outed himself, and his penchant for complex, elitist, faggoty, writing. His voice comes out low and measured, but he feels screechy. Again, his face is flushed. He keeps talking, wants to win the point,

'I think it is really important that as new academics we can write differently too, sometimes I want to speak softer, and sometimes my writing is angry, I guess. In my writing I want to be a living, breathing, human being, who cares about this stuff, you know? I want people to feel it. There needs to be space for that. That is what I think, I guess.'

Kim seems pleased by the contrary points that have emerged and stokes the conversation further.

'So we have two different views here about what good writing is, any other perspectives?'

Several people raise their hands. They each largely disagree with Lew, and direct their responses to Kim who notes their contributions on the whiteboard. It reveals an outline of writing as a tool, which merely transmits.

Lew considers replying again. He feels passionate, defensive. His own experience is that standard advice for academic writing would leave it deadening, always a carbon copy of the writing before it. Ultimately, he can't be bothered going back for thirds. It's a tough crowd.

The final session is the thesis examination process. Lew prepares bullet points in anticipation. He wonders why he has never really thought about the end of his thesis, which is supposed to be only two years away. He does think about the possible examiners though. He likes searching for their photos, on university websites, Academia.edu, Twitter accounts…

The day is to conclude with a session on library and computer skills. He follows the rest of the students down the flight of stairs, spots Maria and nods, she flashes him a weary smile. He has already been marked present for the second half of the day so he decides to bunk it. He walks up the facilitator and explains he is having a migraine and needs to lie down. He waves to Maria and Amanda on the way out, but they don't see him, already busy undertaking the set of searches given to them by the librarian.

Once outside of the computer room his mind turns to booking his English test. Maybe he'd have time if he got there before four? He has to find the office first and that might take a while because it is somewhere across campus, and it's still raining. But first he needs to pee. He walks to the bathrooms one floor down from the doctoral lounge. He moves quickly, eyes cast downward. Lew enters the cubicle and locks the door. Sitting on the toilet he reaches for his mobile but knows it hasn't buzzed. There is no one to message, he just has to wait. He lets out a sigh and can feel it coming. A wave. Of what? Grief? Shame? Anger? Despair? In the end it is something more ordinary. The desire to just keep moving. He gathers himself together and decides to get the English test over and done with. At least it'd be another thing off the list.

CONCLUSION

It is my hope that this story has resonated with readers in some way, moving them to consider how students might experience aspects of contemporary doctoral education. In closing the chapter I do not intend to offer any final take on what the story means, or does. Instead, I wish to pose some questions in order to provoke further debate. What might the story teach us about the affective practices of *doing* 'doctoral student'? For example, are there resonances between the ways Lew enacts 'worthy' doctoral subjectivity, and the ways intelligible 'academicity' (Petersen, 2007) increasingly means 'keeping ahead of deadlines, juggling workloads… supporting new 'initiatives', making good use of our time, even at the point of catastrophic health crises' (pp. 241–242). Secondly, what might the affective practices visible in the text teach us about the politics of doctoral education? Perhaps, like academics, doctoral students are at an affective and embodied 'breaking point'. Yet as the story suggests, this might manifest itself as a muffled whimper, rather than a loud 'snap!' Indeed, as Lew 'gathers himself' and contemplates sitting his compulsory English test, I wonder whether he evokes *something* about doing emotion work in doctoral education's present moment. The story offers a view of 'doing doctoralness' that is often about compartmentalising, coping, muddling along, and moving to the next thing on your list.

ACKNOWLEDGEMENTS

An earlier version of "Doctoral Induction Day" received one of the *Contemporary Ethnography Across the Disciplines* (CEAD) PhD essay prizes. This assisted me to travel to present at the 2012 CEAD conference in Hamilton, NZ. I thank the CEAD committee for their support and encouragement of doctoral researchers in this way. I am also grateful to a kind mob of readers who have generously offered their reflections on the story.

REFERENCES

Burford, J. (2014). A meditation on the poetics of doctoral writing. *Higher Education Research and Development, 33*(6), 1232–1235.
Burrows, R. (2000). Living within the h-index? Metric assemblages in the contemporary academy. *The Sociological Review, 60*(2), 355–372.
Carr, A. D., Rule, H. J., & Taylor, K. T. (2013, Winter). Literacy in the raw: Collecting, sharing, and circulating graduate literacy narratives. *Computers and Composition* (online).
Elizabeth, V., & Grant, B. (2013). 'The spirit of research has changed': Reverberations from researcher identities in managerial times. *Higher Education Research and Development, 32*(1), 122–235.
Gill, R. (2010). Breaking the silence: The hidden injuries of the neoliberal university. In R. Ryan-Flood & R. Gill (Eds.), *Secrecy and silence in the research process: Feminist reflections*. Abingdon, England & New York, NY: Routledge.
Gray, R. (2004). No longer a man: Using ethnographic fiction to represent life history research. *Auto/Biography, 12*(1), 44–61.
Nöbauer, H. (2012). Affective lanscapes in academia: Emotional labour, vulnerability, and uncertainty in late modern academic work. *International Journal of Work Organisation and Emotion, 5*(2), 132–144
Pelias, R. (2004). *A methodology of the heart: Evoking academic and daily life*. Walnut Creek, CA: Altamira Press.
Petersen, E. (2007). Negotiating academicity: Postgraduate research supervision as category boundary work. *Studies in Higher Education, 32*(4), 475–487.
Richardson, L. (1994). Writing: A method of inquiry. In N. K. Denzin & Y. S. Lincoln (Eds.), *Handbook of qualitative research* (pp. 516–529). Thousand Oaks, CA: Sage.
Saltmarsh, S., & Randell-Moon, H. (2014). Work, life and im/balance: Policies, practices and performativities of academic well-being. *Somatchnics, 4*(2), 236–252.
Sparkes, A. (1997). Ethnographic fiction and representing the absent other. *Sport, Education and Society, 2*(1), 25–40.
Sparkes, A. (2002). Fictional representations: On difference, choice, and risk. *Sociology of Sport, 19*(1), 1–24.
Sparkes, A. (2007). Embodiment, academics, and the audit culture: A story seeking consideration. *Qualitative Research, 7*(4), 521–550.
Tierney, W. (1993). The cedar closet. *Qualitative Studies in Education, 6*(4), 303–314.

James Burford
Faculty of Learning Sciences and Education
Thammasat University, Thailand

BARBARA GRANT, CATHERINE MITCHELL, EDWARD OKAI,
JAMES BURFORD, LINLIN XU, TONI INGRAM AND
VANESSA CAMERON-LEWIS[1]

10. DOCTORAL SUPERVISOR AND STUDENT IDENTITIES

Fugitive Moments from the Field

Doctoral supervisor and student identities are embodied and intricate. They are lived in the thick of human lives, in among other identities we simultaneously hold. Because of the high stakes attached to doctoral education, these identities often include heightened vulnerabilities, excitements, tensions, affects and uncertainties. And so, while supervisors and students often experience the excitement of research, the thrill of creating new knowledge, and the fun of working together, both may also find themselves plunged back into difficult – even painful – states of unknowingness, of 'learner-ness', of uncertainty.

In this chapter, we offer a series of fugitive moments in the lived experiences of doctoral students and supervisors.[2] In crafting our narratives and juxtaposing them in a simple linear sequence, we hope to offer the reader a feeling for the rough but fertile texture of these heterogeneous identities in ways that might help us to think more deeply about what it means to be a doctoral student or a supervisor: to think about how we enact the identities we occupy in relation to ourselves and the difficult work we are doing – and towards the others of our supervision relations. While institutions might idealise particular identities for their doctoral supervisors and students, we do not have to simply accept those on offer. We can enact ourselves in ways more particular, more interesting, more ethical, more political, more *nuanced*, than our institutions can dream of.

To produce the following narratives of identity, six doctoral students and one of their supervisors met for a half-day workshop. We are used to meeting together as a group to talk about our work and to review each other's writing, so this mode of interacting was familiar and usually generative of ideas and energy. The workshop brief sent out by the supervisor was this:

> Think about an important *formative* incident in your experience as a doctoral student … Select some objects (or images of them) that were connected to, or entangled with, this incident and be prepared to tell your story including the role played by these objects. (Email, 25 January 2015)

We began the workshop with a round of talking about our objects/images – this activity was inspired by the supervisor's current work on doctoral supervisors as assemblages enfolded with 'other humans, objects, forces, procedures' (Rose, 1996: 182). She wondered how objects would be expressed as aspects of student and supervisor identity. The round was followed by fast-writing,[3] and a brief peer review of the writing in pairs. At the end of the workshop, we each had some rough writing – this chapter was on its way!

In the end, the final narratives are variegated: some concern objects (in which case, images are provided), while others do not, although they do involve Rose's 'other humans, … forces, procedures'; two are written in the third person, four in the first. This variety might provide a bumpy ride for the reader but this is, indeed, our intention. Student and supervisor identities are themselves bumpy rides for those who inhabit them.

Figure 10.1. Coffee making supplies

MAKING YOUR OWN COFFEE/DOCTORAL STUDENT IDENTITY 1

Day 1

It is a sunny day, a warm beginning for the winter.

I arrive early, probably too early. I go to the kitchen at the end of the corridor to make myself a coffee. It tastes horrible. I just learned to use this coffee machine yesterday and it's an entirely new experience for me with my strong tea culture. In half an hour, I will meet my supervisor for the first time. I keep looking at my watch. While counting the minutes, I cannot help imagining the scenarios: What will she say? Will she like me…?

Her office is at the beginning of the corridor. Now it's seven minutes before the meeting. I am unsure if it's appropriate to arrive this early for an appointment. I wait outside for another three minutes, then knock. My mind goes blank. Somehow I find myself sitting on a small red sofa, talking about my settlement in this country. We have begun talking about my proposed research when I catch her word, 'however':

'However, because I don't have the expertise in your research area, you probably will have to change your main supervisor in your second year …'. I am frozen: my blood turns into ice, despite loads of her comforting words. I don't remember how this conversation ended. I get out of her office and walk to my own; I cannot feel my legs.

I am in turmoil and have that bitter coffee taste again, from mouth to heart. I go to my desk and pin the character '静' to the wall. It means calm, quiet and tranquil. To change the supervisor in one year, when everything has taken shape, brings a great deal of risk and uncertainty. I will go through another round of adaption with the new supervisor, which may involve much change in the research design. It's a sword hanging over my neck and I don't know whether or when it will cut off my head. What should I do? It's my second week in this country and my first week in the university. I barely know anyone. I don't know where I can seek advice. My husband and I walked about ten kilometres per day around the city the whole of last week to find a place to stay, and he is trying desperately to get a job in this foreign land to support us. My seven-month old daughter is in China with her grandparents.

Day 2

The next morning, I come to my supervisor again and say: 'I don't want to change supervisor in one year; however, I could change my research topic.' This is a difficult and bold decision, but it's what I can think of to remedy the situation while not ruining the relationship by confronting the supervisor with a direct refusal. Being a Chinese student, I have been raised in a culture of collectivism and high power distance, in which harmonious relationship is expected. When harmony is threatened, people of low power bear the responsibility to restore it. Therefore, I should make the concession since teachers are to be respected and students are to be obedient.

Year 2

Today, I may not do the same if it happened again. I gradually realize my taken-for-granted epistemology doesn't always work here. Instead, it sometimes adds bitterness to my PhD experience. I start adapting. While remaining Chinese, I adopt the take-and-give-up strategy between my host and home cultures, although how much to take and how much to give up remains mysterious. Likewise, I try to make my coffee enjoyable by adding the 'right' amount of sugar and milk.

I'm still trying.

MERRY CHRISTMAS!/DOCTORAL STUDENT IDENTITY 2

It's Christmas Day, the carols are playing and we're sitting around the table amidst the festive remnants of food, wine and Christmas crackers. The post-Christmas pudding conversation moves onto my PhD. It's early days and I'm explaining to my family what I plan on researching. 'You're studying what? What's the point of *that*?' My uncle asks in a tone more critical than curious.

My research is in the area of gender, sexuality and schooling. For my uncle (think forestry and farming), education is about, or rather should be about, mathematics, literacy and science. Teaching kids how to read and write, that's what's important. And he's not shy in expressing his opinion. The idea that I was more interested in the ways young people also learn about gender and sexuality at school was just not on his radar. Sadly, he's not alone.

So I found myself attempting to explain (probably not as articulately as I would have liked) my research topic or, more specifically, defending its worth, to the sound of Frosty the Snowman. Even with the much-appreciated support from other family members, I don't think I succeeded. The conversation reached an impasse: I was left thinking my uncle was a dinosaur, he thought my doctorate was a waste of time and my Nana was in need of more wine. She had the right idea.

In the days following, I felt a lingering sadness and disappointment. While my uncle and I are very different, I was disappointed that he didn't appear to see the value in what I was doing. Or at the very least appreciate that other people might see the value in it. I also clearly needed to get better at articulating it!

There are a few things that I've taken away from this experience. It has raised questions for me about the idea of a PhD and what is deemed worthwhile knowledge. My masters research was in the same area yet I do not recall a similar conversation with my uncle. Is there something about the public perception of a PhD that invites and incites critical opinion? Is it a public commodity and therefore subject to particular ideals and standards? If so, whose? My uncle certainly had clear ideas about what knowledge he considered worthy of a PhD in Education. Alas, mine fell short.

It was also an important lesson in being able to describe my PhD topic in a way that is succinct and accessible. I can now appreciate what all the doctorate advice books mean about the 30-second elevator pitch. Like a doctoral thesis, though, that pitch is a constant work in progress. After broaching this topic with one of my supervisors who shares similar research interests, I've also come to realise that sometimes a vague description can be prudent. This I find liberating: some people just aren't going to get it!

Note to self: Next Christmas when Frosty the Snowman comes on, feel free to press skip.

FIND THE PERFECT PEN, FIND THE PERFECT WORD/DOCTORAL STUDENT IDENTITY 3

She has full hands. She has picked up a bundle of pens from the messy pile sitting next to her. Her narration begins. Her fellow students and supervisor sit quietly around the table as the pens begin to fan out in front of her, row after row. This row, she says, is a particular collection of fountain pens: one black, one silver, and another

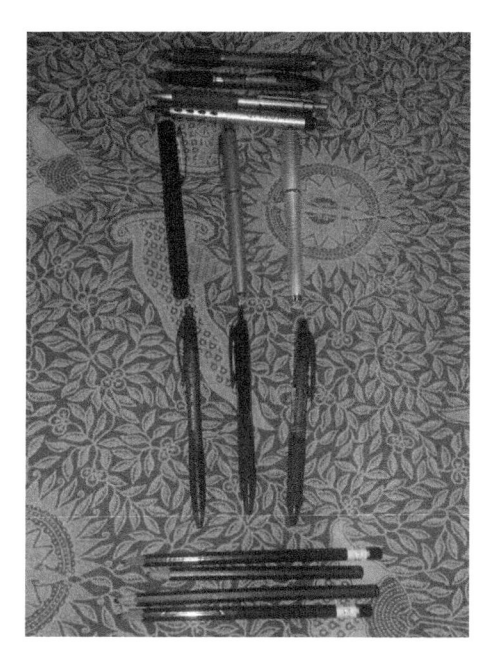

Figure 10.2. Writing implements

finely wrought in carved silvery-white metal. Each has a different nib, a particular weight and grasps the page in different ways. The next row is of cheap plastic pens. All super lightweight, they run easily along the page with only a gentle push of the writer's hand. Although inexpensive, they were nonetheless chosen carefully, with time spent testing and analysing the particular qualities of each before purchase. Choosing a pen can be a complex business. She knows sharing her approach to this choosing may reveal a little too much of her particular fascination (her fetish?) with writing implements.

The pens in the third layer bear the insignia of several universities, her own and others further afield. These are used less, but collected and kept together in her workspace. Each represents some kind of moment or event, and offers her a sense of belonging to the academic community. They signify her academic cosmopolitanism: she is, for the time being, a doctoral student/academic on the move. The few she has brought along today are just a sample of many, received in conference packs or workshops: organised together, they are tangible reminders of her time and place within academia. They also provide a physical means to hold onto those places lost in time. She knows this particular subset of pens, these souvenirs from local and international universities, may not grow much in the future. Her doctoral candidature is coming to a close and her academic future is open-ended, to say the least. She says she is not quite sure how to account for the impermanence and uncertainty of her doctoral student experience and that storing these souvenir pens together in a precious place seems like a good idea.

The last row of writing tools holds black wooden pencils – exclusively black, she tells her listeners. She is not able to fully explain for this requirement, but it speaks a little of her fastidiousness and the intensity she brings to the smallest academic decision. The blackness of the pencils, perhaps, also speaks to her desire for simplicity, even within her own complex constructions. The pencils are located in the bottom row, nearest to her reach; these are the most organic of her writing implements and she finds their simple design, colour and materiality reassuring. They are close to her of late because she has been wrapped in a cycle of re-working and editing her own work. Pencil is capable of being quickly erased, a useful quality in the painstaking process of textual changes on drafts that seem to refuse to resolve themselves into any kind of completed form.

These pens and pencils, and the careful choices made in their acquisition, are symbolic of the careful decisions she has to make navigating the complex world of the PhD. They bring a reassuring materiality to her desire to write, if in a somewhat old-fashioned way, and help her to construct a 'writerly' identity as she strives, hopefully and hopelessly, towards her aspiration of crafting a scholarly thesis and, perhaps, finding a place in the academy.

The pencils and pens assembled here, and the many others not on show, are tools of practice and intellect. She hopes, just a little bit, that by finding the right pen, the *perfect* pen, she might also find the perfect word. The kind of word fit for a writerly doctoral thesis.

AN UNDONE ACTIVIST/DOCTORAL STUDENT IDENTITY 4

I tell few people I am writing a PhD. I don't like the reverence a PhD invokes, the separation it creates. I am separated enough writing on my own in this small room. Instead my identity is that of a never quite present mother. Seldom do I turn up for playgroup, our house is never tidy, there is no baking and I am too tired to go out at night or invite people over. I still cling to identities once claimed as a young Pākehā activist: middle-class with anarco-feminist tendencies; heterosexual but queer; an anti-capitalist, cis-gendered female seeking allies to support minority struggles everywhere. This advertisement of myself belongs to a postmodern society where oppositional difference structures the world.

But my identity is shifting as I do my PhD. I am, in Elizabeth Grosz's (2011) words, 'becoming undone'. Theory is unravelling me. Rosa Braidotti (2012) shows me my world is structured on a concept of difference where different-from necessarily means worth-less-than. Postmodernity does not undo this logic of oppositional difference, but only confuses the flow of power associated with the self/other dichotomy. This is not to be underestimated: in New Zealand, this has allowed a woman to become prime minister; Māori immersion schools have been established; homosexuals are allowed to marry. (The examples go on.) But these increasingly visible subjectivities, with their rights now seemingly equal with those of the original One, still uphold the dichotomy where the original One is affirmed as male, white, heterosexual. As a woman, I am weary of being Other; as a middle-class hetero Pākehā, I am weary of affirming my privilege. I am an undone activist. I need a different logic to traverse this monological system of sameness.

This is the work of my PhD: to teach me how to think 'otherwise'. The process of unbecoming began with a shift from thinking difference as relative and logical to thinking difference as *ontological*. Ontological difference understands difference as the generative force of the universe (Deleuze, 1994), a difference both internal and external, a movement or force that makes the world. This notion of 'pure difference', as Grosz (2011) explains it, 'is that movement of self-differentiation, that movement of internal differentiation that separates itself from difference that surrounds it' (2011: 93). This difference is the movement of differing from itself and, in differing from itself, it becomes differentiated. But this difference is not different *from*, because it is still *in relation to* the difference it was. Yes, this takes slow repeated reading to comprehend: to reconsider what I previously took as truth.

Grosz's words take us back to identity: 'This pure difference in itself, this process of self-differentiation that has no self before it begins its becoming, is the undermining of all identities, unities, cohesions' (2011: 93). Modern identities rest on oppositional difference, but difference as ontological undermines this kind of identity: how one can name oneself when one is always in the process of becoming? The pretence of unity that modernism affords us – and the possibilities for equality – is derailed by pure difference. Such a complicated undoing of my concept of self as separate draws my attention away from my past, from those static identities, to an awareness of my constant movement of self-differentiation in relationship with the world, a process of un/becoming. Instead of naming myself as different-from, as a 'doctoral student' in contrast to those who are not, or as one kind in contrast to another, I am drawn to think of the effects of my differing and how I can best be in relationship.

WEARING DOCTORAL IDENTITY/DOCTORAL STUDENT IDENTITY 5

I tell myself I've got this. A deep breath in and, as I release, I count out loud: *one, two, three…*

I'm locked inside the toilet cubicle, seat down, head resting in my hands. My face is hot and flushed. The bathroom is familiar despite being far from home. Same chipped door. Same thin loo paper. Same pink liquid hand-soap. Part of me thinks I'm being stupid. I should be milling about like everyone else, finding the people I've come all this way to meet. But I'm also trying to be gentle with myself. Sometimes you've just gotta do what you gotta do and, for me, that means disappearing when I'm close to completely losing it.

I'm hoping it's a good crowd. It's a symposium on queer theory and higher education. I made the trip because my two intellectual worlds so seldom collide like

Figure 10.3. On my hands

this. I think it's the collision sparking the anxiety. I'm not yet sure who, or how, to *be* here. Before I left home, I created fantasies about the audience I'd be speaking to. Sometimes I'd imagine a caricature of 'HE types', other times a tribe of radical queer grad students. The difference matters in terms of what I'd say, of course, but also for how I'd choose to present myself.

In higher education worlds, I restrain my sartorial exuberance. In the buzzing whirl of a conference, I often can't handle the added emotional labour of embodying sexual/gender trouble. Looking down, I notice my outfit's a work of compromise: dark-brown leather boots could pass for tidy rural-esque footwear but, to the right audience, they might code the business-butch I'm getting at. The rest is pretty plain. Dark-blue jeans, black tee, and a thick woolen coat that can easily pass for grey (if you get close enough, it's a lovely shade of deep purple).

In my pocket, I have two rings.

I snatched them as I left my hotel room. If I wear them, they will be the most excessive part of my outfit by far. I originally bought them as homage to a hero of my adolescence, the writer Dame Edith Sitwell. I came across the dangerous dame while at the peak of the mystery about what to do with my own embodiment. Well recognized as a literary presence, ferocious critic and stubborn eccentric, Sitwell was also known for her physical presence. Once described as a 'high altar on the move', she was known for her brocade gowns, turbans, furs, but especially for her beautiful hands festooned with enormous chunks of aquamarine or amethyst. There is something about the leonine Dame Edith that abides with me, even though I am rather timid, and ambivalent about my desire to stand out.

The objects that bring me closest to her spirit, these two rock-encrusted rings, remain in my pocket.

I'm still not sure what to do. I'm still worrying about what to communicate in my talk and on my body. My bigger-than-usual response must mean something. This symposium, and the way I am received at it, must matter a lot to me, I guess. I shove my hand in my pocket and feel the weight and texture of the stones. I take in another deep breath, exhale, and count *one, two, three...*

PHD WRITING: THE YOKE OF MIND-FREEZE/DOCTORAL STUDENT IDENTITY 6

Translating my ideas and thoughts into writing has always been a struggle for me. In undertaking a PhD, the challenge is compounded by my lack of confidence that my writing is of the high quality expected from doctoral students. I feel in constant battle with the yoke of mind-freeze (my term for what others call 'writer's block' – see Bane, 2012 or Rose, 2009, for example). I begin every piece of writing with zeal, and a plan for the expected outcome, but I get stagnated after a few sentences. The quest to be original *and* practical in the process of knowledge recycling and creation demands I engage with theory to explicate relationships and variables involved in my study. However, it is so challenging to use abstract concepts in a simple and practical way, especially when I have to relate them to my research questions. My identity as a writer struggling for space and voice in a highly contested field (doctoral education) is being challenged by my struggle to work with theory at a high level of understanding and mastery: working with theory dims my confidence in my writing since I feel unable to assert myself through theory in a creative way.

The recurrent mind-freeze I experience in writing has led to many unfinished or discarded drafts. Though I know the writing process is gradual and subject to periodic amendment, I discard such writings because I judge them as not fitting the PhD standard. These self-sabotaging behaviours (which others may refer to as 'perfectionism') sap my enthusiasm to return to those drafts. However, pressure from supervisors – as well as knowledge sharing within the supervisory space, or positive feedback on my draft – sometimes acts as a catalyst to return to unfinished work. The supervisory relationship has been a space where I can discuss my challenges and get suggestions for how to go forward. To help me deal with mind-freeze, one supervisor gave me a sample outline of a piece of her writing she had done to take cues from. Though I have now adopted the use of outlines for my writing, I still contend with mind-freeze when trying to develop the themes and sub-themes within the outline. Symbolically speaking, by activating my thinking to flow in relation to my writing, the friendly discussions serve as a 'source of heat' to 'melt the ice' of my mind-freeze.

The pressure I get from the supervisory space to submit writing by a certain deadline may be challenging but it is positive for my writing process because it compels me to write despite the mind-freeze. The thought of getting an email from my supervisors asking why I have not sent them promised writing – not wanting to disappoint them – helps me to sustain the writing process. So requests for writing function as positive stressors and, despite a lack of confidence and the tyranny of mind-freeze, these requests help me persist in my PhD becoming and to meet my goals for each year.

PARTNER IN BONDAGE/DOCTORAL SUPERVISOR IDENTITY

Mistress B (MB) feels the handcuffs. Encased in scarlet artificial fur, they are soft to the touch. MB's first doctoral student sent them to her, along with a sequined black eye-mask, after submitting her thesis. At the time, MB thought they were a funny reference to her own master-slave work but, on second thoughts, maybe there was more to them, even than the student 'knew'. After all, they are only soft to touch *on the outside*. For the preceding 18 months, MB and the student had been bound together in arduous exchanges of writing and feedback. They had both slaved over long draft chapters lavish with theories, insights, data. But MB's enslavement had been of the masterful kind – the hardest work was done by the student, as it needs to be. The student (who was also a friend) had not complained nor told MB just how painful it had been.

Today, though, MB is thinking about another kind of bondage she experiences as a doctoral supervisor: that with co-supervisors. Since 2001, her institution has required more than a single supervisor in doctoral supervision; the most common arrangement in her Faculty is the inclusion of a co-supervisor. The co-supervision bond is regularised through the Doc 6, which carries many signatures formalising the framework of a doctoral student's education.

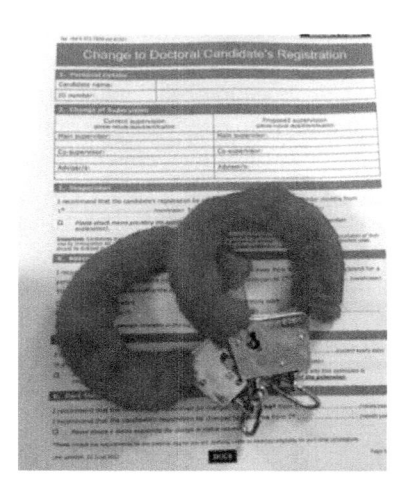

Figure 10.4. Handcuffs

For MB, the bondage of co-supervision is a treasure chest: new collegial relationships; creative ideas for supervision conduct; vibrant three-way discussions; fresh ways of thinking about theories, methodologies, writing. Sometime she finds consolation in sharing anxieties about students and/or their work. Supervision can be a lonely experience for supervisors too. And other, darker pleasures are also found in bondage, as Michel Foucault (1989) reminds us: 'There's so much pleasure in giving orders: there's also pleasure in taking them' (p. 55).

But co-supervision has also been a Pandora's box. Some little demons have been loosed to unpredictably disturb her sense of self – and her work – as a supervisor. Unsettling questions, tricky to ask of a colleague, hover over her co-supervisions at times ('why do you do that?', or worse, 'why haven't you done that?'). Then there's moments of slowly dawning realisation that she and a co-supervisor have wildly different assessments of a student's ability. And worrying uncertainties over how to address a co-supervisor when she disagrees with something they contribute to the supervision. And anxieties about offending co-supervisors by exceeding her authority and somehow diminishing theirs. In the most difficult moments, her bondage in co-supervision leads to a feeling of losing her grip as a supervisor qua expert with something to offer, and that the student's work is somehow endangered.

MB settles into her chair and carefully composes (and recomposes) an email to the doctoral student and co-supervisor. In the end, she simply says: "I don't really understand this work but, also, I don't really understand the (co-supervisor's) feedback. Something is not working here. I need to do things differently." She feels vulnerable in her ignorance, not like a supervisor at all. But she sends the email out into the ether anyway. She sits back; she stretches her tight and painful shoulders. She's relieved, she has gripped onto something, she is no longer in free-fall. She has no idea what will happen next. While she is waiting, she teaches, writes, worries, laughs, cries, fills out forms, goes to meetings, reads manuscripts, and deals with millions of emails.

IDENTITIES LIVED IN (MATERIAL) MOMENTS

> Narrative is both a mode of reasoning and a mode of representation ... explanation in the narrative mode is contextually embedded ... (Richardson, 1997: 28)

Our identities as doctoral students and supervisors are formed as assemblages: we are, as Rose says (1986: 182), enfolded with other humans (supervisors, family members, co-supervisors, conference goers, academic colleagues), with objects (food and drink, pens, jewelry, drafts of writing, institutional documents), with forces (new ideas, supervision relations, personally felt compulsions, deadlines), and with procedures (reading and thinking academically, writing academic texts, meetings with students and supervisors, presenting conference papers, institutional approvals). These other 'things' make us who we are as students and supervisors; as these 'other humans, objects, forces, procedures' move in and out of our experience and consciousness, and as new things enter, we become different, if only sometimes fleetingly.

We wrote the seven narratives of doctoral student and supervisor identities knowing who the other authors were, including that one is a supervisor of the other six. This knowledge will have shaped – consciously and unconsciously – our choice of moment to focus on, for our identities are always somehow strategic, as Stuart Hall argues (1996). Our identities also always exceed us. Of circumstance and necessity, then, the narratives are fragments of how we think of ourselves as doctoral students and supervisor. Yet fruitfully, each narrative rivets attention on a particular formative context or aspect of experience within the doctoral zone that is not entirely peculiar to the individual who recounts it: the traumatic shock of arriving in a new place with different rules; a painful episode of family refusal to recognise the seriousness of that which we take so seriously; complex links between choice of writing implement and a sense of writerly self; powerful impacts of new theories on existing identities; gut-wrenching possibilities that rise up when we prepare to present ourselves to strangers; difficult struggles to write when we feel as if we cannot produce an appropriately doctoral voice; demanding mixed-bags of effects arising from new institutional mandates for supervision practice. The narrative form permits close attention to the embeddedness (Richardson, 1997) and concreteness of moments of identities, just as it reveals some of the reasonings and affects inside those moments.

In a sense, what we offer here is a collective story that 'gives voice to those who are silenced or marginalized in the cultural narrative' (Richardson, 1997: 32): we are not suggesting that we are silenced and marginalized subjects of the university per se because, despite alienating experiences that we could each recount, easy arguments can be made for both our importance and our privilege. Rather, the voices we offer here come from marginal, usually silenced, places *within* our overflowing identities as doctoral students (international and local) and supervisor (local, white) within an anglophone research-intensive university in a post-colonial setting. We offer moments of vulnerability and uncertainty, of hope and good will, of zaniness and creativity, with the intention that others will find their foibles here too and, knowing something more about how others struggle, be heartened for their work in the doctoral zone. For, alongside the bumpiness of the ride, there are many distinctive and delicious pleasures to be had for both supervisors and students.

NOTES

[1] Authors are ordered alphabetically by first names.
[2] The weight of the chapter falls towards the 'student', as six of the authors write from that standpoint.
[3] Fast writing is a technique suggested as a composing strategy by Peter Elbow. His very useful instructions are: 'The idea is to simply write for ten minutes (later on, perhaps 15 or 20). Don't stop for

anything. Go quickly without rushing. Never stop or look back to cross something out … to wonder what word or thought to use, or to think about what you are doing. If you can't think of a word or thought, just use a squiggle or else write, '"I can't think of it". Just put down something' (1973: 1).

REFERENCES

Bane, R. (2012). *Around the writer's block: Using brain science to solve writer's resistance*. London, England: Penguin Books.
Braidotti, R. (2012). Interview by Rick Dolphijn and Iris van der Tuin. *New materialism: Interviews and cartographies* (pp. 19–37). University of Michigan Library, MI: Open Humanities Press.
Deleuze, G. (1994). *Difference and repetition* (P. R. Patton, Trans.). New York, NY: Columbia University Press.
Elbow, P. (1973). *Writing without teachers*. New York, NY: Oxford University Press.
Foucault, M. (1989). Michel Foucault interviewed by French radio. *Impulse, 15*, 50–55.
Grosz, E. (2011). *Becoming undone: Darwinian reflections on life, politics and art*. Durham, NC & London, England: Duke University Press.
Hall, S. (1996). Introduction: Who needs identity? In S. Hall & P. Du Gay (Eds.), *Questions of cultural identity* (pp. 1–17). London, England: Sage Publications.
Richardson, L. (1997). *Fields of play: Constructing an academic life*. New Brunswick, NJ: Rutgers University Press.
Rose, M. (2009). *Writer's block: The cognitive dimension*. Carbondale, IL: Southern Illinois University Press.
Rose, N. (1996). *Inventing our selves: Psychology, power and personhood*. Cambridge, England: Cambridge University Press.

Barbara Grant
School of Critical Studies
University of Auckland, New Zealand

Catherine Mitchell
School of Critical Studies
University of Auckland, New Zealand

Edward Okai
School of Critical Studies
University of Auckland, New Zealand

James Burford
School of Critical Studies
University of Auckland, New Zealand

Linlin Xu
School of Critical Studies
University of Auckland, New Zealand

Toni Ingram
School of Critical Studies
University of Auckland, New Zealand

Vanessa Cameron-Lewis
School of Critical Studies
University of Auckland, New Zealand

GINA WISKER

11. TOIL AND TROUBLE

Professional and Personal Expectations and Identities in Academic Writing for Publication

I've done my 4 pieces for the REF so I don't have to write any more.
(Colleague)

Writing is about danger for me: it's like life – you can go under.
(Toni Morrison, cited in Reynolds & Noakes, 2003: 6)

Academics are subject to confusing sets of values in a marketised higher education system which sees students as co-producers of knowledge and also consumers, customers and products. In the turmoil of competing drives to re-orientate, academic identities are also in turmoil. This paper focuses on tensions between intrinsic and extrinsic motivation which drive writing for academic publication, and the tangled personal and professional academic identities which relate to these tensions.

LITERATURE REVIEW

Established and current research into academic identities often concerns balancing acts of managing the personal, professional and a range of academic demands (Clegg, 2008; Henkel, 2005a, 2005b; Fanghanel, 2007), while research into writing for academic publication often focuses on doctoral students, and writing development (Aitchison & Lee, 2006; Aitchison, Kamler, & Lee, 2010). Research writing is seen as a 'complex struggle for identity in intertwined and often contradictory discourses' (Kamler & Thomson, 2006). Previous research into writing blocks and breakthroughs for academics who write and publish (including PhD students) (Wisker & Savin Baden, 2009; Wisker, 2013; Wisker, 2014a and b) suggests some blockages are caused by factors relating to time management including being realistic in determining the amount of time needed and insisting on it being available for writing; lack of or inappropriate support for the writing process, and problems with having a 'right' to speak professionally on a topic. Each of these issues is also tied up with a sense of identity and academic identity in particular. It is argued that a major value of higher education is producing 'Socratic citizens who are capable of thinking for themselves, arguing with tradition, and understanding with sympathy the conditions of lives different from their own' (Nussbaum, 2002: 302) and influential thinkers in higher education also focus on values so that in

Imagining the University (2013), Barnett argues for dialogue between views and the right to debate, that we require 'a proliferation of ideas of the university, if only to demonstrate that things could be other than they are'. He argues for an ecological university existing positively in relation to the 'other', to which it should be a gift. In the light of these values statements it is useful to explore the mix of demands, expectations, support, reward and tensions experienced by those whose academic writing is a mix of the professional and the personal, in terms of their contribution of time, concern about articulating their research and their views, and the tensions they feel in their own academic identities, referred to, above, as a kind of dubious, witchy mix ('hubble bubble, toil and trouble' referencing the three weird sisters/ witches in Shakespeare's Macbeth, where power operates, identity is in confusion, and things are never as they seem).

This chapter combines work across academic identities and writing for publication, now a major feature of academics' professional lives. This exploration of academic writers' perception of relationships between personal and professional writerly and other identities takes place the context of neoliberalism and the matching of expected, deliverable outputs in universities. In this context, workload models are increasingly being used to determine what is done, how it is seen to be done, and its outputs measured according to explicit formulae. The amount and kind of publication output is particularly important, especially in the context of the Research Excellence Framework (REF in the UK). Writing for publication is accompanied and driven by expectations, targets, while recognition is attached to 'quality' and to production rhythms of regular, high quality outputs or perhaps 'churn', its compliant but less high scoring sibling. However, writing is for many academics and practitioners much more than a mechanical production of outputs and is intrinsically tied up with their sense of identity, as professionals and people who seek communication through writing. Writing for publication also depends on the development of a 'discoursal voice' (Maybin, 2001) which explores, discusses, evidences and argues with a level of confidence in the discourse of the discipline, at an academic level, in the genre for which publication is sought. The term discoursal voice derives from Bakhtin (1986). Here, situated meaning-making is sought between writers who enter the discourse community who make sense of the established use of words in this community, and make them their own. Bakhtin refers to spoken word and speakers but earlier (Wisker, 2015b) I argue that we can see this as transferable to the written word, in an academic writing context. Words are experienced and used in three ways, first, the neutral word of a language then, 'as an other's word, which belongs to another person and is filled with echoes of the other's utterance, and finally my word', 'imbued with my expression', (Bakhtin, 1986: 88). Comfort and confidence or lack thereof when producing academic writing and entering conversations with others is, I argue, a matter for induction and development (and struggle) and then interaction with the receptiveness of gatekeepers: managers, peer reviewers, editors and readers. Academic writers work with 'the word of authority, of constraint, of precedent' (1986: 88). To keep 'imposter syndrome' at bay (Kearns, 2014) we need to feel we have a right to speak using 'the authoritative word' (Bakhtin, 1981: 342), with confidence.

My experience as an academic writer has produced a range of joys and tensions in my writing practices and the rest of my professional and personal life. It has also caused me to look at my own often conflicted and sometimes celebratory sense of a writerly identity. The demands, processes and outputs of writing can, in my experience, offer rewards and development opportunities which might well enhance my sense of academic identity, but they can also produce tensions, burnout, and other extreme responses. These are sometimes associated with trying to fit writing in when the time it demands seems more elastic than anything else, the writing process itself including blocks and breakthroughs (Wisker, 2014a), and peer review judgment (Wisker, 2014b). Alongside my research work, I lead activities on writing for publication, and review and edit for academic journals. It is clear that many colleagues find academic writing 'high stakes' work. It is seen as stressful and rewarding; the amount of time and persistence needed for academic writing is rarely calculated realistically and there is a great deal of covert or tacit, often unshared knowledge about how to go about it effectively. Sustained publication success is seen as an enviable mystery, like living to a healthy old age. In my workshops and teaching, I try to demystify academic writing practices and success in publishing by sharing advice concerning planning, research on successful writing habits and outputs, publishing and publication expectations and norms. Nonetheless, critical feedback and unpredictable outcomes are felt as stressful by colleagues. Within the university context, writing for publication is now expected, and expected to be of high quality, produced regularly. The insecurity and indefinability coupled with personal reflection led me to enquire about the experiences of others in relation to their academic writing identities.

METHODOLOGY AND METHODS

This research focuses on the tangles and tensions, the hubble and bubble, of personal and professional identities in writing for publication gained from experiences in the UK, Ireland and South Africa. It builds on re-scrutiny of earlier projects: 'Doctoral Learning Journeys' and the parallel international project (Wisker et al., 2010), (1); writing projects (Wisker & Savin Baden, 2009; Wisker, 2012; 2014a, 2014b, 2015a), (2, a, b, c) and new work undertaken for this chapter involving interviews with academics who write for publication (3). Each set of data concerns interview comments related to professional and personal academic identities, tied up with writing for publication. I decided to scrutinise the earlier data first because writing and identity emerged as an interesting relationship in both the doctoral research journeys and the writing research data, for which there was little space in reports at that time. The doctoral learning journeys work was focused on research processes but also reported personal experiences, and writing was seen as both a struggle and an achievement. In the writing research (2009; 2013; 2014a, b) the focus was on writing blocks and breakthroughs, and more on strategies than feelings, although these were always bound up with blockages, strategies and achievements.

In re-scrutinising the work from 2007–2014 I found under-reported themes concerning professional and personal writing identity and tensions. The re-scrutiny paid particular attention to writers' experiences of professional and personal writing identity and tensions as related to the production and reception of writing. (referred to throughout as 1 and 2 a, b, or c followed by respondent number/letter). I built on this earlier work by conducting a new small-scale, highly focused study using face to face or email interviews with UK and international academic writers in 2015b (n=7). This explored their experiences of relationships and tensions between the professional and the personal in terms of their academic writing production and reception (referred throughout as 3 followed by respondent number /letter.) The emerging themes, below, are clear in responses from both the earlier work (1 and 2 a, b, c) and the recent work

DATA AND DISCUSSION

By re-analysing earlier data and combining it with the fresh study, a new dataset was constructed which was coded and thematically analysed. Four key themes emerged:

- Time management;
- Expectations of role;
- Confidence; and
- Identity and writing, and these are explored further below.

Time Management – Balances, Allowances, Prioritisation, Tensions between Professional and Personal Time

Most respondents mentioned some problems with having enough time to write, and/or managing writing time. Even those who had been allotted sabbatical time or had chosen to step back from other roles and write (with or without losses in income to do so) reported issues with managing the time to be productive as a writer whose work resulted in publication. Some respondents reported tensions between expectations that they would write and publish on a regular basis and unrealistic timetabling and workload, often related to the idea that those who construct and manage timetables do not themselves write for publication. In these cases, managers could be unrealistic in expectations of output, stemming from unawareness of the variable, often unpredictable amounts of time needed to carry out research, draft and re-draft through to producing a published piece. Some who allocate time, expect and count outputs, do not themselves either conduct research or publish, so are unaware of the personal as well as professional time and angst it takes up. Whether they wrote at home or at work, most acknowledged that the time required would not fit in to a normal working week. Time was always required outside this, eating into other activities such as domestic and other personal time. Some chose to write at home as well as or instead of at work, partly because of the opportunities to write at night, or to fit it in round a variety of other activities such as marking or preparatory reading, where all of these activities were seen as difficult in a shared office space or when beleaguered by email traffic or visiting colleagues and students. One commented, 'You are doing a working day but you are doing it in a home space' (3, F).

Another raised the issue of working hours when no office would be open anyway, and said that they naturally write in hours considered antisocial. Asked about working a 'normal' working day at home they said, 'I don't, I do different hours' (3, A). Another respondent tries to separate professional and personal writing but notes 'they do kind of bleed into each other' (3, F). Of time and location they variously note that either 'professional writing is a bit nine to five' or conversely, 'I can't write in my office' (3, F). I ask workshop participants to consider when they write best so that they can identify good times to focus on their writing, and times to focus on other activities and the preferred choice is what could be defined as anti-social hours, i.e., the late evening until early hours of the morning or 5am until the working day starts. Some say this is when other demands lessen, the house is silent, and the email is not making demands on them. Others suggest that they learned to work at these times as students, or when they had young families. Whatever the explanations, that these two timespans are by far the most popular says something important about the relationship between professional demands on time, and personal time/space management. It causes me to ask questions about a variety of issues related to the personal and the professional dimensions. How can academics be expected to write in noisy shared office spaces? If they are doing a 'normal' working day teaching and in meetings, should universities expect them to write at home in the evenings, early hours and weekends, or is this work unseen, unheard, something about which early career researchers are rarely informed, a hidden factor outside any workload planning model, and in some cases, a silent contributory factor in terms of burnout?

One respondent who writes, edits, publishes and teaches comments about time management issues and the experience of constant pressure:

> Oh god, so yes. Work/life balance? Not in an academic job! I regularly find myself checking and answering emails at 11pm at night (including at weekends). If I try to 'write' and not deal with the mundane realities of academic life (admin, email) the result is so punishing after a few days that I don't even try that anymore… It's ridiculous. Academics have all summer off? Ha. Not the ones I know… (3, C)

Another from an earlier study talks about 'managing the writing energy' which returns a sense of control to the management of time for writing, whenever it occurs. He notes 'I only have so much writing energy, and if it is expended on bureaucratic documents, then it's gone' (2 a, P). A blogpost (Wisker, 2014b, doctoralwriting. sig. August 14, 2014) on the topic of recognising and managing writing energy, acknowledging choice and lack thereof, suggests that academic writers need to be aware of demands on time and work to our strengths, which involves managing our writing energies in terms of professional and personal time.

Expectations of Role, Recognition and Support (or Lack of Support)

There seems to be a shared or hidden quota of writing outputs expected, and differences in the amount and kind of support, and knowledge of that support for writing for publication. One respondent clarified their feelings about the varieties of professional writing they were expected to produce, differentiating between bureaucratic documents such as strategies, reports and policy documents, and the more creative research and experience based writing. They noted:

> The whole summer which rained the whole summer which I devoted… to writing strategy documents I did it as a political commitment because I had to and I knew that it would be a foundational political commitment. I never want to do that again because it was just so awful, I have never hated writing so much. I can do it now a lot better than I could when I spent that whole summer doing it, and I can teach other people to do it. Because it's not about anything to do with you at all. (3, G)

This identifies a clear split between genres of and motivations for writing. It highlights differences between time-sapping bureaucratic documents and the rewarding writing that feeds back into creative, critical thinking energies, most often perceived to be at odds with output models. This split could cause a conflict in terms of motivation and time management, as well as writing identity. The notion of getting 'enough' written springs from the idea of a quota of writing. I argue that this notion fits with current views about outputs, workload models, and utilitarian views of measurability and matrices by which academics are judged, but that fail to take account of and so undermine the issues of sustainability, continuity and identity attached to an academic's investment of their personal and professional identity (as well as time) in the writing process. Publications seem to be sometimes taken for granted, produced and producible to order. Some of my respondents report hearing the following comments: 'Oh, another one of those, you must do them in your sleep'; 'Is this the same as the last one?'; 'You do so many of them'; 'I need three 3* or 4* REF pieces';'This isn't up to scratch'; 'Why hasn't she/he finished another 4 star REF piece in the time available?' (3, varied). Plumbing this issue further, and it is complex, surfaces a relationship between academic time, commitment and the experienced reality of the actual time academic writing and other tasks take if done properly. The amount of time to research, overcome impostor syndrome and angst, wrestle with the planning and writing, submit and correct and re-submit and so on, is also not easily calculable, and even less a topic of public knowledge or workload modelling. The undefinable processes can lead to a constant sense of mystery, guilt and insecurity – or over-confidence (see the final theme, below).

One respondent felt their time and identity undermined in the context of university insistence that they publish fast and high quality REF material. They reported:

> feeling used and nothing more than research writing fodder to boost the school's REF rating. Poor advice early on set the bar unnecessarily high regarding the scholarly journal to pitch my writing to which meant I was perpetually engaged in a cycle of self-doubt about my ability to reach the standard required. It was never good enough. Deadlines that were set for completion of first, second, third articles were unrealistic so the cycle of failure continued to expand and overwhelm. (3, C)

Their writing self felt undermined because of the insistence:

> to write for the School, having to write for the Research Centre. I found myself paralysed. I was constantly frustrated by a self that wasted so much time, by allowing myself to be perpetually distracted by the more pressing demands of my everyday work role. (3, C)

Another respondent emphasises the importance of support for academic writing processes since otherwise it is rather a lone job:

> Writing is a challenge because unlike teaching, which is often given, we have to plan and organize writing and publishing all ourselves. This is why the commitment of the individual academic and collaboration with others locally is so important. (3, A)

Writing workshops, courses, and critical friendships were all mentioned as helpful support, but in the context of unrealistic expectations, mystifying processes and the lack of understanding of the time taken to produce publishable outputs remain.

Confidence in Writing – Importance of Right to Speak, Facility with Discourse – Disciplinary, Academic, Publication

While some respondents are very confident about their credibility to speak on a topic through writing, others are less so. They report being unsure of their right to speak, their mastery of the subject discourse, and the discourse of academic publication and argument. They have doubts about their control of the discourse of academic writing, arguing that the rules seem hidden, the ways through the complexities of writing for publication unclear, models unavailable. This has been identified by Kearns (2014) as an example of 'imposter syndrome' (Clance & Imes, 1978; Topping, 1983; Clance, 1985; Ward, 1990; Kearns, 2014). 'Imposter syndrome' was first identified as a feeling among high flying women, and others have researched and developed the notion as found in ethnic minority students, undergraduates, actors, and a range of people in successful careers. Kearns thought its combination of fear of discovery and sense of false pretences in a high stakes role perfectly described the experiences of doctoral writers. My contention is that it also perfectly describes academic writers more broadly, since high investment in their research, their right to speak, their control of their academic discipline based voice and the importance of their publishing from a basis of credibility makes them ideally recognisable as potential sufferers of imposter syndrome. We are forever afraid of being caught out for our research practices, our expression and structure, and our right to write and enter the academic dialogue. One of the PhD candidates (also an HE staff member) spoke of overcoming their sense of insecurity in academic writing by seeing their contribution not so much as about asserting their incontrovertible answer to major issues, which would have been rather a hubristic stance, but rather as taking part in an ongoing conversation which has lent more confidence to their writing and their conference engagement:

> A big learning experience for me has been that doing a doctorate is not a search for the truth but is really just taking part in a conversation. This doesn't stop me thinking that an 'expert' knows all of the answers and I suppose this is about confidence on my part... [But they don't have my experience] So how can they know everything? and what I have to offer is just as important as theirs, and I suppose that is also a learning experience in that when I sit with the 'learned' in a conference I feel confident in challenging them as I now see myself as a peer. (2, a, K)

Some felt that they were wasting time, hadn't the right to speak, but that sometimes these more hesitant moments led to breakthroughs in their thinking, especially if they got on with the writing themselves, reviewed it and shared it with others, noting:

> how frustrated I get with my writing when I seem to spend hours just when I look back at what I have done in maybe two hours of work, it's been focused in on one paragraph that I can't let go of and you know and – and it's not necessarily just getting the sentence structure right, it is just the amount of thinking that has to go into that paragraph and I think re-drafting is such a challenging thing to do, you know getting it out of my system's one thing, the sort of head dumping is one thing but then the re-drafting of that is such a time consuming process. (2, a, J)

The following respondent's notion is of writing as a journey in which they gradually appreciate that the work is academic enough, acceptable, and that they can have some confidence in it:

> I think it (the writing journey) is about accepting that you will go through different phases of feeling confident and you know if I was setting out on my journey again I think I'd probably have to do it in a similar way really you know I was influenced by the writing of others and how things...you know that it was academic enough. (2, a, J)

Identity and Writing – Confirmation or Unsettling through Professional and Personal Reasons for and Approaches to Writing

Writing is bound up with a sense of identity (Ivanic, 1998), self-worth, creativity and autobiography. It is not always easy to offer it for scrutiny and evaluation in league tables related to high impact journals and internal university ratings. Some noted the heightening or undermining of self-worth in relation to publishing when writing is felt to be a major part of identity. Respondents discussed the tensions between a professionally-orientated and a personal sense of writing identity, where the professional demands and the personal commitment, expression, and sense of achievement (or not) were sometimes seen as in a tension, sometimes less than positively. One comments that:

> I realised I had always written for me, written because I chose to write, written when I found time to write. On reflection the need to control why I wrote wasn't completely egotistically driven the need was related to an internal locus of control, a need to own my professional role activity. I have always determined what I do as a lecturer. I design my own roles. I create opportunities. My strength is my ability to drive forward new ways of thinking about teaching and learning. I am passionate about my identity as a lecturer, as a scholar, as a promoter and enabler of development within others. The changing goal posts within the research secondment led to my sense of loss of control of the process. It was no longer what I had signed up to. It (ME) had become a tool for a political end, one that didn't seem to care whether I learnt from the process or not, a dispassionate place… I was suffering from reality shock and felt shaken by the cold, emptiness of a cherished aspiration. (3, C)

In some circumstances the writing identity is hidden. Sometimes writing is seen as not a proper role (for those in, for instance, administrative posts) and so is carried out in secret, and at other times writing is a supportive activity for which others get credibility and reward (contributors not even included). This latter situation was reported by research colleagues whose writing was a form of 'ghost writing' for academics who produced data which they wrote up for publication which academics published under their names alone.

Another participant notes the difference in their confidence in relation to different forms of writing:

> I think I'm much more confident in doing research that's involved in my pedagogy. I'm much more confident in that than actually producing a research paper out of my PhD. And I think that's just because I feel that I don't know what I'm doing it's that sort of lack of confidence, I'm not quite sure I've mastered the language, the modes. (2, a, J)

Some develop writing split selves, separating the personal from the professional, using reflective and creative writing to infuse professional writing. Others develop hybrid habits and modes of expression, separating the personal, creative, disciplinarily different and academic. Much of the judgment of what we do is entirely outside our control lying with peer reviewers and editors, and respondents noted that having your writing refereed and re-written massively affects your sense of self-worth:

> My active work to do with writing is to do with me. (3, F)

> I think there's quite a lot of messiness through the middle where they definitely seep into each other. There is a lot of movement at that very far end the formal strategic stuff, if you're thinking about that stuff you're thinking using all of yourself, so other elements creep in. It all feeds one way but not so much, the strategic work feeds into the other stuff and sometimes the other way. (3, G)

Keeping the two identities, professional and personal, separate is important for some. One notes that:

> I think I am working to keep them separate because I like that distinction but at the same time they don't stay separate immediately. So yes I am dredging the imaginative and using it in my professional writing fairly constantly really... But it's something that I'm musing on so I keep a record of it so I am using that stuff all the time. In terms of time and actually physical work I try to keep them separate so I have a full working day and then I try to have evenings that are for other kinds of writing or just family time and weekends. (3, F)

Another talks about the importance of working with others, and reflecting on their process as she reflects on her own. The energy she expends supports confidence in writing identity.

> Personally, I fight the same demons, but I'm more stroppy. At conferences, people call me refreshing! They remember what I have to say because I have 'stimmung' ...– voiceness. But I'm the maverick. They know that I'm right when I tell them that everyone wants to read something interesting and vibrant that says something, something memorable, but then there's the fear again... They leave my sessions having found out what they wanted to say it in the first place. They are enriched by the enthusiasm of their subject. We don't get paid very much in academia – and academic publishers barely pay anything at all – so it has to be about love. (3, G)

CONCLUSIONS

Writing for publication is a part of the academic role, something early career researchers discover early in their careers. But now it can come with unrealistic expectations, accompanied by time management, anxiety and right to speak issues which accompany the production of publishable work. Research reported here unearthed 'toil and trouble', tensions between professional and personal worlds, reasons for writing, demands on time, and writing identities. Workload models and institutional managers who lack an understanding of the publishing process undermine publication goals. Writing bleeds into personal time, antisocial times. For some this led to a sense of control of their own production and for others a real tension in terms of balance and identity, and where there was imbalance they commented that it could lead to resentment and burnout. Many indicated that recognition and reward rarely match the time and energy put into writing, but that a sense of achievement offered by the lasting importance of getting into print is very important and, for some, compensates the identity conflicts encountered. If writing was a named role, enabling freedom and time to prioritise writing, different stages in the academic professional journey would be supported. Alongside the tensions reported, the right to speak, to communicate and a delight in publication could, to some extent, mitigate against over-work and confusion about expectations, in a management led model which failed to recognise the complex conceptual work, the investment of identity and of personal angst and time, in any published piece. Development of a writerly identity was an important issue for those consulted in the study. Participants see writing for publication as a complex issue with regard to their academic identities, an intertwined mix of the personal and professional that can be understood using a lens informed by academic identities theories, since being in the world concerns personal and professional identities that intersect in writing.

REFERENCES

Aitchison, C., & Lee, A. (2006). Research writing: Problems and possibilities. *Teaching in Higher Education, 11*(3), 265–278.

Aitchison, C., Kamler, B., & Lee, A. (Eds.). (2010). *Publishing pedagogies for the doctorate and beyond.* Abingdon, England: Routledge.

Bakhtin, M. (1981). *The dialogic imagination: Four essays.* Austin, TX: University of Texas Press.

Bakhtin, M. (1986). *Speech genres and other late essays.* Austin, TX: University of Texas Press.

Barnett, R. (2013). *Imagining the university.* Abingdon, England: Routledge.

Clance, P. R. (1985). *The imposter phenomenon: Overcoming the fear that haunts your success.* Atlanta, GA: Peachtree Publishers.

Clance, P. R., & Imes, S. A. (1978). The impostor phenomenon in high achieving women: Dynamics and therapeutic interventions. *Psychotherapy: Theory Research and Practice, 15,* 241–247.

Clegg, S. (2008). Academic identities under threat. *British Educational Research Journal, 34*(3), 329–345.

Fanghanel, J. (2007). *Investigating university lecturers' pedagogical constructs in the working context.* London, England: The Higher Education Academy.

Henkel, M. (2005a). Academic identity and autonomy in a changing policy environment. *Higher Education, 49,* 155–176.

Henkel, M. (2005b). Academic identity and autonomy revisited. In I. Bleiklie & M. Henkel (Eds.), *Governing knowledge: A study of continuity and change in higher education: A festschrift in honour of Maurice Kogan* (pp. 145–167). Dordrecht, The Netherlands & New York, NY: Springer Verlag.

Ivanic, R. (1998). *Writing and identity: The discoursal construction of identity in academic writing.* Amsterdam, The Netherlands & Philadelphia, PA: John Benjamins.

Kamler, B., & Thomson, P. (2006). *Helping doctoral students write: Pedagogies for supervision.* Abingdon, England: Routledge.

Kearns, H. (2014, April). 'Dr Who. Frauds in research education – The imposter syndrome explained.' *Proceedings of the Quality Postgraduate Research* Conference, Adelaide, Australia. Retrieved from http://www.qpr.eduau/wp-content/uploads2015/05//QPR_Proceedings_3KL.pdf (Accessed June 1, 2015).

Maybin, J. (2001). Language, struggle and voice: The Bakhtin/Volosinov writings. In M. Wetherell, S. Taylor, & S. J. Yates (Eds.), *Discourse theory and practice: A reader* (pp. 64–71). London, England: Sage.

Nussbaum, M., (2002). Education for citizenship in an era of global connection. *Studies in Philosophy and Education, 21,* 289–303.

Reynolds, M., & Noakes, J. (2003). *Toni Morrison: The essential guide.* London, England: Random House/Vintage Books.

Shakespeare, W. (1601). *Macbeth* (11th ed.), *Muir, Kenneth* (1984) [1951], The Arden Shakespeare Second Series.

Topping, M. E. H. (1983). The impostor phenomenon: A study of its construct and incidence in university faculty members. *Dissertation Abstracts International, 44,* 1948–1949B.

Ward, G. R. (1990). *The relationships among attributional styles, motivational orientations and the impostor phenomenon among high achieving undergraduate students* (Unpublished dissertation). Mexico, NM & Albuquerque, NM: University of New Mexico.

Wisker, G. (2012). *Voice, vision and articulation.* Presentation at the international threshold concepts conference, Dublin, OH.

Wisker, G. (2013). Articulate – Researching writing and publishing our work in learning, teaching and educational development. *Innovations in Education and Teaching International, 50*(4), 344–356.

Wisker, G. (2014a). Voice, vision and articulation: Conceptual threshold crossing in academic writing. In C. O'Mahoney, A. Buchanan, M. O'Rourke, & B. Higgs (Eds.), *Proceedings of the National Academy's 6th Annual Conference and the fourth biennial threshold concepts conference threshold concepts from personal practice to communities of practice.*

Wisker, G. (2014b). *Managing the writing energy.* Retrieved August 14, 2014 from http://doctoralwriting.sig

Wisker, G. (2015a). *Getting published: Academic publishing success.* London, England: Palgrave Macmillan.

Wisker, G. (2015b). Developing doctoral authors: Engaging with theoretical perspectives through the literature review. *Innovations in Education and Teaching International, 52*(1), 64–74.

Wisker, G., & Savin-Baden M. (2009). Priceless conceptual thresholds: Beyond the 'stuck place' in writing. *London Review of Education, 7*(3), 235–224.

Wisker, G., Morris, C., Cheng, M., Masika, R., Warnes, M., Lilly, J., … Robinson, G. (2010). *Doctoral learning journeys: Supporting and enhancing doctoral students' research and related skills development through research evidence-based practices.* Final report of the NTFS funded project. Retrieved from http://www.heacademy.ac.uk/resources/detail/ntfs/Projects/Doctoral_Learning_Journeys

Gina Wisker
University of Brighton, UK
and
University of the Free State, South Africa

PART IV

ON SUPPORTING ACADEMIC IDENTITY DEVELOPMENT

VIRGINIA KING AND JENNIE BILLOT

12. CREATIVE RESEARCH STRATEGIES FOR EXPLORING ACADEMIC IDENTITY

INTRODUCTION

In this chapter, we encourage the exploration of academic identity using less conventional research strategies which involve metaphor. The first examines metaphors used within narratives to delve deeper into participants' academic stories, while the other employs visual metaphors to represent academic identity. Academic identity itself is complex, and forming an identity can be troublesome (Churchman, 2006). Those who enter the academic profession are faced with multiple understandings of what an academic does and who an academic is. How can these encounters be better understood in an environment of shifting and competing influences (Billot et al., 2013)?

The experiences of academics, both less and more experienced, provide insight into how academic identity is constructed and the existing tensions between the individual and their particularised workplace. However, a traditional questionnaire or interview might direct participants towards the researcher's conceptualization of identity; while a focus group could capture shared aspects of identity yet fail to reveal each individual's sense of self. We therefore suggest the use of research strategies which are open to the multiplicity of ways in which identity within the academy is experienced. By adding metaphor analysis to the use of stories and pictures, we enhance how situations and relationships can be explained, for story structure and pictures can reveal, display and inform more than we can view directly (Eisner, 1997). Affirming that one's identity is embedded in the way the professional role is enacted (Billot, 2010), these strategies help to illuminate a personal interpretation of an experience. As such, they can work alone or in combination with other data collection techniques, encouraging an insightful and ethically responsible exploration of academic identity. While participants focus on the creative techniques employed, their internalized understandings of identity reveal themselves unasked. The results can surprise both researcher and participant.

We begin this chapter by questioning the concept of academic identity and considering metaphor as a means of revealing consciously and unconsciously held understandings of identity. We then draw on examples from our own research into academic identity, to demonstrate our creative strategies without being prescriptive as to their use. We conclude with a brief review of the strategies' strengths and limitations.

J. Smith et al. (Eds.), Identity Work in the Contemporary University, 157–167.
© 2016 Sense Publishers. All rights reserved.

IMAGINATION AND REALITY AT ODDS

From Kingsley Amis' *Lucky Jim* (1954) to Julie Schumacher's *Dear Committee Members* (2014), numerous fictional works portray academic life as difficult. One explanation for this difficulty is the disjunction between the imagined life in the academy and the reality that is experienced. Amis' comic novel follows 'Lucky' Jim Dixon's angry rejection of the life he had sought in a provincial English university for which he is entirely unsuited. Schumacher uses Professor Jason T. Fitger's many letters to recruitment committees to juxtapose his academic ideals with his failing career in a failing department in an American college. These two fictional characters exemplify the tension between their expectations of an ideal professional life (Henkel, 2000) and the reality that academics frequently experience in their workplace. Research into academic identity reveals more nuanced, but equally interesting, accounts of individuals' lives where the imagined and the real collide.

Novels make it easy to understand that academic identity is socially constructed (Billot, 2010; Henkel, 2000). In other words, as academics, we perceive ourselves in relation to those we work with and for; and we alter our self-view in response to our interaction with other people and the social structures they represent. Indeed, the way characters interact with each other in novels often gives readers insight into characters' true feelings. Furthermore, the plots of both Amis' (1954) and Schumacher's (2014) fictions depend upon their (anti-) heroes' often ludicrous attempts to distinguish themselves from certain colleagues, superiors and processes, and to align themselves with other ones. Research into academic identity goes further than any fictional account. In our own research, we seek to understand identity as a phenomenon and to theorize its importance within higher education generally and in specific contexts by exploring the ways that individuals interact with each other and their social setting.

The well-established notion of a three-part academic identity derived from one's institution, discipline and personal interpretation of what an academic 'should' be like (Taylor, 1999) exemplifies the difficulties of reconciling imagination and reality. As the fictional Dixon and Fitger illustrate, the institutional aspect of identity provides a focus for disjuncture as soon as institutional values are interpreted in the light of personal values. However, institutional values change. Much recent research builds on Mary Henkel's (2000) suggestion that academic identities are under threat from governmental and institutional policy because an academic's perception of their professional self and standing is contextually positioned. While higher education institutions are increasingly focused on performance and managerial imperatives, the individual academic is more likely to prioritise their own academic endeavours (Mårtensson, Roxå, & Olsson, 2011), or to invoke their own contrasting values (Winter, 2009). For example, in the UK, Bolden, Gosling and O'Brien (2014) report individuals' feelings of 'ambivalence', 'dissonance', 'vulnerability' and 'exclusion' (p. 763) resulting from their institutions' policy focus. While some academics may adapt to managerialism, others will resist it (Henkel, 2000). Furthermore, there is often tension between the academic self and the institutional structures and requirements that are directed towards a more collective identity (Le Roux, 2014). This lack of alignment can affect academic motivation, self-efficacy, commitment, job satisfaction and effectiveness (Billot, 2010). Thus the role of the academic is one of compromise in a context which is constantly changing (King, 2013). The outcome is that individuals may experience a plurality of identities as they learn to juggle roles, shift priorities and position themselves within the academic domain (King et al., 2014). In addition, the challenges they encounter may be compounded by an unclear understanding of the rules of the academy, which may be tacitly understood by colleagues (Bolden et al., 2014; Boyd & Smith, 2014). Our own research interest centres on the disjunctures implicit in individuals' social settings; and the ways in which academics perceive, negotiate, ignore or dismiss them.

CAPTURING IDENTITY THROUGH METAPHOR

Metaphor enables us to 'make a connection between things' (Knowles & Moon, 2006: 3); however, Lakoff and Johnson (1980: 235) argue that '[m]etaphor is not merely a matter of language. It is a matter of conceptual structure', hence metaphor-usage can reveal participants' unconscious conceptualisations as well as conscious ones. For example, orientational metaphors are subsumed into language so that the metaphorical conceptualization that 'HIGH STATUS IS UP; LOW STATUS IS DOWN [goes unnoticed in phrases such as] ... She'll rise to the top [or] He's at the peak of his career' (Lakoff & Johnson, 1980: 16, capitalization as in original). The focus on metaphor has been widely applied in previous studies, (see for example González, 2008; Hughes & Tight, 2013; Juntrasook, Nairn, Bond, & Spronken-Smith, 2013) and the metaphorical process has been helpfully critiqued, particularly by Schmitt (2005). Being cognisant of their potential limitations, we nevertheless claim that these research strategies add to the bank of qualitative methods that can be used to explore identity. They are no less rigorous for being creative, indeed while they can be used on their own, they also constructively support and align with other methods of inquiry.

Our study of metaphor also helps to uncover what participants might not feel able to express directly or even realise about themselves. We contend that it is important to explore, rather than ignore, the emotional aspects of the academic self (Vincent, 2004), even though emotion may make this kind of research uncomfortable for the researcher and the participant. Identifying the struggle to be an academic is as informative of the context as it is of the individual, as our exemplars demonstrate. When we examine metaphorical use within narratives, we gain access to 'professional craft and experiential knowledge otherwise invisible to those who participate in it' (Clandinin, 2007: 355). As Billot et al. (2013) identified in their study, metaphors can be a natural (or even unconscious) way of structuring meaning, while alternatively, metaphors can be purposefully constructed to (consciously) convey a clearer understanding of a concept or experience. Equally, visualisation is illuminative since it provides the means 'to come to know the self, and to better understand the self's relationship to the world and the relationships within the world' (Serig, 2006: 244). Thus our research approach reflects Eisner's (1997) contention that by using an 'alternative form of data representation' (p. 7) we may enlarge our understanding of the concept under study.

NARRATIVE METAPHOR

Narratives provide rich and informative landscapes of human perceptions and experiences and the first strategy draws on metaphors used by participants within their written narratives. Narrative analysis is strongly interpretive and is 'rooted in a social constructivist paradigm in which behaviours and their meanings are socially situated and socially interpreted' (Cohen, Manion & Morrison, 2011: 581). So analysing the metaphors within academic stories provides an opportunity to understand how academics act and react in certain circumstances, and whether the actions are positive or negative. Conclusions can inform how the reactions and behaviours of academics may impact on staff engagement and professional harmony in the academic workplace.

The narrative approach was used in a study of academic leadership in universities across North America, Europe and Australasia (Billot, et al., 2013). Thirty-eight academics described an encounter with a colleague holding a position of responsibility using prompts to guide the content of the narrative (such as context, what happened, personal reactions experienced and later reflections on the encounter). They were encouraged to use metaphors since this can add depth to such stories. Within the final narratives, sentence structure ("I feel like ...") 'scare quotes' and the placing of metaphors at the end indicate that some metaphors were intentionally used while others were more unconsciously employed. Examples of the latter include references to those acting like a *'bull in a china shop'*, being a *'roadblocker'* or *'pouring oil on troubled waters'*, while other phrases contain metaphorical elements- *'she stared [at me] with a look of glacial disdain'*. Such expressions have common understandings and provide a description that moves beyond the normal vernacular. Other metaphors are less common and can provide greater insight into personalised reactions to the behaviour of others, *'I dreaded being seen as a stirrer'*; and *'we felt like frightened chastened children and scurried from the room'*.

Writing about an experience with a colleague (or any particular episode) provides an individualised descriptive textual picture of how an academic situates themselves within that event. Hager (2008) has noted that 'humans seem to be unable to think about learning without employing metaphors of some kind' (p. 679) and when selecting a metaphor for description, the storyteller is trying to make sense or give meaning to their explanation (Gabriel, Geiger, & Letiche, 2011). The language that is used (and how it is used) offers an avenue for understanding an experience, while the metaphors employed provide extra insight into the participant's understandings and perceptions of their levels of power and agency. One study participant explained their reactions in this way:

> The behaviour that was dished out to me was a powerful message in silence, a message of oppression [...] Our conversations about progress [of] changes and working in a team are hampered by the elephants in the room; we have a whole herd now. I do still feel like a deer in the spotlight, startled and overexposed.

Researchers who choose to focus on the use of metaphors, have at least two options for analysis. Text can be examined for unintentional metaphors (see Lakoff & Johnson, 1980) such as those often used in daily language (*'My team leader bulldozed his way through the meeting'*) or those purposefully constructed in order to give new understanding to a concept or experience (*'a deer in the spotlight'*). In both cases, a process for metaphor identification and analysis needs to be developed in order to provide research transparency (Pitcher, 2013). As in our study, researchers should devise a tailored, systematic yet flexible process for analysis. Categories identified by an individual researcher can be charted, cross-checked and compared with those developed by other team researchers, after which commonalities, patterns, and relationships across the metaphors can be identified and themed. This practice, supplemented by participant checking, is supported by experienced researchers such as Gonzales and Rincones (2013), Pitcher (2013) and Schmitt (2005).

The metaphors used in the study provided an extra vehicle for the academics to describe their feelings. After analysis, checking and theming, it was possible to identify a continuum of reactions in which feelings and perceptions ranged from an ongoing positive reaction to a leader's style through to feelings of disengagement, distrust and resistance (Billot et al., 2013). It is left to the reader to consider how far metaphor-usage in the following examples illustrates this continuum:

> By acting as a 'peacemaker' and creating a 'sea of tranquillity', this supportive, caring and nurturing approach has been to make me feel very much at ease in my role.

> In the constant push-me-pull-you role of manager it's a constant juggling act to keep the people above and below you happy.

> Our team leader is always looking for 'handmaidens' to do the 'leg work'. (3 staff members then refused to do the leaders' work).... I thought it was a horrible mess but I had no trouble distancing myself from it.

> I was really angry at my leader for not sticking to the decisions made at the previous meeting. I felt undervalued and ... felt like I was in a twilight zone. I have become more wary of him and don't trust him as much as before.

> She displayed bullying tactics, acting like a 'tiger bulldozer', leaving me feeling a lack of trust and disempowered. The whole experience has left me with a lot of cynicism on business plans for [university] change.

For researchers searching to understand the particular, rather than aiming to gain a generalised picture of a setting, narrative inquiry allows an examination of the links between the thoughts and actions of academic professionals (Clandinin, 2007), as well as the connections between the lives of teachers and their pedagogy (Elbaz-Luwisch, 2007). As teachers, academic work involves interaction with colleagues which naturally has an impact on relational dynamics. In the study of teachers and their experiences with academic leaders, metaphors within narratives usefully contributed to an understanding of encounters and subsequent actions and reactions in the higher education context.

Schmitt (2005) provides an informative critique of metaphor analysis and emphasises the need for a transparent and rigorous process to reduce the limitations of using this research strategy. When analysing metaphors there are bound to be cultural differences in the use, interpretation, and perceived value of metaphors (e.g., Schmitt, 2005) and there is a risk of interpreting perceptions out of context. For example, an academic might use a negative metaphor, but their overall narrative could display a positive attitude toward their situation/encounter. This lack of alignment signals that care is needed when making interpretations and that metaphors need to be interpreted in the setting of the fuller story. Eisner (1997) further identifies that multiple interpretations are possible with complex data and the researcher needs to be their 'own toughest critic' (p. 9). Despite these potential limitations, metaphors offer the researcher an extra window through which to view an academic's experience.

METAPHORICAL ISLAND MAPS

Underpinned by the metaphor "ACADEMIC IS AN ISLAND", this research strategy helps to 'perform the magical feat' (Eisner, 1997: 4) of making participants' thinking visible. The use of visual methods in educational research is increasingly accepted (Barrett & Hussey, 2015; Leavy, 2009) despite a lack of integration of results and practice between researchers (Pauwels, 2011). The genesis of this particular strategy is documented in King (2013) where it is demonstrated autoethnographically; and in King et al. (2014) where it is explored collaboratively. Creating an island map promotes understanding academic identity through creation of – and reflection on – a visual metaphor of self. Participant reflections are informed by academic identity theory (for example, Henkel, 2000). The participants, working alone or in small groups, think of themselves as an island which has attributes that define their academic identity. These attributes are visualized as features placed on a map of that island as in Figures 12.1 and 12.2 which were created as part of a recent project researching academic identity amongst aspiring researchers. Not unusually, the creator of the map in Figure 12.1 found that it was *'quite different'* from the image she had expected to produce. She was surprised to find that her map did not split into industry-related and academic attributes. Instead, she found that *'most attributes were ... used in both [sectors] and instead the map evolved into groupings of supportive attributes'*. Two months after creating this map, the participant resigned from her academic post in order to return to industry. The unconscious alignment of the two sectors' identities in this map may have represented a preliminary step in this significant career move.

Figure 12.1. Example of an academic identity map (transcribed from hand-drawn image)

Participant visualizations can illuminate understanding (Leavy, 2009) for example, in terms of the elements that have been included and excluded (in Figure 12.1, home-life is excluded), the way the elements are positioned (here the attributes 'passion' and 'organised' are on opposite sides of the island), and their relative prominence (here 'Professional' is the only attribute capitalized). When accompanied by a reflexive analysis written by the participant, the creative process can transform a participant's understanding of their role and relationships at work, and, in some cases, outside work. For example, in the study underpinning King et al. (2014), one participant commented that the highly integrated work and home-identities he had depicted as an interconnected archipelago reflected an academic career in which he had '*no down-time*' (p. 264), while another used the opportunity to develop a series of drawings which helped her understand her career aspirations. Neither of these participants has a creative background: one is an electrical engineer, the other a specialist in aviation and aerospace.

Whether expressed through language or other means, conceptual metaphors can clarify thought, synthesize insights and highlight particular aspects of one thing by relating it to something else (Lakoff & Johnson, 1980). For example, when another participant drew his island as a volcano from which an explosion of work 'lava' overflowed into every aspect of his life, he was highlighting the uncontrollable nature of the academic workload (King et al., 2014). His images, before and after the explosion, are a powerful commentary on the fate of early career academics, highlighting his love of his subject, the importance he attributes to his home-life, and the responsibility he feels for dealing with all aspects of work. He exemplifies a uniquely higher education 'form of self-regulation that is extremely compelling and seductive, and which renders academics over-committed and yet simultaneously falling short of an idealized, and by definition impossible, set of managerial, peer and self-induced expectations' (Knights & Clarke, 2013: 352). The commentary that accompanies the volcano images critiques the influence that organizations have on individual identities through the provision or withholding of resources (King et al., 2014), implying that this academic has, rather like the fictional Lucky Jim and Professor Fitger, adopted an identity and a work ethic suited to another kind of organization than the one in which he now finds himself.

Figure 12.2. Beryl's academic identity map

In Figure 12.2, 'Beryl' depicts an island of academic identity she does not yet inhabit. She confirms that she has consciously employed the metaphor that 'BECOMING AN ACADEMIC IS A JOURNEY' by reflecting that she is '*still on the boat ... striving to reach the island*'. Beryl seems anxious to become a better academic in the future, suggesting a confident yet aspirational academic self rather than one beset by 'imposter' insecurities (Knights & Clarke, 2013). She says '*I wanted to express my feeling of having to constantly keep moving; hence I began to view the island as a destination, rather than somewhere I currently reside*'. In her drawing, Beryl sits in a motor-boat which she has left to drive itself while she focuses on preparing teaching materials. She is '*currently pressured for time*' and notes that in her picture '*even the compass for the map became a clock*'. This suggests a demanding level of self-regulation (Knights & Clarke, 2013). While she considers the sea around the island to be calm, its relative size does suggest some sense of isolation. Beryl comments that she knows from '*recent past experience ... that sharks can lurk*'. Indeed, a shark's fin is discernible to the right of the island in the 'Sea of HE', suggesting the metaphor 'HIGHER EDUCATION IS A DANGEROUS SEA'. This brief analysis serves to illustrate the kinds of insights that can emerge with this research strategy, as well as showing the influence on the analysis of the researcher's chosen theoretical lenses (here, Knights & Clarke, 2013). While questions remain regarding Beryl's identity, this map and commentary support Serig's (2006) contention that art provides a way of understanding one's place in the world better.

Practical criticisms of this research strategy include the view that individuals' drawing skills may be inadequate to express their subtlety of conception, although this is not a response that we have encountered amongst participants. This visual strategy could also exclude those with sight impairment, however, the initial stages of creating an identity map – beginning with a list of one's attributes and then clustering them – are open to all. Nevertheless, we recognise that this strategy will not appeal to all academics. It is also possible that some participants could produce maps which are inaccessible to researchers and hence cannot be independently analysed. These are issues to consider when planning research, as is ensuring that the researcher obtains publication copyright for images created by participants (Pauwels, 2011).

Although our participants' frequently-expressed surprise on reviewing their maps confirms this strategy's power to reveal unconscious thought, from a methodological viewpoint, it could be argued that the maps provide only limited insight into participants' sense of academic identity. For example, Figure 12.1 conveys nothing with which others could empathize, no sense of the particular social location, no dimensions of personality – nothing that Eisner (1997: 4) among others, would have us seek in 'alternative' data representation. Yet, this is exactly what Figure 12.1's author intended. She wanted the map to convey nothing of her private self and little of her professional interactions. Such decisions are 'inherently interpretive' (Eisner, 1997: 8) and the very emptiness of Figure 12.1 is hence significant. The researcher's role is therefore to explore such unusual features – here unearthing the participant's decision to leave academia. Creating metaphorical island maps, like other arts-based strategies, provides a means of highlighting interesting aspects which might be overlooked using a conventional method (Leavy, 2009).

REVIEW

Our two strategies provide alternative ways of exploring academic identity which have enabled us to creatively 'see' academic identity in new ways and find previously unperceived meaning (Eisner, 1997; Leavy, 2009). While we found them successful in enabling participants to express thoughts and feelings about their working life in ways that have surprised even themselves, we do not prescribe any particular way of implementing them. We contend that the key strength of these strategies is that they encourage the participant to focus on the creative aspect of the narrative or map and thereby allow metaphors to emerge unasked. For us, each strategy concludes with a reflexive stage in which the participant reviews their contribution: this affords the opportunity to add conscious metaphors to the narrative or to consciously revise the map if wished. This reflexivity also enhances the ethical dimension of the research since it ensures that participants are happy to share their edited contribution, which admittedly, may now be incomplete. Nonetheless, the strategies provide authentic insight into how colleagues make sense of their academic selves, the context in which they operate and the interactions they find significant. These strategies also offer the opportunity for research *with* participants; for example, the paper produced as King et al. (2014) developed from collaboration between staff and student-colleagues undertaking a UK university teaching and learning qualification.

Our research strategies elicited some strong emotional responses from participants. Some expressed a sense of powerlessness within the academy, others gained an awareness of misdirected effort or experienced the revelation that their values were at odds with those of colleagues or institution. On the other hand, some participants felt empowered by having gained an understanding of their place in the academic landscape. Nonetheless, it is important that participants feel confident that their data will not be misused (Pauwels, 2011). Since examining the complexity of academic reactions can inform our understanding of academic identity, being creative in our research approach can enhance the inquiry. Our creative approach (like Loads and Collins, this volume) has provided scope for 'illuminating rather than obscuring' (Eisner, 1997: 8) the distinctive elements of each experience. We have found that these strategies have each assisted the exploration of particular facets of academic identity despite the key limitation that multiple interpretations are possible with such complex data. Combining either strategy with other research methods (such as interview or reflective commentary) could assist the researcher's understanding of context and thereby enhance confidence in their interpretations. Used within a carefully crafted research design, either strategy would facilitate the exploration of academic identity.

REFERENCES

Amis, K. (1954). *Lucky Jim*. London, England: Victor Gollancz.
Barrett, T., & Hussey, J. (2015). Overcoming problems in doctoral writing through the use of visualisations: Telling our stories. *Teaching in Higher Education, 20*(1), 48–63.
Billot, J. (2010). The imagined and the real: Identifying the tensions for academic identity. *Higher Education, Research and Development, 29*(6), 709–721.
Billot, J., West, D., Khong, L., Skorobohacz, C., Roxå, T., Murray, S., & Gayle, G. (2013). Followership in higher education: Academic teachers and their formal leaders. *Teaching and Learning Inquiry, 1*(2), 91–103.
Bolden, R., Gosling, J., & O'Brien, A. (2014). Citizens of the academic community? A societal perspective on leadership in UK higher education. *Studies in Higher Education, 39*(5), 754–770.
Boyd, P., & Smith, C. (2014). The contemporary academic: Orientation towards research work and researcher identity of higher education lecturers in the health professions. *Studies in Higher Education*. doi:10.1080/03075079.2014.943657
Churchman, D. (2006). Institutional commitments, individual compromises: Identity-related responses to compromise in an Australian university. *Journal of Higher Education, 28*(1), 3–15.
Clandinin, D. J. (2007). *Handbook of narrative inquiry: Mapping a methodology*. Thousand Oaks, CA: Sage Publications.
Cohen, L., Manion, L., & Morrison, K. (2011). *Research methods in Education*. London, England & New York, NY: Routledge.
Eisner, E. W. (1997). The promise and perils of alternative forms of data representation. *Educational Researcher, 26*(6), 4–10.
Elbaz-Luwisch, F. (2007). Studying teachers' lives and experience: Narrative inquiry into K-12 teaching. In D. J. Clandinin (Ed.), *Handbook of narrative inquiry: Mapping a methodology* (pp. 357–382). Thousand Oaks, CA: Sage Publications.

Gabriel, Y., Geiger, D., & Letiche, H. (2011). The marriage of story and metaphor. *Culture and Organization, 17*(5), 367–371.

Gonzales, L. D., & Rincones, R. (2013). Using participatory action research and photo methods to explore higher education administration as an emotional endeavor. *The Qualitative Report, 18*(64), 1–17.

González, M. M. (2008). Feminist praxis challenges the identity question: Toward new collective identity metaphors. *Hypatia, 23*(3), 22–38.

Hager, P. (2008). Learning and metaphors. *Medical Teacher, 30*(7), 679–686.

Henkel, M. (2000). *Academic identities and policy change in higher education*. London, England: Jessica Kingsley Publishers.

Hughes, C., & Tight, M. (2013). The metaphors we study by: The doctorate as a journey and/or as work. *Higher Education Research and Development, 32*(5), 765–775.

Juntrasook, A., Nairn, K., Bond, C., & Spronken-Smith, R. (2013). Unpacking the narrative of non-positional leadership in academia: Hero and/or victim? *Higher Education Research and Development, 32*(2), 201–213.

King, V. (2013). Self-portrait with mortar board: A study of academic identity using the map, the novel and the grid. *Higher Education Research & Development, 32*(1), 96–108.

King, V., Garcia-Perez, A., Graham, R., Jones, C., Tickle, A., & Wilson, L. (2014). Collaborative reflections on using island maps to express new lecturers' academic identity. *Reflective Practice: International and Multidisciplinary Perspectives, 15*(2), 252–267.

Knights, D., & Clarke, C. A. (2013). It's a bittersweet symphony, this life: Fragile academic selves and insecure identities at work. *Organization Studies, 35*(3), 335–357.

Knowles, M., & Moon, R. (2006). *Introducing metaphor*. Abingdon, England: Routledge.

Lakoff, G., & Johnson, M. (1980). *Metaphors we live by*. Chicago, IL: The University of Chicago Press.

Le Roux, C. (2014). Towards attaining academic habitus in an intimidating academic environment – An auto ethnographic case study. *Proceedings of the International Conference on Humanities Sciences and Education ICHE2014* (E-ISB: 978-967-12022-1-0) 24-March 25, 2014, Kuala Lumpur, Malaysia. (Organized by worldresearchconference.com).

Leavy, P. (2009). *Method meets art: Arts-based research practice*. New York, NY: Guilford Press.

Mårtensson, K., Roxå, T., & Olsson, T. (2011). Developing a quality culture through the scholarship of teaching and learning. *Higher Education Research & Development, 30*(1), 51–62.

Pauwels, L. (2011). An integrated conceptual framework for visual social research. In E. Margolis & L. Pauwels (Eds.), *The Sage handbook of visual research methods* (pp. 3–24). London, England: Sage.

Pitcher, R. (2013). Using metaphor analysis: MIP and beyond. *The Qualitative Report, 18*(68), 1–8. Retrieved from http://www.nova.edu/ssss/QR/QR18/pitcher68.pdf

Schmitt, R. (2005). Systematic metaphor analysis as a method of qualitative research. *The Qualitative Report, 10*(2), 358–394. Retrieved from http://www.nova.edu/sss/QR/QR10-2/schmitt.pdf

Schumacher, J. (2014). *Dear committee members*. London, England: The Friday Project.

Serig, D. (2006). A conceptual structure of visual metaphor. *Studies in Art Education, 47*(3), 229–247.

Taylor, P. G. (1999). *Making sense of academic life: Academics, universities and change*. Buckingham, England: SRHE & Open University Press.

Vincent, L. (2004). What's love got to do with it? The effect of affect in the academy. *Politikon, 31*(1), 105–115.

Winter, R. (2009). Academic manager or managed academic? Academic identity schisms in higher education. *Journal of Higher Education Policy and Management, 31*(2), 121–131.

Virginia King
Coventry University, UK

Jennie Billot
Auckland University of Technology, New Zealand

DAPHNE LOADS AND BRIGID COLLINS

13. RECOGNISING OURSELVES AND EACH OTHER IN PROFESSIONAL RECOGNITION

We begin this chapter by inviting readers to eavesdrop on a group of university educators engaging in arts-enriched identity work as part of their professional development. We then look at one aspect of the context in which this work is taking place: the current focus on recognition for university teachers. While welcoming this new interest we warn of the risks of too heavy a reliance on external standards and normative frameworks. We propose the practice of arts-enriched development as an opportunity for academic colleagues to make sense of who they are as teachers without reducing their development to a series of predetermined, measurable outcomes with no room for discovery, surprise or critique. Finally we suggest an expanded and differentiated understanding of *recognition* as the key to meaningful identity work for university teachers.

EAVESDROPPING

Arts-enriched development activities involve active engagement with collage, sculpture, poetry, photography and other creative ways of prompting deep thinking about teaching practices and teacher identities. Today, fifteen participants from all over the UK have gathered together for a full day to experience and evaluate arts-enriched activities. Some are lecturers, some are staff developers. All are concerned with how academics can learn to develop themselves and their teaching. The workshop is entitled 'Surprising Spaces' and is funded by the Higher Education Academy (HEA), the national body for enhancing learning and teaching in higher education (HE) in the United Kingdom. It is one of a series of HEA events highlighting the United Kingdom Professional Standards Framework for teaching and supporting learning in higher education. The UKPSF is a set of professional standards and guidelines that sets out key areas of activity undertaken by university teachers, the core knowledge they need and the professional values that they should exemplify. We begin with poetry. I ask a small group to respond to Tell all the Truth by Emily Dickinson (Johnson, 1955):

Tell all the truth but tell it slant
Success in circuit lies

I ask what strikes them as surprising or significant about particular words. What connections can they make with their teaching?

Meanwhile my colleague, Charity McAdams introduces Theme for English B by Langston Hughes (1994: 409):

> The instructor said,
> Go home and write a page tonight.
> And let that page come out of you–
> Then, it will be true.

Her group gets to talking about notions of truth, frustration, their expectations of the workshop and what it feels like to be plunged into uncertainty.

Brigid Collins is an illustrator, artist and educator. Brigid welcomes us into a room filled with an abundance of "stuff." There is paper of all kinds, ribbons, wool, sheets of coppery and silvery metal, spools of wire and paperclips. There are enticing tools and 'toys' including hammers and blocks of print, scissors, knives and needles, as well as paintbrushes and pots of ink and paint. Brigid works between poetry and images, creating what she calls 'Poem-Houses', (Collins & Grisoni, 2012), Brigid has prepared a brown paper bag for each of us that contains more treasures: fragments of maps, pages torn from old books, photographs, a glue stick, bits of wall paper. Each bag also contains a blank postcard and a small flat pack box. Drawing on our earlier encounters with poems we are asked to find words, cutting them or tearing them from books, stamping them on metal labels, or printing them with wooden blocks.

Next we move into three-dimensional collage and use the cardboard boxes to make a house for our words to dwell in. Brigid draws our attention to the dialects of the inside and outside of the box, to how we foreground particular aspects or move them into the background. She speaks of the potential of collage for creating unexpected juxtapositions, the learning from taking risks and from making and redefining what we deem to be mistakes. Soon the room is filled with the hum of purposeful activity. People are hammering, cutting, holding their boxes up to the light, laughing, pausing, deep in thought. As we work, Brigid tells us about how David Bowie used the cut-up technique to write his lyrics, inspired by William Burroughs and Brion Gysin, how Dadaists such as Tristan Tzara created found poems, how Eisner (2003) talked about 'thinking with our hands.'

After a shared lunch we spend some time in contemplation and discussion of our poem houses, noticing ambiguities, patterns and questions, and making connections with our identities and practice as educators.

IDENTITY WORK FOR 21ST CENTURY ACADEMICS

So how does this workshop relate to identity work, and to the context in which university teachers are constructing their identities?

> Identity work involves the mutually constitutive processes whereby people strive to shape a relatively coherent and distinctive notion of personal

self-identity and struggle to come to terms with and, within limits, to influence the various social-identities which pertain to them in the various milieux in which they live their lives. (Watson, 2008: 129)

Watson's halting, cautious definition captures beautifully the painful awkwardness we often experience in trying to make sense of who we are in the 21st century. As academics, we must carry out this striving, struggling and shaping in the face of serious challenges to our values and traditions (Henkel, 2005), and yet it is possible to create and sustain robust academic identities if we can make or find 'spaces for the exercise of principled personal autonomy and agency' (Clegg, 2008: 329). In this chapter we explore an aspect of the current HE context that has potential both to challenge academics' sense of who they are and to open up spaces for meaningful identity work: interest in professional recognition for university teaching.

In many parts of the world, quality assurance for higher education focuses on accreditation at the level of the institution (see, for example US Department of Education, 2015; Council on Higher Education South Africa, 2015), whereas in the United Kingdom and Australia individual university teachers are being asked to demonstrate the quality of their professional practice so that they may be recognised for their teaching (Higher Education Academy, 2011; Office for Learning and Teaching, 2015). This attention to tertiary level learning and teaching and the associated focus on professional development for university teachers are both very welcome and overdue. We take a broad view of professional development, including all of those experiences and processes that enable professionals, in this case university lecturers, to learn, grow and flourish. Systems of professional recognition make it possible for the fruits of that learning, growth and flourishing to be acknowledged and fairly rewarded. However, external standards and frameworks have the potential to hamper identity work, as well as to support it. The UKPSF has proved to be influential as a way of both 'asserting one's identity as a teaching-focused academic'; and as 'a means of recognising teaching' (Staff and Educational Development Association, 2013: 31). The Framework was developed by the Higher Education Academy (HEA) in order to provide guidance for individual practitioners, academic developers and institutions. Proposed in the Government White Paper *The Future of Higher Education* (2003), published in 2006 and revised in 2011, following widespread consultation with the sector, the UKPSF was one among a number of measures intended to address concerns that the UK Higher Education system was under-resourced, uncompetitive, detached from the concerns of business and the economy and failing to address social exclusion. It was claimed that teaching in particular was poorly regarded and insufficiently rewarded, resulting in some cases in 'poor provision' and 'problem areas' (p. 50). The UKPSF emerged three years later.

The shifts in emphasis from the White Paper to the UKPSF already show signs of the tension between different ways of understanding university teachers' professional development and the place of identity work. Whereas the White Paper had advocated a focus on *standards, skills, training, competences, performance management, scrutiny* and *rewards* in response to these shortfalls, the new Framework referred to *demonstrating understanding* and *engaging in practices*. Instead of *updating skills*, practitioners were encouraged to *engage with areas of activity, with core knowledge and with professional values*. Whereas the White Paper had called for reform through standardisation, the UKPSF suggested a more open-ended approach, embracing 'creativity, innovation and continuous development' (p. 2). And yet despite the softening of language, the UKPSF performs, quite appropriately, a regulatory function. It delineates what a good university teacher should know, what s/he should be able to do, and the values that should underpin practice. It was intended as a guide for making equitable decisions about recruitment, promotion and disciplinary action and is concerned with prediction, control and consistency. The UKPSF can be easily misread and misused as reductionist and narrowly instrumental. There is a place for clarity, particularly since the role of the university teacher is widely misunderstood and undervalued, but too heavy a reliance on external standards and normative frameworks may suppress some valuable aspects of academic identity work. In the next section, the concept of artistry is introduced. We suggest that through artistry we may be able to complement the UKPSF and bring it to life.

ARTISTRY IN UNIVERSITY TEACHING

By artistry we refer to a way of being that is

> riddled with uncertainties, marked by surprise, motivated by the satisfaction of discovery, supportive of innovation and prized for the experience it makes possible. (Eisner & Powell, 2002: 134)

It was Schön (1983) who introduced the concept of professional artistry, claiming that for the professional practitioner in any field, science and technique are not enough. Practitioners thus embody a distinctive way of knowing, often indescribable in words, revealed in action and irreducible to a mere set of rules or procedures. Artistry is the hallmark of those practices that are required in 'unique, uncertain and conflicted situations' (p. 9). It follows that artistry is required in areas characterised by unpredictability, doubtfulness and contradictions. One notable example is university teaching.

Eisner (2003) identifies *artistry* as a quality missing from much contemporary practice and provides a convincing rationale for moving beyond narrowly instrumental accounts of professional development. For him, artistry is not confined to the fine arts; the products and processes of any human endeavour requiring skill, commitment and imagination can embody artistry. Nor is artistry concerned only with feeling: it has a significant cognitive dimension, as implied by his identification of a number of forms of 'artful thinking'. One of the hallmarks of artistry, according to Eisner, is the pursuit of surprise. He advocates this active seeking out of the unexpected as a counterbalance to current preoccupations in education with standardisation and control. He associates the pursuit of surprise with Dewey's (1938) notion of flexible purposing – a readiness to change our plans in the light of what we are learning from our current experiences. It is the nature of educational practice that we have to make judgements relating to ill-structured problems where there are no universal rules and no definitive solutions. In creating and responding to artwork it is important to slow down our processes of perception so that we may reflect on how we make meanings and come to judgements. Eisner suggests that we must learn to trust and develop our feel for what is the right thing to do at a particular time in a particular situation. We need to integrate form and content, and accept that our practices, and the process of developing them, cannot be fully translated or explained in words. It is important that we immerse ourselves in the pleasurable absorption of creating. Finally, he says, we must become the architects of our own education, shaping the learning environments that will in turn shape us.

Greene's (1995) notion of releasing the imagination has much in common with Eisner's concept of artistry. She, too is interested in the unexpected, and also draws on Dewey, proposing surprise as a remedy for the inertia of habit. Unlike Eisner she makes explicit links with action for social justice. She sees engagement with the arts as a way of breaking through habitual ways of seeing, thinking and acting. Such engagement may bring about empathy with others' experiences, allowing us to move beyond the preoccupations of our own private worlds. The startling insights we gain may lead us to reconsider what we had understood as settled certainties, and this may be the first step towards acting for social change. Greene's account also has some affinity with Mezirow's (1997) claim that transformational learning happens when we are able to dismantle our familiar and limiting frames of reference. Social action may be both a catalyst for, and an outcome of transformational learning. Mezirow claims that a disorienting dilemma – a surprising experience or insight that disrupts our assumptions – could lead us to change not only our point of view on specific topics, but also our more deeply-ingrained habits of mind. He refers to the imaginative use of metaphors as one method of stimulating such transformations (Mezirow & Associates, 1990). Both Greene and Mezirow challenge us to look beyond the technical aspects of university teaching to its moral and political dimensions.

Empirical investigations of artistry in the professional development of university teachers are rare. A recently published collection of case studies of arts-enriched university pedagogies (MacIntosh & Warren, 2013) does show practitioners embodying Eisner's concept of artistry in their teaching. They bring poetry, drama, imagery, movement and cinema into their learning and teaching activities with student doctors, nurses, social workers, economists and managers. But what of the development of the university teachers themselves? We think there is a strong case for extending Eisner's artistry of teaching to arts- enriched professional development for university teachers.

ARTS-ENRICHED IDENTITY WORK IN PROFESSIONAL DEVELOPMENT PRACTICE

In my role as facilitator I (Daphne) invite colleagues actively to engage with the processes, artefacts and ways of thinking associated with the creative and expressive arts. I invite them to read a poem as a starting point for reflection on their teaching, or to write their own poem to communicate what they have learned. They listen to music, make sculptures or take photographs. We often use art materials – paint, paper and crayons – but sometimes it is artistic sensibilities that are most salient: the exploration of subjectivity or the valuing of ambiguity. In these cases we may use materials that are not usually associated with art, such as everyday objects or policy documents. I locate my practice of arts-enriched professional development for university teachers in relation to three distinct traditions: arts-based research, the expressive therapies and adult education.

Arts-Based Research

By arts-based research practices we refer to methodologies that draw on music, poetry, painting and other media in order to address research questions, create and analyse data, represent findings and disseminate interpretations and understandings. For those academic colleagues who may be wary of my approach, the growing acceptance of arts-based research practices in the world of qualitative research provides reassurance: practitioners and proponents offer a rationale for their methodologies and engage with critique in ways that seem acceptable in the academy. Their arguments are also relevant to professional development: it is helpful to think of academics' identity work as a form of research.

Leavy (2009) lists the strengths of arts-based research practices as attention to process, immediacy, consciousness-raising, giving voice to overlooked perspectives, promoting dialogue, particularly with wide audiences, the evocation of meaning and the ability to work with multiple meanings. Arts-based researchers have engaged with critiques of the validity and trustworthiness of these practices, recommending a move from rigour to vigour (Sinner et al. cited in Leavy) and acknowledging the limitations of alternative forms of representation with regard to precision, acceptability and ease of publishing.

Smart's (2014) work provides an example of how a practice associated with research can be modified for the purposes of academic development. Smart (2014) has introduced poetic transcription with a twist in order to support early career academics' transition into role. Drawing on the research technique of poetic transcription, whereby interview data are distilled in to poems, Smart invites colleagues to rewrite in poetic form a critical incident shared by one member, before presenting their new version to the group. The rules are that whilst words can be removed, none can be added, and the chronology must be maintained. Changes of punctuation are allowed to create emphasis, and each version is given a title. Smart suggests that 'poetic transcription with a twist' may have the potential to create conversations about early career academics' lived experience so that their transitions are 'less painful, less isolating, enabling, in turn, their sense of identity, agency and community to thrive' (p. 69).

Expressive therapies

This approach may be defined as the therapeutic use of artworks of all kinds in the context of an established relationship between an individual or group with psychological, emotional or other significant issues and a qualified therapist who is bound by a code of ethics. It is now used by non-therapists who have successfully applied concepts and practices from art therapy in professional development contexts with health workers, counsellors and teachers (Silverstone, 1997). Artwork has traditionally been seen as an alternative medium for those who experience barriers to verbal communication – children, people with learning disabilities, individuals or groups who are distressed or disadvantaged. Artwork can also be understood as a way for articulate individuals to by-pass familiar, routinised, or ossified ways of thinking, speaking and seeing. For academics, who are only too familiar with speaking and writing, alternative ways of representing their ideas and experiences are well worth exploring. The expressive therapies provide a language and a way of thinking that are very valuable in professional development work. They can help us to think about academic development, and how language can be used in open-ended and generative ways.

An approach to the use of metaphor that may prove useful for academic staff developers is found in the therapeutic literature (for example, Angus & Rennie 1988; Sims & Whynot, 1997; Sims, 2003), and is characterised by three principles. First, participants are supported to linger a little longer than usual with ambiguity and uncertainty. Rather than moving quickly from connotative meanings to categorisation, they are urged to slow down their meaning making so that they can come to a considered, nuanced understanding of themselves as teachers. Secondly, Sims and Whynot (1997) place emphasis on participants' interpretation of their own metaphors and the value of staying with the individual's own imagination. Attention paid to their idiosyncratic expressions can demonstrate the value placed on them as individuals, deepen the relationship between facilitator and participant and encourage further metaphorical expression. Thirdly, the spirit of playfulness and involving others, through the sharing of artwork and invitation for feedback is also important. They caution against 'premature closure' (p. 343) where one group member may be inclined to supply a definitive explanation or translation, rather than living with multiple possibilities.

Adult Education

'Educators are learners' (Cranton, 1996:1) and continuing professional development, including the identity work carried out by university teachers can be understood as a form of adult education. Lecturers, claims Cranton, are adults who are learning about their teaching, and as such can helpfully be understood as engaging in the kinds of learning that are potentially transformational (Mezirow, 1997). Transformative learning theory places great value on individuals' capacity and need to make sense of their own experience. Transformative learning is said to occur when an individual becomes aware of an assumption that shapes or colours their thinking, reflects critically on that assumption, finds it wanting, and discards it in favour of a new understanding. Cranton (1996: 91) suggests that 'immersion in an aesthetic or artistic experience can lead to imagining alternatives, especially for people who normally think in linear problem-solving ways'. It makes sense to think of academic development as transformative learning (TL) because the centrality of autonomy and criticality in TL sits well with academic values and practices. The role of the developer as facilitator who learns alongside the 'developee' is also appropriate in the university context.

One example from Higher Education is the work of Upitis et al. (2008) who examined the weekly art-making sessions of a group of university colleagues over five years. They interviewed six group members and one observer to find out how the art making group had evolved, what kept it going, and what impact it had on the personal and professional lives of participants. Upitis et al. (2008) showed that art making in groups can provide more than temporary reprieve from the pressures of work. Through art making the participants they studied were able to transcend their everyday work and were able to take care of themselves, to deepen and equalise their relationships with colleagues, manage difficult experiences and have a positive impact on their workplace.

UNDERSTANDINGS OF RECOGNITION

Let us return to our colleagues hammering, sticking, laughing and talking in the 'Surprising Spaces' workshop. What exactly is going on here? These activities will attract credits in many institutional Continuing Professional Development (CPD) frameworks. The workshop is firmly located within the structures set up for the recognition of university teaching. But what exactly do we mean by recognition in this context? Who or what is being recognised, and by whom? In my role as academic developer in a large Scottish university, I am often called upon to offer support and guidance to colleagues who want to gain recognition as Fellows, Associate, Senior or Principal Fellows of the HEA, categories that map directly on to the UKPSF. Although we commonly conflate a whole variety of processes under the term, I find it helpful to distinguish between four interconnected but distinct acts of recognition. First, at a basic level colleagues come to accept that they are teachers. This is by no means straightforward for many academics who for a range of reasons may be unwilling to take on, or to be seen to take on, a teacher identity. At this point they *recognise* themselves as teachers in the sense of becoming aware of, or accepting the role that they play in the education of others and the privileges and responsibilities that this involves. Secondly and more interestingly for me, is when they go beyond the question of 'Am I a teacher?' to 'Who am I as a teacher?' Here they *recognise* idiosyncratic aspects of themselves as individuals as well as becoming aware of differences and commonalities with others in terms of class, gender, sexuality, disability and other aspects of their identities. Thirdly, in my mentoring role it is important for me to *recognise* what they do, know and value in relation to agreed criteria. I need to know the required standards and to know them again (re-cognise them) when I see them embodied in my colleagues' practice and to make comment when they are missing. The assessor relies largely on applying agreed standards, although in a well-crafted submission, with a sensitive assessor, there may be room for appreciation of the candidate's identity as a teacher. Finally, formal *recognition* is given when the awarding body accepts that standards have been met and employers and others accept the value of the piece of paper as standing for something meaningful. In all of these acts of *recognition,* clearly articulated standards and frameworks are useful. However when individuals ask "Who am I as a teacher?" and the mentor (or developer or critical friend) is helping them to find meaningful answers to that question, something more nuanced and open-ended is also needed. An approach to professional development based entirely on the apparently settled certainties of the UKPSF, for example 'knowledge of the subject material', 'appropriate methods' and 'effective environments' cannot adequately prepare academics for the unpredictability, exploration and discovery that are a vital part of learning for students and teachers alike. What external standards and normative frameworks fail to capture is that vital dimension of a teacher's identity that we know as artistry and that can be fostered during arts-enriched identity work. Here are the comments of three of the workshop participants:

> This workshop helped me to gain a clarity about where my role as teacher fits within my wider work/life picture.

> It made me feel re-energised and quite inspired! With universities becoming increasingly bureaucratic and focussed on their 'business models' it was really refreshing

> to do something so creative and reflective, something useful in the sense that it had real content (a box-making as opposed to a box-ticking exercise) that I am able to apply it in my own work with students and colleagues. In fact, I took my box along to show my postgraduate teaching skills class – they really liked the idea – and I hope to get a group making one next semester.

> Getting involved in creating artefacts and discussing poetry were both very powerful experiences which allowed me to engage with my senses and most profound beliefs, ideas and understandings, and to share them in an unconventional way.

It seems to us that the Surprising Spaces workshop shows how university teachers and academic developers can challenge the reductionism implicit in normative frameworks by introducing an element of artistry. In my practice and research I have found that arts-enriched professional development activities focusing on identity work allow lecturers to break out of habitual, guarded modes of communication, in order to go deeper than everyday talk and to encompass feelings, values and intuition. Workshop participants explore previously unconscious material so as to see something new in themselves as teachers, or to see familiar aspects in fresh ways. They find time for listening and reflection, seek out surprise, create fresh metaphors and explore their sense of who they are (Loads, 2009). Artwork and exploration of metaphors enables them to reflect on who they are as teachers, and what teaching means to them. They are able to stay with ambiguity, re-embody their thinking and find time and space for rest and refreshment: a restorative space (Loads, 2010) In activities that are less overtly "artistic" but that nevertheless show aspects of artful thinking, for example collaborative close reading of academic texts or policy papers on learning and teaching, I have found that colleagues are willing to engage with powerful metaphors, intriguing ambiguities and questions that make them think deeply about their teaching practice and teaching identities (Loads, 2013).

This workshop was previously reported on the Higher Education Academy blog at https://www.heacademy.ac.uk/surprising-spaces-arts-enriched-reflection-professional-development-academics-teaching-arts-and

REFERENCES

Angus, L., & Rennie, D. (1988). Therapist participation in metaphor generation: Collaborative and noncollaborative styles. *Psychotherapy, 25*(4), 522–560.

Clegg, S. (2008). Academic identities under threat? *British Educational Research Journal, 34*(3), 329–345.

Collins, B., & Grisoni, L. (2012). Sense making through poem houses: An arts-based approach to understanding leadership. *Visual Studies,* 27(1), 35–47.

Council on Higher Education, South Africa. (2015). *Accreditation framework.* Retrieved from http://www.che.ac.za/ (Accessed August 12, 2015).

Cranton, P. (1996). *Professional development as transformative learning: New perspectives for teachers of adults.* San Francisco, CA: Jossey-Bass.

Dewey, A. (1938). *Experience and education.* Indiana, IN: Kappa delta Pi.

Eisner, E., & Powell, K. (2002). Art in science? *Curriculum Inquiry, 32*(2), 131–160.

Eisner, E. (2003). Artistry in education. *Scandinavian Journal of Educational Research, 47*(3), 373–384.

Future of Higher Education. (2003). Retrieved from http://www.dfes.gov.uk/highereducation/hestrategy/pdfs/DfES-HigherEducation.pdf (Accessed March 4, 2015).

Greene, M. (1995). *Releasing the imagination: Essays on education, the arts, and social change,* San Francisco, CA: Jossey-Bass.

Henkel, M. (2005). Academic identity and autonomy in a changing policy environment. *Studies in Higher Education, 49,* 155–176.

Higher Education Academy. (2006/2011). *Professional standards framework.*

Hughes, L. (1994). *Collected poems of Langston Hughes.* New York, NY: Vintage.

Johnson, T. H. (Ed.). (1955). *The poems of Emily Dickinson.* Cambridge, MA: The Belknap Press of Harvard University Press.

Leavy, P. (2009). *Method meets art: Arts-based research practice.* New York, NY: The Guildford Press.

Loads, D. (2009). Putting ourselves in the picture: Art workshops in the professional development of university lecturers. *International Journal for Academic Development, 14*(1), 59–67.

Loads, D. (2010). I'm a dancer and I've got a saucepan stuck on my head: Metaphor in helping lecturers to develop being-for-uncertainty. *Teaching in Higher Education, 15*(4), 409–421.

Loads, D. (2013). Collaborative close reading of teaching texts: One way of helping academics to make sense of their practice. *Teaching in Higher Education, 18*(8), 950–957.

MacIntosh, P., & Warren, D. (Eds.). (2013). *Creativity in the classroom*. Bristol, England: Intellect.

Mezirow, J., & Associates. (1990). *Fostering critical reflection in adulthood*. San Francisco, CA: Jossey-Bass.

Mezirow, J. (1997). Transformative learning: Theory to practice. *New Directions for Adult and Continuing Education, 74*, 5–12.

Office for Learning and Teaching. (2015). Retrieved from http://www.olt.gov.au/about-olt (Accessed March 4, 2015).

Schön, D. (1987). *Educating the reflective practitioner*. San Francisco, CA: Jossey-Bass.

Silverstone, L. (1997). *Art therapy the person-centred way: Art and the development of the person* (2nd ed.). London, England: Jessica Kingsley.

Sims, P. (2003). Working with metaphor. *American Journal of Psychotherapy, 57*(4), 528–536.

Sims, P., & Whynot, C. (1997). Hearing metaphor: An approach to working with family-generated metaphor. *Family Process, 36*, 341–355.

Smart, F. (2014). Poetic transcription: An option in supporting early career academics? *Journal of Perspectives in Applied Academic Practice, 2*(3), 66–70.

Staff and Educational Development Association. (2013). *Measuring the impact of the UK professional standards framework for teaching and supporting learning (UKPSF)*. Retrieved from https://www.heacademy.ac.uk/sites/default/files/resources/UKPSF_Impact_Study_Report.pdf (Accessed March 4, 2015).

Upitis, R., Smithrim, K., Garbati, J., & Ogden, H. (2008). The impact of art-making in the university workplace. *International Journal of Education and the Arts, 9*(8), 1–24.

US Department of Education. (2015). *Accreditation and quality assurance*. Retrieved August 12, 2015 from http://www2.ed.gov/about/offices/list/ous/international/usnei/us/edlite-accreditation.html

Watson, T. (2008). Managing identity: Identity work, personal predicaments and structural circumstances. *Organisation, 15*(1), 121–143.

Daphne Loads
University of Edinburgh, UK

Brigid Collins
Independent Artist, Scotland, UK

KARLA BENSKE, CATRIONA CUNNINGHAM
AND SAM ELLIS

14. THE METANOIA OF TEACHING

Translating the Identity of the Contemporary Academic

As increasing numbers of academics align their practice with the UK Professional Standards Framework (UKPSF), there is a growing requirement for them to engage with pedagogical research in higher education and become what Weller (2011) calls 'scholarly teachers'. Trowler (2013) has demonstrated that most of this research employs qualitative social science methods. This research slant means that, currently, a large number of academics must articulate their teaching experiences in a disciplinary language that does not belong to them. They are forced into an interdisciplinary conversation (Strober, 2011) without necessarily being given an opportunity to use the tools and skills that helped to shape their identity as academics in their own discipline.

Conversely, the use of arts-and-humanities methodologies in the scholarship of learning and teaching now seems to have gained irresistible traction, having been well established for more than a decade (see, for example, Hubbard & Power, 2003). Representative examples of this approach include textual interpretations (Chick et al., 2009) and confident advocacy for content analysis (McKinney, 2007). Others have developed bespoke taxonomies of thinking set unashamedly in their own discipline contexts – and made close readings of subsequent student work to inform evaluation and course design (Ciccone et al., 2008).

Following these pioneers, we wanted to experiment with methodologies from the arts to see what other forms of 'data' we could collect and analyse that would enable academics to engage with their teaching in ways that resonated more deeply with the arts and humanities. The three authors of this chapter came from three different disciplines in the arts and humanities and yet in our interdisciplinary conversations about methodology and teaching and learning, it became clear that we were seeking to explore the experiences of academics in ways which could provide more satisfaction than our forages into the scholarship of learning and teaching to date.

In this chapter, therefore, we interrogate the often terrifying ambiguity that encapsulates what it means to teach (and research) in higher education. From the outset our aim was to delve into uncanny in-between spaces of the academy, to identify fears and the unfamiliar landscape that teaching can create. We wanted to explore to whom we may 'confess' our sins without fear of repercussions, who may be able to provide absolution (Foucault, 1998; Wolff, 1950), and what can be learned through confessing and by sharing confessions with other academics. Participants in this study were asked to submit an anonymous note briefly describing a critical incident that they had experienced as university teachers, but may never have dared to 'confess' to anybody. Each participant was given a slip of A5 paper, with the instruction to 'spend five minutes writing about a critical incident in your teaching' or to 'note down words or expressions you associate with that experience.' These 'confessions' were placed into a black box – an idiom with connotations of a confessional booth, but also a source of information (in an aero-mechanical sense) when something has gone wrong. The act of confessing further evokes the Ancient Greek 'metanoia', meaning 'turning right around' or 'changing one's mind', and (mis)translated in the English bible as 'repentance'. Were our participants repentant (with all the associated connotations of contrition and regret), or were they practising metanoia in the truest sense, by reflecting on a critical incident and committing to personal change?

The vocabulary of academic development has challenged the performative agenda of New Public Management with variable success over the past twenty-five years. However, Macfarlane and Gourlay (2009: 455) have observed that new lecturers engaging in mandatory teaching qualification programmes (PGCerts) are routinely required to enact their 'penitent sel[ves]' by emulating 'tearful admissions of inadequacy' in the manner of contestants on reality TV shows; thus 'educational developers have created their own set of dogmas' (p. 458). In appreciating the value of a single chosen incident, our reflective apparatus provides an opportunity for a more authentic engagement with the metanoia of teaching.

Bass and Linkon (2008) urge practitioners to use textual analysis as a tool to explore our pedagogical practice. They suggest using critical and analytical skills to 'read' the classroom, and to examine how students are learning by reading their work in this context. A similar approach has been adapted here, using the collected 'confessions' as reading material of a different kind. We also encouraged our participants to consider an arts-enriched approach to confessing (Loads, 2009): rather than writing confessions, we invited them to draw the incident they were describing. For some of our participants this seemed like a step too far into the liminal space of confessions; however, a few ventured into this unfamiliar and counterintuitive terrain.

Our exploration of methodology drew on the authentic learning movement to inform our own development as researchers and practitioners (Lombardi, 2007). We set out to work with real contexts and experiences, draw on relevant literature, collect multiple perspectives, interpret collaboratively, reflect on our process, and support one another towards conclusions and identifying next steps (Herrington & Herrington, 2006). Crucially, we followed a course of open-ended inquiry and engaged in social learning throughout (Rule, 2006). Reflecting this developmental process, this account first details our curiosity and initial questioning, followed by the messy process of trial and error, and finally our reflections and procedural revisions.

The linguistic and cultural challenges highlighted above are evident in all the data we collected. Whether as researchers who have become teachers, as non-native teachers who are learning to adapt to the UK HE system, or as experienced practitioners who are now teaching their craft, our participants were all in some way crossing borders, migrating into new territories. To help us explore this 'in-between' space it has proved helpful to turn to translation studies where, of course, the movement across and between languages is much explored. Questions around the invisibility and power of the translator are important (Venuti, 2008; Bassnett and Lefevere, 1996) as well as the ethical dimension of what one is translating and for whom. The leap into another language or culture is described by the Canadian author Nancy Huston as a 'Mutilation. Censorship. Guilt.' (Huston, 1997: 22). These words describe the fear of entering another language, and also capture the sense of potential exposure faced by academics as they cross the different languages and borders of the academic space.

CURIOSITY AND INITIAL QUESTIONING

We began our discussions by exploring issues of identity through the frequently-shared vocabularies of academia and religion. Shadowy figures known as 'deans' and 'provosts' continue to patrol common room and sacristy alike. The University of Paris is rare in being able to trace its lineage directly back to an individual cathedral school; nevertheless, the emergence of places of 'higher thinking' from the sixth century onwards was bound with the Latin church through the centrality of monasteries in commercial and intellectual life. Most of the early universities fell under the aegis of Rome to some extent, and in northern Europe, theology was placed at the heart of the emerging curriculum. The lens of religion is most striking when we consider the vocabulary commonly used to describe officials in higher education. The dean, for example, was originally 'a leader of ten' (decanus) in a medieval monastery, with monks organised into clerical platoons for administrative purposes. Now the academic dean serves a similarly senior executive function. Further, the rector is the 'ruler', and the provost is 'set over' (praepositus) those beneath him.

Against this background, some broad questions began to emerge. Does the retention of religious vocabulary underline certain restrictions within the fully-financialised modern academy? Do the monastic robes of academe reinforce the deference of the medieval church? As a result, do our senior managers (literally) patronise us? What are the implications for our sense of identity? Taking the shared heritage of academia and religion as a starting point, we began to devise ways of interrogating the ambiguities that encapsulate what it means to teach at university.

An initial collection of 25 confessions was sampled – six of which were drawings – and some general observations were made. Following Macfarlane and Gourlay, we began by considering whether each of the confessions contains vocabulary which could be described as repentant; whether the tone of the confession is contrite and remorseful, seeking to atone for some heinous perceived error. Perhaps surprisingly, given the nature of the task (submitting a confession to a black box), only three of the 25 confessions communicate this level of regret. However, a majority of the confessions contain what Macfarlane and Gourlay label 'the dramatic appeal of the "quick fix"'. 14 of the 25 respondents identified, without prompting, a key lesson that had been learned from the critical incident. Whether or not these achievements are merely 'exaggerated mirage[s]', this does at least suggest that a genuine transformation (perhaps as the result of reflection) had occurred; that a moment of metanoia, of rethinking one's practice, had caused the participant to head off in a new direction.

Interestingly (but perhaps not surprisingly), the overwhelming majority of confessions (21 of 25) described a student-facing situation. The remaining specific situations included the lecturer assessing alone, in a CPD environment, in conflict with a senior manager, and designing a virtual learning environment. Where open conflict (with students as well as senior managers) was depicted, a Jungian form of metanoia also became evident: a momentary meltdown towards self-reparation, an existential crisis leading to an abandonment of a former persona.

TRIAL AND ERROR

Our aim is to demonstrate that applying arts-and-humanities approaches – particularly interpreting and 'translating' – not only adds depth of meaning, but also stretches the canvas by allowing multiple readings through embracing the subjectivity of the interpreter and tolerating the ambiguity and ambivalence of diverse interpretations. One specific confession was interpreted in two different ways to showcase two different approaches and how this both liberates the interpreter and deepens our understanding of the confessions. Secondly, two additional confessions were chosen for interpretation on the basis that they were created by an arts-enriched approach, in this case containing drawings combined with some text. As such they demonstrate poignancy achieved through arts-enriched 'creation', and the additional multiplicity of meaning made possible by 'opening up' the array of interpretation approaches available to the authors.

This process is a messy one: by embracing the ambiguity and uncertainty of this approach the authors themselves could not be sure how the outcome would unfold. On the contrary, the emphasis lies squarely on the process of creation, interpretation and learning, leaving possible insights or understandings to be identified by the reader. This would also be the case for anyone replicating this methodology with a view to enriching academic development through arts-based approaches combined with arts-and-humanities-based interpretations of qualitative data.

Confession 1 – Poetic Translation

By poetically transcribing (or translating) this confession, it becomes twice removed from the actual incident thus opening it up further to a detailed close reading. The emotions expressed in the confession informed the participant's decision on how to act and, together with the rationalising of the series of events that formed part of the incident, allowed the interpreter to appreciate the confession more thoroughly. This activates a wider range of perspectives, in-depth emotions and considerations that may have been lost without the poetical translation of the text. Transforming the confession into a poem allows the translator to shift, change and counterbalance the stresses and foci presented in the text.

During the act of translating the text into a poem, the translator 'becomes' the poet, stepping into the shoes of the academic who experienced the incident, re-living it, and thus empathising with the 'confessor'. In this instance, the translator's choice is to take liberty by omitting only some of the words, but not to change the order of the words (Aultman, 2009). The poetic format, however, allows a shift in emphasis due the freedom of choosing different formats for the verses. The original text of confession 1 is given below in full.

> I entered the room not a little overwhelmed by the prospect of teaching a class on Lacanian theory to a class of uninterested first year undergraduates. I don't remember exactly what happened, as is often the case in traumatic events, but one of the lads, rebelling against authority/showing off asked me to get him a coffee. Driven by a deep-seated desire to flee, which I justified by telling myself that getting the bloody coffee would somehow show him up, and make the rest of the class a bit cross with him, I left. I came back 10 minutes later with a coffee and carried on with the class. I can dress it up as a pedagogical strategy, but basically I ran away.

The poetical translation of confession 1 reads as follows:

Confession 1

>   Not a little overwhelmed
>   by the prospect of
>   teaching Lacanian theory
>   to a class of
>   uninterested
>   first year undergraduates.

>   I don't remember what happened,
>   as is often the case in
>   traumatic
>   events,
>   but one of the lads
>   rebelling against authority/showing off
>   asked me to get him
>   a
>   coffee.

Driven by a deep-seated desire to flee,
telling myself that
getting the bloody coffee
would somehow
show
him
up,
I left.

I came back
later
with a coffee and carried on with the class.
I can dress it up as a
pedagogical strategy,
but basically

I
ran
away

The poem starts with a voice making an under-statement, admitting to being only 'not a little overwhelmed', hinting towards a feeling of unease, underpinned by both feeling insecure about teaching as well as 'confessing'. 'Not a little overwhelmed' can also be expressed as 'feeling a lot overwhelmed', but the use of a negation and the adjective 'little' highlights the unease, the uncertainty of facing an unknown, new situation. It marks the crossing of a threshold, or entrance into a grey, ambiguous area, not previously experienced. This sensation is followed by the 'prospect' of teaching, counterbalancing the insecurity with a notion of hope, a vista, a positive way of looking forward to a task. However, the prospect here is that of 'teaching Lacanian theory | to a class of | uninterested | first year undergraduates'. The complexities of Lacanian theory represent a challenging prospect for teachers and first-year undergraduates alike, and the poetic voice's judgement or view that the first-year undergraduates are 'uninterested' introduce the reader to the dilemma faced by the teacher: how to engage students with as complex a topic as Lacanian theory?

Verse two relates to a 'traumatic | event', during which the teacher is asked to fetch 'one of the lads | [...] a | coffee', signalling a shift of power from the teacher to the student. Here is metanoia in the Jungian sense of crisis and self-surrender. However, the fact that the speaker refers to the student as a 'one of the lads' is a way of denigrating the student's position in class. It is a negative view of a student who is deemed to be a rebel, not interested in studying and prone to disruptive behaviour. The power balance between teacher and student has shifted to 'lad' and (female?) teacher, in which the lad undermines the teacher's position and 'downgrades' the teacher to the role of a servant, asked to fetch a coffee. The response is unexpected in the sense that within the context of teaching it stands out as a perceived exception rather than what is viewed as the norm. The two options of action are to fight or to flee, in other words to confront the 'lad' and attempt to regain the power in class or leave the classroom. One could argue that the 'perceived norm' is that teachers should stay and either ignore the challenge, or attempt to state calmly that getting coffee does not form part of teaching.

The poem's speaker, however, states that 'Driven by a deep-seated desire to flee | […] | I left.' This admission is extremely resonant, emphasised by using the poetic format of leaving it as a stand-alone line. The attempt to rationalise the action of 'getting the bloody coffee | would somehow | show | him | up' pales against the deeply-felt sensation of fear and the decision to escape the situation. Neither the poetic voice nor the reader knows what happened in class during the teacher's absence and no one can tell what the consequences of this action are for future sessions. The resonance of the decision to 'flee' reverberates through the remainder of the poem, like ripples in a pond, pointing towards the emotions felt by the teacher, still remembering the 'traumatic | event', wondering, worrying, looking for justifications and answers. The fact that the teacher 'came back | later | with a coffee and carried on with the class' may leave readers and fellow teachers perplexed, but it is also a deeply moving confession, opening up a rarely witnessed vulnerability felt by teachers who find themselves in difficult situations. In the poem, the voice belittles its own competence by referring to 'pedagogical strategy' as a 'dress […] up' rather than an achievement. The feeling of failure is visceral, even more so in the poetical translation in which the judgement of self is unrelenting and unforgiving to the very end: 'I | ran | away'.

The poetic translation humanises the teacher's voice and emphasises the importance for creating a space to 'confess', speak about fears and perceived failures in order to learn, develop confidence and strategies for dealing with critical incidents; or as Jones (2010) puts it: '[t]hrough the metaphors, the tension between the multiple and messy and our endeavours to contain it are illustrated, for example by the idea of the velvet box, the shrink-wrapped package, the props and compartmentalising juxtaposed against the importance of play, *the explosions, dishonesty and experiments that go wrong*' (603, our emphasis). Writing the confession has opened the 'shrink-wrapped package' and allowed a critical incident to be shared honestly, not impinged by the need to 'conform' to an accepted discourse of penitence and reflection (MacFarlane & Gourlay, 2009), and thereby enabled the participant, the translator and the reader to learn from the experience. The academic identity has thus been reconstructed. Self-reparation has followed a moment of despair; metanoia has truly been enacted.

Confession 2 – Interpretation

Our analysis of the images enabled us to translate the confessions in a way that led to more unexpected or surprising interpretations than we had found many of our written confessions which were lacking in a liveliness or simply expressed in a language that was embedded in the academy, rather than a language that conveyed the emotion of the moment. We had once again reached the 'wet, woolly wall' (Loads, 2013). In her account of learning the French language, Huston expresses the difficulty of finding the right words, using the right tools to express herself clearly. The following quotation illustrates the fear this can evoke:

> Les dictionnaires nous induisent en confusion, nous jettent dans l'effrayant magma de l'entre-deux-langues, là où les mots ne veulent pas dire, là où ils refusent de dire, là où ils commencent à dire une chose et finissent par en dire une tout autre. (Huston, 1997: 13)

> Dictionaries lead us astray, throwing us into the terrifying magma of being in-between two languages in the very place where words don't mean anything, or refuse to say, where they start meaning one thing and end up saying something completely different.

In academic development we have no dictionaries to help us speak the different languages of our disciplines, and yet this quotation resonates because the UKPSF has emerged as our 'manual'. We are accustomed to the language of pedagogical research, but do we translate it well for our colleagues? For some of our research participants, this 'language' is so alien that it could be perceived to be what Weller (2011) calls the 'gobbledy-gook' sentences, or what Loads (2013) describes as the 'wet woolly wall' of pedagogical research language. So, there is every possibility that just as Huston describes above, they start meaning one thing but end up saying another. For Huston, this space 'in-between' languages is terrifying. But what if being led astray like this, unknowingly, could take us somewhere rather productive?

If one were to 'read' the picture in Figure 14.1, according to the methods described above, there are many striking aspects to this confession. Foremost is the contrast between the academic writing on the board and the child-like figures represented, hinting at a clash of cultures. It is interesting that the word 'pornography' is capitalised in contrast to the small letters of the other words, which seem less legible. Indeed, is this perhaps a deliberate misspelling of 'feminist', making it look like 'femenist', thus evoking 'semen'? This capitalisation also makes 'pornography' stand out more than anything on the page, suggesting the female lecturer is feeling objectified in some way. This feeling is emphasised by the almost doll like image of the lecturer with her long, fair hair and frilly collar. Yet, her look feels far removed from the stereotypical image of the porn star – this lecturer is approachable with her large smile. It is interesting to note that one of her eyes is covered – does she not want to see or is she blinded by a strand of hair?

The portrayal of the students in this picture is also noteworthy: with the exception of the long-armed (male?) student, who has hair, all of the others are bald. This gives them an androgynous look but also suggests nudity, thus creating a possible vulnerability. Is it the subject under discussion that makes them seem naked, bare, exposed? None of the people represented in the picture has a nose – emphasising

THE METANOIA OF TEACHING

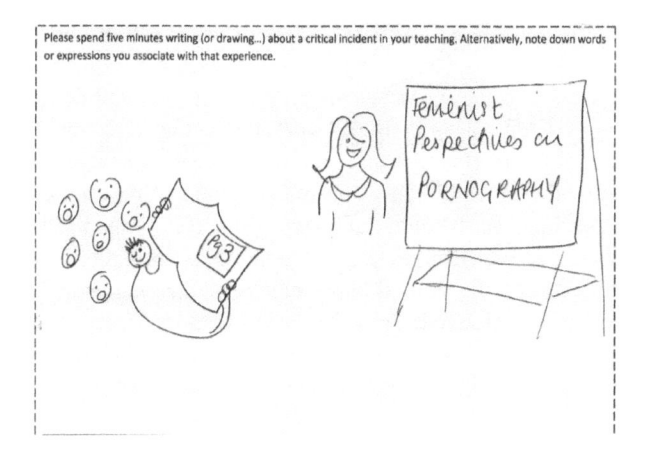

Figure 14.1. A critical incident arising from a difficult topic

their mouths and eyes. The contradiction between the sophistication of the topic and the childlike picture creates a conflicting mood – there are tensions here, layers of meaning lurking under the surface. Or is it their open-mouthed shock (or delight?) in the picture on Page 3 that is actually making them vulnerable? Their number suggests peer pressure, forcing them to conform to a societal expectation that is so very radically different to the topic in their class. Considered within the context of growing 'laddism' in the culture of higher education (Jackson, Dempster, & Pollard, 2015), this image is even more striking. What words could articulate with such clarity such a contradictory, almost ironic commentary of the tensions in teaching academic ideas in mainstream culture?

What can this tell us about academics' reflections on their teaching? What is striking is that underneath an often comical and arguably infantile representation, in the case of the drawing, and the humorous tone of the narrative account is a strong sense of contradictory tensions, and also of fragility and vulnerability. The words and images reveal what is often hidden in our usual public accounts of teaching at conferences or in journals where practice is described differently, in a way that is – one might argue – more sterile.

Confession 3 – Interpretation

The text in this image reads:

> Taught a writing class for a subject lecturer. I was given all guidelines for the dissertation prior. I tailored the class to the guidelines. Mid sessions it became clear guidelines and supervision instructions didn't match at all. Students were melting down!! Chaos ensued!! I was one blamed for causing problems and criticised by subject academic.

The image on this confession presents a state of crisis, of an unbearable conflict within a scary in-between place, the grey area where everything seems lost and nothing appears to make sense. We see an image of an 'unravelling' person, shouted at by disproportionately large (female?) mouths – faceless, just lips, teeth and tongue. The central figure also looks like a figure from a board game or a body stuck in a sarcophagus, the latter hinted at by the presence of bandages woven around the figure and reaching out beyond the canvas. This can be read as close to feeling 'dead', something that has been related to the phase of liminality by Turner (1967), with the subject entering the liminal phase having to die, vanish or be lost before a metamorphosis can be achieved. The association with the image of a mummy also denotes a feeling of being 'bounded' (Meyer & Land, 2003), stuck inside a set of boundaries and not being able to transcend or cross the threshold.

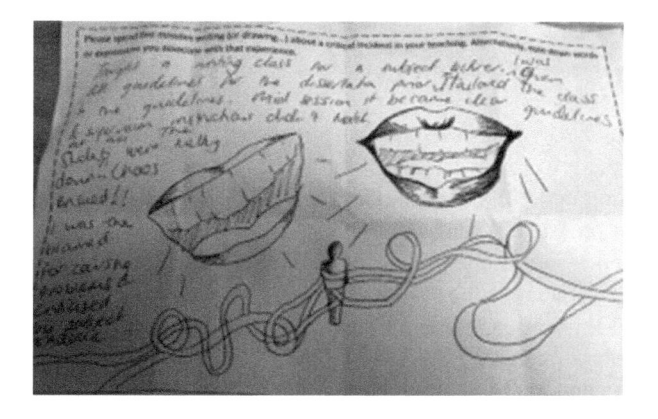

Figure 14.2. A critical incident arising from staff misunderstandings

The figure's size is significant, especially in comparison with the faceless open mouths. It is small enough to be swallowed by either of the mouths, emphasising the powerlessness felt by the participant about the critical incident that is described and drawn on the confession. There are two mouths, painted in quite some detail, with teeth and a tongue and carefully drawn lips. The lines reverberating from the mouths appear to denote sound or maybe speech (shouting?), although there is no hint as to what they may be saying. We do not know who these mouths represent. Is it the students? Is it the colleagues? Or both? The scapegoating of the subject for the 'failure' of the class is felt more intensely because of the difference in size and the position of the mouths on either side of the figure.

The image can be interpreted as a representation of a complete 'unravelling of identity', confounded by the bandages that, paradoxically, symbolise both the loss of structure or 'unravelling' and being bound up or tied up, not being able to escape. Against the background of Lacanian psychoanalysis the subject who 'confessed' this incident could be seen as to find themselves in a position where the loss of identity is matched with a loss of approval from the colleague as well as the students (Fink, 1997). It also reminds of the Jungian form of metanoia, the moment of meltdown that leads towards personal change.

REFLECTIONS, REVISIONS AND CREATIVE RESPONSES

The process of data analysis encouraged us to reflect on our emergent methodology and to suggest some refinements for the future. A case emerges for nuancing the confession generation process – to elicit descriptions of interactions with peers and managers, moments in preparation and assessment, as well as the predominantly student-facing incidents we collected. One solution might be to use our anonymised images and confessions in academic development sessions and explore the 'readings' which surface in group discussions (Smart, 2014). Different interpretations could be a powerful way for academics to become more aware of their own assumptions, expectations and practice. It could also open up more discipline-specific ways of academics approaching their own pedagogic research. Critically, too, this may provide a forum for discussing the productive adaptations (the 'changing one's mind' of metanoia) which generally follow a traumatic episode.

Offering our participants the freedom to use an arts-enriched approach to present their 'confession' enabled those who provided us with drawings to communicate the emotions experienced during the critical incident more intimately. Our approach to interpreting the images, and also in applying an arts-and-humanities-based approach to analysing one of the written confessions, has demonstrated that this process can indeed enrich the data analysis. It enables the interpreter to bring to the fore the emotions encountered by the participants and to highlight the fact that these incidents are a) integral to academic identity and b) essential in order to learn and continuously 'evolve' as a teacher in higher education. Our approach has also shown that allowing the participants to 'confess' anonymously has generated mainly genuine reflections, untainted by an accepted discourse of 'penitence' (Macfarlane & Gourlay, 2009), something which has been disoriented by the introduction of measurable 'key performance indicators' and objectives. The process of 'confessing' offered our participants an opportunity to face the fear of failure, but without needing to express the contrition of repentance.

These interdisciplinary probings of confessions have enabled us to examine critical moments in the professional practice of academics, and have laid bare the vulnerability of teaching in higher education. Through the conversations involved in preparing this chapter, we have at once surprised, delighted and challenged one another as we confronted our own disciplinary ways of being and thinking. In a sense, then, this process has also exposed (and helped to clarify) our own identities as three authors working in different roles in academic development. Interdisciplinarity may well be a complex beast, accused of being 'underthought' (Liu, 1989 quoted by Ellis, 2009), yet our approach and dialogue led to much thinking. Our academic politeness and mutual goal sustained our dialogue, and we would recommend this methodology of translation to other colleagues to try, not least as a way of examining one's own academic identity. Confessions, whether drawn or written, open up a space for discussing the wildernesses of the classroom. Above all, the confessions convey the emotion, fear and fragility of what it means to examine one's own practice, to contemplate fresh possibilities, and to assume a professional identity with teaching at its core.

REFERENCES

Aultman, L. P. (2009). A story of transition: Using poetry to express liminality. *Qualitative Inquiry, 15*(7), 1189–1198.
Bass, R., & Linkon, S. L. (2008). On the evidence of theory: Close reading as a disciplinary model for writing about teaching and learning. *Arts and Humanities in Higher Education, 7*(3), 245–261.
Bassnett, S., & Lefevere, A. (1996). *Constructing cultures: Essays on literary translation*. Clevedon, England: Multilingual Matters.
Chick, N., Hassel, H., & Haynie, A. (2009). Pressing an ear against the hive: Reading literature for complexity. *Pedagogy, 9*(3), 399–422.
Ciccone, A. A., Meyers, R. A., & Waldmann, S. (2008). What's so funny? Moving students toward complex thinking in a course on comedy and laughter. *Arts and Humanities in Higher Education, 7*, 308–322.
Ellis, R. J. (2009). Problems may cut right across the borders: Why we cannot do without interdisciplinarity. In C. Balasabramanyam & S. Fallows (Eds.), *Interdisciplinary learning and teaching in higher education* (pp. 3–17). New York, NY & London, England: Routledge.
Fink, B. (1997). *A clinical introduction to Lacanian psychoanalysis: Theory and technique*. Cambridge, MA: Harvard University Press.
Foucault, M. (1998). *The will to knowledge: History of sexuality* (Vol. 1, R. Hurley, Trans.). London, England: Penguin. (First published in French in 1976.)
Herrington, J., & Herrington, A. (2006). What is an authentic learning environment? In J. Herrington & A. Herrington (Eds.), *Authentic learning environments in higher education* (pp. 1–14). Hershey, PA: IGI Global.
Huston, N. (1997). *Perdre le nord suivi de douze France*. Arles, France: Actes Sud.
Jackson, C., Dempster, S., & Pollard, L. (2015). 'They just don't seem to really care, they just think it's cool to sit there and talk': Laddism in university teaching-learning contexts. *Educational Review, 67*(3), 300–314.
Jones, A. (2010). Not some shrink-wrapped beautiful package: Using poetry to explore academic life. *Teaching in Higher Education, 15*(5), 591–606.
Loads, D. (2009). Putting ourselves in the picture: Art workshops in the professional development of university lecturers. *International Journal for Academic Development, 14*(1), 59–67.
Loads, D. (2013). Collaborative close reading of teaching texts: One way of helping academics to make sense of their practice. *Teaching in Higher Education, 18*(8), 950–957.
Lombardi, M. (2007). *Authentic learning for the 21st century: An overview* (Educause Learning Initiative Paper 1).
Macfarlane, B., & Gourlay, L. (2009). The reflecting game: Enacting the penitent self. *Teaching in Higher Education, 14*(4), 455–459.
McKinney, K. (2007). *Enhancing learning through the scholarship of teaching and learning: The challenges and joys of juggling*. San Francisco, CA: Jossey-Bass.
Meyer, J., & Land, R. (2003). Threshold concepts and troublesome knowledge: Linkages to ways of thinking and practising within the disciplines. In C. Rust (Ed.), *Improving student learning – Theory and practice ten years on* (pp. 412–424). Oxford, England: Oxford Centre for Staff and Learning Development (OCSLD).

Smart F. (2014). Poetic transcription: An option in supporting the early career academic? *Journal of Perspectives in Applied Academic Practice*, *2*(3), 66–70.

Strober, M. (2011). *Interdisciplinary conversations*. Stanford, CA: Stanford University Press.

Trowler, P. (2013). Can approaches to research in art and design be beneficially adapted for research into higher education? *Higher Education Research and Development*, *32*(1), 56–69.

Turner, V. (1967). *The forest of symbols: Aspects of Ndemu ritual*. Ithaca, NY: Cornell University Press.

Venuti, L. (2008). *The translator's invisibility: A history of translation* (2nd ed.). Abingdon, England: Routledge.

Weller, S. (2011). New lecturers' accounts of reading higher education research. *Studies in Continuing Education*, *33*(1), 93–106.

Wolff, K. H. (1950). *The sociology of Georg Simmel*. New York, NY: The Free Press.

Karla Benske
Glasgow Caledonian University, UK

Catriona Cunningham
University of Stirling, UK

Sam Ellis
Glasgow Caledonian University, UK

TAI PESETA AND DAPHNE LOADS

EPILOGUE

Continuing the Conversation

To close this work, we provide an epilogue that looks towards the implications of academic identities research in university contexts internationally. As is customary in an epilogue, here we take stock of the contributions to this volume, and offer comment about what might be ahead for those who remain concerned about, and interested in, the state of academic identities and its attendant practices, research and scholarship. In our title we suggested that being an academic in the contemporary university could be thought about as 'uneasy' work. We opened up a space to consider the challenges, pleasures, and affects involved in being a teacher, a researcher, a doctoral student, a supervisor, an educational developer, a scholar and writer. These 14 chapters exemplify how this work appears and feels *now* at a time when the modern academy has become subject to multiple narratives of its purpose. It should be no surprise that these narratives about the university are apparent in this volume. Across each of the four parts, we are reminded time and again that efforts to better understand academic identities are intimately bound up with changing ideas of what the university is and can be. And so, if we dig a little deeper, we find connections to lines of inquiry advanced by Barnett – an idea of the university that is both super-complex (Barnett, 2000) and imaginative (Barnett, 2013); we encounter Shore's (2010) argument that the university has become 'schizophrenic' in orientation, and in ways that are consistent with fast capitalism and all its effects; and we confront Barcan's (2013) notion that the university can be thought of as a palimpsest – with several logics at play: a scholarly society, a bureaucracy, and a corporation, and that each one 'brings with it a particular set of expectations, demands and regimes of academic practice' … and 'creates particular relations to and experiences of *time'* (pp. 13–14, original italics). Clearly, these are not the only feasible diagnoses available about the university but they do point us to urgent questions about a renewed conceptual, policy and research agenda for those who are committed to doing, and inquiring into, academic life in ways that offer more meaning than what seem to be universities' current preoccupations with branding, marketing and international rankings. While there is plainly no shortage of scholarship available about academic identities (Clegg, 2008; Fanghanel, 2012; Gill, 2009; McWilliam, 2004) – in all its forms, settings and complexities – the demand before us is this: how can we build a research agenda that confronts the challenges ahead? Although there has been a proliferation in the online *I Quit Literature* (narratives of leaving the university), this volume demonstrates that current and aspiring academics remain fully committed to the idea of the university despite the toll on their weary bodies (Barcan, 2013), an impoverished work-life balance, and fundamental systemic issues (Lyons, 2015). In our view, the chapters signal that the idea of the university is still worth thinking hard about, and that an academic life is worthy of serious examination.

As we see it, there are at least three prospective (and perhaps contradictory) impulses governing the broad direction of academic identities research: first, the unbundling of academic work; second, the emergence of third-space hybrid academic identities; and third, a call for the integration of academic work (represented through scholarship and stewardship). We take each one in turn below.

UNBUNDLING ACADEMIC IDENTITIES: ON PARA-ACADEMICS

Macfarlane (2011: 59) is not alone in lamenting the demise of a 'holistic concept of academic practice'. In the place of the academic who pursues the integration of teaching, research and service, he argues that for some time, we have been witnessing the emergence of 'para-academics' – those who 'specialise in one element of the tripartite academic role' (p. 59). In this category, he names the following types: 'student skills advisors, educational developers, learning technologists, and research management staff' (p. 59) but suggests it does not stop there. A para-academic might also be someone employed on an academic contract to engage in research, teaching, and service but who for structural or resource reasons has a teaching load that makes it difficult for them to conduct research, or a head of department in an academic leadership role who no longer teaches but is expected to maintain their research performance.

While Macfarlane (2005) was critical of the effects of unbundling upon an integrated notion of academic citizenship, the drivers of the para-academic effect are reasonably well understood and documented across the global university sector. In Australia, as in other jurisdictions, governmental commitment to mass (and potentially) universal access to higher education evident (DEEWR, 2008; Dearing [NCIHE, 1997]) brought with it a funding obligation to support widening participation initiatives. Alongside that, a raft of new para-academic positions designed to support student transition, retention and academic success expanded rapidly. In addition, the decline in government funding in many Westernised higher education systems has led to the inevitable consequence of universities looking for new sources of revenue. Chasing the international student market has been one response; another has been refreshing courses and curricula for a more flexible, open and digital education environment targeted not only at those same markets, but also at markets identified by industry. A third has been to concentrate research priorities in order to maximise and leverage institutional performance in national audit exercises and international rankings. The sheer scale and pace of these changes has accelerated at precisely the same moment that there are increasing demands on universities to be more accountable, transparent, regulated, and cost-effective. The higher education 'market' has also been prised open by for-profit providers, a strategy welcomed by governments who want to stimulate competition and to keep universities on their toes.

Across western nations, this narrative is fairly typical. The effects, however, mark an ambivalent space for many academics. On the one hand, it might be said that para-academic positions provide opportunities to inhabit the university in new ways engendered by a flexibility that releases an academic from trying to do, and be, everything, especially as the speed of work intensifies. For example, rather than taking on the responsibility for all of the curriculum design, assessment-setting, teaching, marking and grading, and consulting with students within a single subject or module, the activities are divided up and can thus be outsourced. Yet while the focus on disaggregating teaching tasks in this way may on the face of it, propose a more efficient form of organisation, it advances an impoverished and technical view of teaching and learning – where the hermeneutic relation between the teacher and student is broken. The teacher becomes a content provider and the learner comes into view via their digital footprint. Questions also remain about the impact on the quality of the student learning experience.

Whitchurch (2012) has claimed that much of the scholarship about academic identity has so far focused on research and teaching for those on academic appointments. While this volume appears to represent that same general direction, Whitchurch (2008) also reminds us that there is a plethora of research and teaching-oriented activities being carried out by those not on academic appointments – those whom she calls third-space professionals.

HYBRID ACADEMIC IDENTITIES: ON WORKING THE THIRD-SPACE

In the contemporary university, the third space marks 'an emergent territory between academic and professional domains, which is colonised primarily by less bounded forms of professional' work (Whitchurch, 2008: 377). For Whitchurch (writing from the UK), it has been the growth of institutional projects that has compelled new forms of collaboration between staff with different sets of know-how and expertise. Not only do these projects run across the academic and professional staff divide, they also run across different areas of the university too. While Whitchurch (2008) teases out how professional staff tend to occupy and experience this third space, developing four broad types: bounded professionals (operate within structural boundaries), cross-boundary professionals (use structural boundaries for strategic advantage and to build institutional capacity), unbounded professionals (disregard structural boundaries focus on broad projects for institutional development), and blended professionals (dedicated positions that run across professional and academic work), it is only the final two of these types that work in third space projects.

Our sense is that the third space professional has been active and growing for some time in the modern university, a development that is especially felt by academics as the effects of the casualised academic workforce play out on an expanding higher education system. While the third space professional appears to rely initially on an institutional mandate for its view of the university, academics by and large, tend to remain committed to some notion of the discipline as the source of their intellectual inspiration. This is likely to be because the rewards and recognition associated with their work are focused on pushing the boundaries of knowledge in their discipline via research, and bringing students into conversation with the discipline via teaching. It will be no surprise either that institutional projects (well-intentioned as they can be) may be seen to hinder rather than support academics' judgments about research and teaching. There is acknowledgement of a sense of loss in Whitchurch's (2012) work but there is also a picture of inevitability too, where the third space professional is seen as a pioneer of 'collaboration' and 'new opportunities'. In many ways the concerns of academic staff are represented as futile pining for halcyon days – a point made forcefully by Davies (2005). To our way of thinking, this is a tension that needs fleshing out in future research.

INTEGRATED ACADEMIC IDENTITIES: ON SCHOLARS & STEWARDS

There is a strain of inquiry about academic work and identities that promotes the prospect of integration rather than specialisation and disaggregation. Out of the Carnegie Foundation for the Advancement of Teaching in the United States, there have come at least two significant ideas that have influenced our thinking about the landscape of academic identities research: one is the ground-breaking work by Boyer (1990) on scholarship, and the second is that by Golde and Walker (2006) some years later on the preparation of disciplinary stewards via doctoral education.

On Scholars

Writing in a North American context, Boyer (1990) was concerned about the relatively low status of university teaching in relation to research:

> We believe the time has come to move beyond the tired old "teaching versus research" debate and give the more familiar term "scholarship" a broader, more capacious meaning, one that brings the legitimacy to the full scope of academic work. Surely, scholarship means engaging in original research. But the work of the scholar also means stepping back from one's own investigation, looking for connections, building bridges between theory and practice, and communicating one's own knowledge effectively to students. Specifically, we conclude that the work of the professoriate might be thought of as having four separate, yet overlapping functions. These are: the scholarship of *discovery*; the scholarship of *integration*; the scholarship of *application*; and the scholarship of *teaching* (Boyer, 1990: 16, original italics).

Of the four scholarships, the first three: discovery, integration and application appeared to be reasonably well understood and established. Yet for many, Boyer's clarion call for a joined-up approach to academic work provided an occasion (and policy agenda) to argue more strongly for not only elevating the prestige of teaching but also for authenticating it as intellectual work focused on rigorous inquiry. Years later following Boyer, a number of researchers (Trigwell & Shale, 2004; Hutchings, Taylor Huber, & Ciccone, 2011) supported the addition of 'learning' to make the scholarship of teaching and learning. The supplement signalled that the scholarly activities embarked on by the teacher should carry positive effects on students' learning.

Twenty-five years after Boyer, both the idea of scholarship and the notion of being a scholar still linger, yet they jar in the modern university against the pressures on academics to get 'visible or vanish' (Doyle & Cuthill, 2015:671) Without doubt, Boyer's scholarships were normative – they advanced a view about what the university could be. Yet it is not only that the idea of scholarship carries a range of meanings and consequences (Brew, 1999), it may well be that a new generation of academics will only come to know university life in its fragmented form.

On Stewards

Following Boyer's cue at the Carnegie Foundation, Golde and Walker's (2006) work opened up a number of questions about preparation for academic work. If scholarship remains an important and integrating goal, how might doctoral education programs be reimagined and redesigned for that end? They offered the concept of stewardship:

> Stewards think into the future and act on behalf of those yet to come. A steward of the discipline, then, thinks about the continuing health of the discipline and how to preserve the best for those who will follow. Stewards are concerned with how to foster renewal and creativity. Perhaps most important, a steward considers how to prepare and initiate the next generation of stewards. (Golde, 2006: 13)

Golde (2006) further holds that stewards express care for their practice by demonstrating accomplishment in three domains of a field: the first focuses on *generation* – 'the ability to conduct research and scholarship that make a unique contribution and meet the standards of credible work' (p. 10). The second, *conservation,* involves 'understand[ing] the historical context of the field – how and when important ideas, questions, perspectives, and controversies arose or fell (or were overturned) [in order to] grasp the span and sweep of the field and locate themselves and their work in the disciplinary landscape' (p. 10). Third Golde suggests, is *transformation* with its emphasis on engaging communication of the field's questions to a range of audiences.

Read too casually, educating for stewardship may give the impression that future academics should tie their future loyalty and identities to their disciplines no matter the consequence. While there is clearly a discipline reproduction aspect to stewardship, this is not our only reading of it. A steward is entrusted to care for, and make decisions about the discipline's future. In some cases, this may involve defending the merit and accomplishments of the discipline, yet in others, it will encompass opening out the discipline to conversations designed to transform it. In addition to Golde's (2006) dimensions, a steward displays care by engaging their discipline in informed critical debate and through responsible pushing of its boundaries. For those of us interested in a more integrative approach to academic work and identities, many of the early projects developed by the Carnegie Foundation (especially under the leadership terms of Boyer & Shulman) offered proposals for holding together teaching, research and service in ways we have not seen in recent times.

TWO DIRECTIONS, TWO CULTURES?

The landscape of academic identities research reveals paths that branch in at least two directions. One direction takes the disaggregation of academic work as a global inescapability leading to fragmentation and anxiety. The other direction embodies the search for ways of holding teaching, research and service together in some kind of coherent whole. Whether citizenship, scholarship or stewardship provides a helpful framework remains an open question. While many of the chapters in this volume promote a focus on one aspect of academic identity (we assume for analytical purposes), they each seem to turn towards the latter direction in the quest for an academic life where the work is significant and is personally meaningful. These 14 Chapters point towards both systemic dysfunction and directions for valuable personal empowerment. By highlighting a new 'two cultures' divide, we hope this volume will go some way to soothing the uneasiness that so often permeates the structures and narratives to which academics have become accustomed.

REFERENCES

Barcan, R. (2013). *Academic life and labour in the new university: Hope and other choices.* Surrey, BC & Burlington, NJ: Ashgate.
Barnett, R. (2000). *Realizing the university in an age of supercomplexity.* London, England & New York, NY: Routledge.
Barnett, R. (2013). *Imagining the university.* London, England & New York, NY: Routledge.
Boyer, E. (1990). *Scholarship reconsidered priorities of the professoriate.* Princeton, NJ: Carnegie Foundation for the Advancement of Teaching.
Brew, A. (1999). The value of scholarship. *HERDSA Annual International Conference,* Melbourne, Australia, July 12–15.
Clegg, S. (2008). Academic identities under threat? *British Education Research Journal, 34*(3), 329–345.
Davies, B. (2005). The (Im)possibility of intellectual work in neoliberal regimes. *Discourse: Studies in the Cultural Politics of Education, 26*(1), 1–14.
DEEWR. (2008). *Review of Australian higher education (Bradley review).* Canberra, Australia: Australian Federal Government.
Doyle, J., & Cuthill, P. (2015). Does 'get visible or vanish' herald the end of 'publish or perish'? *Higher Education Research and Development, 34*(3), 671–674.

Fanghanel, J. (2012). *Being an academic.* Oxon, England & New York, NY: Routledge.
Gill, R. (2009). Breaking the silence: The hidden injuries of neo-liberal academia. In R. Flood & R. Gill (Eds.), *Secrecy and silence in the research process: Feminist reflections* (pp. 228–244). London, England: Routledge.
Golde, C. (2006). Preparing stewards of the discipline. In C. Golde & G. E. Walker (Eds.), *Envisioning the future of doctoral education: Preparing stewards of the discipline – Carnegie essays on the doctorate* (pp. 3–20). San Francisco, CA: Jossey Bass.
Hutchings, P., Taylor Huber, M., & Ciccone, A. (2011). *The scholarship of teaching and learning reconsidered: institutional integration and impact.* San Francisco, CA: Jossey Bass & Carnegie Foundation for the Advancement of Teaching.
Lyons, M. (2015). The great betrayal. *History Today, 65*(9), 32.
Macfarlane, B. (2005). The disengaged academic: The retreat from citizenship. *Higher Education Quarterly, 59*(4), 296–312.
Macfarlane, B. (2011). The morphing of academic practice: Unbundling and the rise of the para-academic. *Higher Education Quarterly, 65*(1), 59–73.
McWilliam, E. (2004). Changing the academic subject. *Studies in Higher Education, 29*(2), 151–163.
NCIHE. (1997). *National committee of inquiry into higher education (The dearing report).* London, England: HMSO.
Shore, C. (2010). Beyond multiuniversity: Neoliberalism and the rise of the schizophrenic university. *Social Anthropology, 18*(1), 15–29.
Trigwell, K., & Shale, S. (2004). Student learning and the scholarship of university teaching. *Studies in Higher Education, 29*(4), 523–536.
Whitchurch, C. (2008). Shifting identities and blurring boundaries: The emergence of third space professionals in UK higher education. *Higher Education Quarterly, 62*(4), 377–396.
Whitchurch, C. (2012). Expanding the parameters of academia. *Higher Education, 64,* 99–117.

Tai Peseta
Institute for Teaching and Learning
University of Sydney, Australia

Daphne Loads
Institute for Academic Development
University of Edinburgh, UK

NOTES ON CONTRIBUTORS

Sandra Acker is Professor Emerita in the Department of Social Justice Education, University of Toronto, Canada. She has worked in the United States, United Kingdom and Canada as a sociologist of education, with interests in gender and education, teachers' work, and higher education. Her recent research has focused on changes in academic work, university tenure practices, women academics in leadership positions, doctoral student and doctoral graduate experiences, and research project leadership. She is the author of *Gendered Education* (Open University Press, 1994) and *The Realities of Teachers' Work* (Cassell, 1999) and co-editor (with Anne Wagner and Kimine Mayuzumi) of *Whose University Is It, Anyway? Power and Privilege on Gendered Terrain* (Sumach Press & Canadian Scholars' Press, 2008), as well as numerous chapters and journal articles.

Karla H. Benske is a lecturer at Glasgow Caledonian University's Centre for Learning Enhancement and Academic Development (GCU LEAD). She is responsible for leading the FAIR Curriculum @ GCU Project and for supporting the implementation of the University's Recognition of Prior Learning (RPL) Policy. Before moving to Scotland for her PhD in Scottish Literature at the University of Glasgow, she graduated from the University of Tübingen, where she specialised in British Studies, Sociology and German Literature. Her research interests are equality and diversity, critical pedagogy and learner empowerment.

Jennie Billot is Head of Researcher Development at Auckland University of Technology, leading projects that support and develop academic staff and student researchers. Her university initiatives focus on building researcher capacity and capability, enhancing supervision, supervisor mentoring and doctoral skill development. Jennie's personal research interests and expertise lie in the domain of educational leadership, previously instigating leadership programmes and projects as director of several research centres. She also researches academic identity and developing research communities. As Associate Editor for *Higher Education Research and Development* and reviewer for international journals, Jennie actively contributes to scholarship within higher education. In recognition of her publication and project portfolio, Jennie was awarded the New Zealand Educational Administration and Leadership Society Award for meritorious research and scholarship.

Pip Bruce Ferguson has worked in staff development in various tertiary institutions for over 30 years. Her particular interests are in promoting teaching enhancement with staff, both experienced and novice, and to encourage their publication of their good practice using action research. She enjoys co-writing with like-minded people, who have a passion for education and concerns for social justice and equity. Her recent publications have taken an introspective bent, looking at the 'I who teaches' as Parker J. Palmer puts it. Pip is currently practising as a Teaching and Learning Developer at Dublin City University, Ireland.

James Burford is a lecturer, and founding faculty member at the recently established Faculty of Learning Sciences and Education at Thammasat University, Thailand. His primary research area is higher education studies, where he has used queer concepts to explore the affective-political dimensions of contemporary doctoral education. James has also researched and published in several other areas, including evocative writing methodologies, LGBT issues in education, gender/sexuality in international development, and the cultural politics of fat and transgender embodiment. His work has recently been published in journals such as *Higher Education Research & Development*, *M/C Journal*, and *Development in Practice*.

Vanessa Cameron-Lewis is a doctoral student at the University of Auckland in Aotearoa/New Zealand in the School of Critical Studies in Education. Her background is in preventative sexual abuse education and anti-racist work where she has worked in both paid and voluntary roles in her community. In combining her professional expertise and interests with her academic work, Vanessa has focused on sexuality studies with post-colonial and post-modern theory. Vanessa's doctorate is a philosophical rethinking of sexuality education drawing on the monist proposal offered by the new materialist turn in contemporary social theory.

Brigid Collins is an artist, illustrator and educator. Passionate in her desire to forge relationships between images and poetry, in particular, she creates paintings and assemblages in 2 and 3D - called 'Poem-Houses' - often in collaboration with writers, poets and other artists, or to commission and also exhibits regularly. Underpinning all of her work is the joy of making, of handling materials and responding to their unique qualities and capabilities. She believes in sharing her knowledge and experience and leads creative workshops for all ages and lectures in the Illustration Department of Edinburgh College of Art, at The University of Edinburgh and at Leith School of Art, an independent art school also in Edinburgh.

Catriona Cunningham is a former lecturer in French and in Education at Queen's University Belfast, Edinburgh and the University of the West of Scotland, with a research background in francophone postcolonial literature. She is now a Consultant in Academic Practice at the Higher Education Academy in the UK where she leads the work in Modern Languages. Her most recent research is in the area of internationalisation in HE, particularly its impact on academic identities.

Sam Ellis is a senior lecturer at Glasgow Caledonian University's Centre for Learning Enhancement and Academic Development (GCU LEAD). He took degrees in music and geography at Bangor University, and completed a doctorate in history following a two-year visiting scholarship at Cambridge University. He returned to Bangor for several years as a lecturer in music and history. Sam's primary concerns within the field of education are teacher empowerment, educational leadership and informal learning. He is a Senior Fellow of the Higher Education Academy.

Barbara Grant researches in the field of higher education, where her main area of expertise is the study of the supervision of graduate research students. She has also researched and published in several other areas in the field including researcher identity, academic/educational development, research methodologies, and academic writing. The underlying thread connecting her enquiries is an interest in questions of identity, power and ethics in relation to higher education work, relationships and institutions. Her newest project is a post-critical ethnography of doctoral supervision, in which she studies supervision as one element of academic work in the Arts, Humanities and qualitative Social Sciences. Barbara is an Associate Professor in the School of Critical Studies in Education at The University of Auckland, Aotearoa/ New Zealand.

Toni Ingram is a doctoral candidate in the Faculty of Education at the University of Auckland (NZ). Her research interests include girlhood, young femininities, sexualities and schooling. In previous research, Toni has explored 11–13 year old girls' understandings of themselves as sexual subjects. Her current research project examines the relations between girlhood, sexuality and school ball culture.

Virginia C King is a higher education consultant specialising in project management, peer-review and research evaluation. A visiting lecturer in Academic Practice at Coventry University, UK, she supports academic staff development through postgraduate modules and stand-alone workshops. Her extensive publication portfolio reflects her research interests which include academic identity, research group development, education research strategy and the use of visualisation techniques in educational research. She is a member of the International College of Journal Reviewers for the Australasian journal Higher Education Research and Development. As technical editor for the open access International Journal of Practice-based Learning in Health and Social Care she maintains standards for both editors and authors. Follower her on Twitter: @EdResVCK.

Giedre Kligyte's interests revolve around change in higher education context, including higher education policy, academic practice, academic leadership, academic ethics and collegiality. She is also interested in academics' construction of teaching quality in higher education, as well as the role of professional development programs in the enhancement of academic practice. Currently, Giedre is a Lecturer at the Learning and Teaching Unit, UNSW Australia. She is also completing her PhD at the University of Sydney, focused on the notion of academic collegiality drawing in particular on theories of psychoanalysis and poststructuralism.

Daphne Loads is an academic developer in the Institute for Academic Development at the University of Edinburgh. Daphne studied English Literature, Life and Thought at Cambridge University and has professional qualifications in Social Work, Counselling and Teaching and Course Design in Higher Education. She has taught in a range of formal and informal settings in the UK and beyond. In her current post she mentors academic colleagues across the disciplines in developing their learning and teaching practice and teaches on the masters level Postgraduate Certificate in Academic Practice. Her research interests include arts-enriched professional development and academic identities. She is a Senior Fellow of the Higher Education Academy. Daphne balances her academic work by travelling with her partner and gardening.

Jan McLean is a Senior Lecturer at the Learning and Teaching Unit, UNSW Australia where she leads programs to develop scholarly teaching for academic staff. Her research interests centre around academic work and practice including the processes and practices involved in how we 'become' academics, the role and impact of accredited teaching programs and women and higher education.

Neil McLean is Director of the Teaching and Learning Centre at the London School of Economics and Political Science. His professional background is in teacher education and he has worked with academics on the design and delivery of taught provision since 2004. His research interests are psychological and discursive, focusing on identity positioning and the ways in which people create who they are through their interactions.

Catherine Mitchell (Taranaki) is a doctoral student at the School of Critical Studies in Education at the University of Auckland (NZ). Her research interests are located in the field of higher education and include the experiences of first-generation students, the role of the university in the contemporary context, doctoral education and academic writing. She currently works at Unitec Institute of Technology (Auckland) as a learning development lecturer.

Charles Neame has worked as a teacher in higher education since 1991, moving from a specialism in Environmental Business Management into educational development around 2006. He sees teaching as a scholarly activity which brings together a love of knowledge, care for students and the learning community, and a commitment to rigorous teaching and research methodologies. Charles worked at Cranfield University for 18 years from 1991, eventually as head of the Cranfield Centre for Postgraduate Learning and Teaching. He completed a Doctorate in Education at the Institute of Education in 2009, researching models of professional practice adoption and dissemination in higher education. That same year, Charles moved to the Glasgow School of Art to support educational and staff development there, latterly as Reader in learning and teaching practice development. He now works as an academic developer at Manchester Metropolitan University, with a current focus on ethics in the curriculum, and values-based higher education.

Edward Okai comes from Ghana, where he received his Master of Philosophy degree in Adult Education. He has a Bachelor of Arts in Social Work and Sociology from the University of Ghana. He is presently a PhD student at the School of Critical Studies, the University of Auckland, pursuing education. Edward's thesis focuses on the successful socialisation of PhD students in University of Ghana. His research interests include doctoral socialisation and pedagogies for the socializing PhD students.

Tai Peseta is Senior Lecturer in the Institute for Teaching and Learning, University of Sydney. She is interested in the project of academic development, in particular, the operational and discursive logics that govern the field. Tai is Points for Debate Editor, *Higher Education Research and Development* (HERD) journal; sits on the editorial boards for *Teaching in Higher Education*, and the *International Journal for the Scholarship of Teaching and Learning*, and from 2007-2011 was the Australasian Associate Editor of the *International Journal for Academic Development*. At present, Tai leads two research projects, one exploring access and equity in doctoral education and academics' professional learning, and another which interrogates learning, teaching and curriculum change in academic workgroups in which several academics have completed a postgraduate course in university teaching. In 2015, Tai is co-leading an Australian Office for Learning and Teaching (OLT) grant focused on reframing the future PhD (with Simon Barrie and Keith Trigwell).

Linda Price is a Senior Lecturer in Educational Technology at the Institute of Educational Technology at the Open University, UK and a Professor of Engineering Education at the Engineering Faculty in Lund University in Sweden. She researches pedagogically-driven uses of educational technology in a range of contexts in higher education. Her recent research focuses on investigating and developing models of scholarly practices using technology. Her research is distinguished by its strong synergistic approach to research and practice, traversing the fields of education and educational technology research and scholarship. It brings together the two research areas of conceptions and perceptions of learning and teaching in higher education and technology enhanced learning. Her research has provided theoretical frameworks illustrating the range of complex factors to be considered in digital interventions in teaching and learning, enabling knowledge transfer that transcends national and disciplinary boundaries. She has led the convergence of the theoretical approaches to teaching and learning in HE with the experiential approaches to educational technology. Her research is leading current approaches to evidence-based practice in both learning design and academic development.

Julie Rattray is a lecturer in Education and Psychology at Durham University. Her research interests include aspects of teaching, learning and quality in Higher Education, conceptual development, the affective dimensions of liminality and threshold concepts and early development and learning. In particular she is interested in the ways in which students might conceptualise the learning and teaching nexus in Higher Education. She was recently a member of the UK team of project IBAR working with 6 European partners to explore the potential barriers to the implementation of pan European standards and guidelines for higher education and is a Senior fellow of the Higher Education Academy.

Susan R. Robinson has studied Philosophy at the universities of Tasmania, Illinois and Edinburgh. She has taught Philosophy and/or Intellectual History at the universities of Melbourne, Illinois, Edinburgh, Stirling, Open University (UK), Kingston (London), Middlesex, and Birkbeck College University of London. Between 2004 and 2008, she headed and taught into the Certificate in Higher Education programs in Philosophy and Intellectual History at Birkbeck College University of London. Since returning to Australia in 2008, she has worked in the area of research training, and now works at the School of Management, University of South Australia. Her primary research interests lie in the field of higher education.

Jan Smith is a lecturer in the Centre for Academic Practice, School of Education, Durham University, UK. Her research interests focus on academic identities and practices, postgraduate student experiences and threshold concepts. She co-chairs the SEDA Papers Committee, is a member of the Editorial Board of *Teaching in Higher Education* and a past Associate Editor of the *International Journal for Academic Development*. She is Course Director for the Postgraduate Certificate in Academic Practice at Durham, where she also teaches research ethics and qualitative methodologies to Master's and Doctoral students in the School of Education. She previously co-edited *Threshold Concepts within the Disciplines* (2008) with Ray Land and Erik Meyer (Rotterdam: Sense Publishers).

Dorothy Spiller is a Senior Lecturer in the Teaching Development Unit at the University of Waikato, New Zealand. She has worked for over twenty years in student learning support and teaching development and currently co-ordinates the Postgraduate Certificate in Tertiary Teaching offered by the University of Waikato. She employs an inquiry-based approach and collaborative conversations in her teaching development work. Current research interests include assessment and academic identity.

Paul Sutton is an artisan sociology lecturer who, for 20 years, has laboured at his craft in a provincial UK university. His research interests emerge from his teaching and combine the sociological and the pedagogical. They include: using social theory to understand the relationship between the academic identities of learners and teachers and their academic labour; and academic literacies. Once a staunch post-structuralist, an epiphany concerning the foibles of Foucault (at the 2012 Academic Identities conference) prompted him to re-visit the potential of Marxism, particularly the humanism of Eric Fromm, for researching HE learning and teaching in the twenty-first century. In addition to his passion for teaching sociology and researching pedagogy, the author loves to wander and wild camp on Dartmoor. When not working or wandering, the author is usually to be found wondering at the genius of Bach and the quirky imagination of Jose Saramago.

Simon Warren arrived in academia after sojourning in community and adult education, and community arts for a number of years, as well as training to be a teacher. Simon took a post at NUI Galway in January 2014 following work in various universities including University of Sheffield, Birmingham University, South Bank University, Institute of Education (University of London), and Warwick University. Simon's research has focused on the interrelationship between education policy and identity formation, particularly that of professionals. Simon's current research focuses on two areas. He is inquiring into the materiality of learning in higher education that draws on a combination of practice theory and posthuman philosophy to examine the human-non-human relationship in learning and teaching. Simon is also engaged in his Broken Academic project that uses autoethnography to examine the relationship between academic wellbeing and neoliberal reform in higher education. Here Simon is particularly interested in the way narrative and autoethnographic inquiry can work as forms of 'care of the self'. This project is moving towards follow-on work that curates academics' autoethnographic accounts of living in the neoliberal university.

Michelle Webber is an Associate Professor in the Department of Sociology at Brock University, Canada, where she is also affiliated with the Centre for Labour Studies and the Jobs and Justice Research Unit. She has published on feminist pedagogies and knowledges, the regulation of academic practice, university faculty associations and the work of teaching assistants and contingent faculty members. She has co-edited (with Kate Bezanson) *Rethinking Society in the 21st Century: Critical Readings in Sociology* (3rd edn, Canadian Scholars' Press, 2012) and co-authored (with Bruce Ravelli) *Exploring Sociology: Canadian Perspectives* (3rd edn, Pearson Canada, 2015). Michelle also serves as the Vice-President of the Brock University Faculty Association.

Gina Wisker is Professor of Higher Education & Contemporary Literature and Head of Brighton's Centre for Learning and Teaching. Her principal research interests are in learning and teaching, specialising in postgraduate study and supervision and she has published *The Postgraduate Research Handbook* (2001, 2008 2nd edn) and *The Good Supervisor* (2005, 2012, 2nd edn) (both Palgrave Macmillan). She has just completed *Getting Published* (2015, Palgrave Macmillan). Gina also teaches, supervises, researches and publishes in twentieth-century women's writing, particularly postcolonial writing and popular fictions and she has published *Postcolonial and African American Women's Writing* (Palgrave Macmillan, 2000), *Key Concepts in Postcolonial Writing* (2007, Palgrave Macmillan) and *Horror* (2005, Continuum). In 2012 Palgrave Macmillan published her *Margaret Atwood, an Introduction to Critical Views of Her Fiction*. Gina is currently working on *Contemporary Women's Gothic Fiction* (2015, Palgrave Macmillan).Gina has been chair and co chair of the Heads of Education Development Group, is chief editor of the SEDA journal Innovations in Education and Teaching International and online literary publications Dissections and Spokes. She is currently chair of SEDA Scholarship and Research committee, and the Contemporary Women's Writing Association. Gina is a Principal Fellow of the HEA, a Senior Fellow of SEDA, and a National Teaching Fellow.

Linlin Xu researches in the field of higher education. Her main focus now is on intercultural doctoral supervision, particularly on the feedback dynamics between the supervisor and the supervisee in the context of intercultural supervision. As an international doctoral candidate and a lecturer herself, she is interested in issues of academic acculturation of international postgraduate students and academic writing of second language postgraduates. Linlin is a doctoral candidate in the School of Critical Studies in Education at The University of Auckland, Aotearoa/New Zealand.

INDEX

A
Academic Identities Conference, ix
academic identity
  blended professionals, 18, 19, 26, 196–198
  conceptualization of, vii, viii, xi, 3–55, 158, 159, 170–172, 196–200
  formation of, 4, 9, 11–13, 19, 23–28, 45–55, 91–101, 169–178, 181–192
  hybrid identities, 151–153
  identity maps, 162–165
  and job satisfaction, 61–72
  multiple identities, 47, 48, 151–153
  negotiation of, 45–55, 77–88, 129–140, 143–153, 157–166
  para-academics, 196, 197
  professional recognition, 144–146, 148, 149, 169–178
  scholars vs. stewards, 198–200
  and writing for publication, ix, xii, 18, 26, 67, 69, 143–153
academic values, viii, ix, xi, 3–42, 172, 173
  autonomy, 12, 13, 22, 24–28, 62, 65, 66, 71, 72
  and identity formation, 4, 9, 11–13, 19, 23–28, 158, 159, 169–178
  and performativity, 67–72
  and social character, 36–42
academic workgroups, 77–88
academic writing, viii, ix, 67, 143–153
  autoethnographic writing, xi, xii, 105–111, 112n, 114n, 117–127, 129–140
  fast writing, 140n, 141n
  peer review, 72, 145, 152

publications, ix, xii, 18, 26, 67, 69, 143–153
accountability governance, 61, 63, 66–72
Acker, Sandra, xi, 65, 66, 69, 71, 72, 73n
administration, 61, 62, 66, 67, 73n
adult education, 175, 176
advertising, 50
affect; see emotion
agency, 12, 35, 46, 170, 171
alienation, 34–39, 41, 42
Alvesson, M., 113n
Amis, Kingsley, 158
Amorim, K., 51
Amundsen, C., 48, 64
Antaki, C., 45, 49, 52
Antisthenes, 21
apatheia, 23
Archer, L., 47
Archer, M. S., vii, 51
Aristotle, 29n
artistry, 172, 173
arts-enriched identity work, x, xii, 157–166, 169–178, 181–192
Ashwin, P., 3, 5, 6
audit culture, viii, 17–19, 61–63, 66–72, 73n, 113n, 171, 172, 196–197
Aultman, L. P., 185
Australia, viii, 62, 196, 197
autarkeia, 22, 24–26; see also autonomy
authentic learning, 182, 183
authority, 145, 148–150, 188–191
autoethnographic writing, xi, xii, 105–111, 112n, 114n, 117–127, 129–140
autonomy, 12, 13, 22, 24–28, 62, 65, 66, 71, 72, 170, 171, 176
Axelrod, P., 62

INDEX

B
Bachelard, G., 42
Bain, J. D., 52
Bakhtin, M., 49, 144, 145
Bane, R., 137
Barbalet, J., 35
Barcan, R., 195, 196
Barnes, J., 20
Barnett, R., 4, 5, 8–10, 143, 195
Barrett, T., 162
Bass, R., 182
Bassnett, S., 183
Baxter-Magolda, M. B., 3, 6, 10, 11
Behar, R., 110, 114n
being, 6, 35
Bendix Petersen, E., 78–82, 84, 88, 126
Bensimon, E., 71
Benske, Karla, x, xii
Benwell, B., 45, 49, 50
Bergsma, A., 24
Bernstein, B., 5
Billot, Jennie, x, xii, 157, 158, 159, 160, 161
biophilia, 38, 39, 43n
blended professionals, 18, 19, 26, 151–153, 196–198
Bochner, A. P., 106, 112n
Boer, H., de; see de Boer, H.
Boje, D. M., 93
Bolden, R., 158, 159
Bonnett, A., 114n
Bourdieu, P., 72, 113n
Bowie, David, 170
Boyd, P., 159
Boyer, E., 198, 199
Bozeman, B., 27
BP (British Petroleum), 50
Brady, I., 112n
Braidotti, R., 134
Branham, R. B., 21, 25, 29n
Brenk, F. G., 24, 25
Bridger, A. J., 114n

Britain, viii, ix, 18, 62, 169–172, 176–177
British Petroleum (BP), 50
Bronfenbrenner, U., 92
Bronner, S. E., 39
Brookfield, S., 33, 34, 39
Bryson, C., 17
Bullard, J. E., 52
Burford, James, ix, xi, xii, 118–126
Burke, P. J., 46
Burroughs, William, 170
Burrows, R., 117
Butcher, J., 84
Butterwick, S., 67

C
Cameron-Lewis, Vanessa, ix, xii
Canada, viii, xi, 61–72
capitalism, 34–39
career progression, 7–11, 26–28
  annual reviews, 69–72
  tenure, 62, 63, 65, 66, 72n, 73n
Carnegie Foundation for the Advancement of Teaching, 198–200
Carr, A. D., 118
Cassim, B., 29n
Chalmers, D., 79
change, 17–19, 34, 35, 37–42, 48, 51, 81, 82, 86, 173, 196, 197
Chick, N., 181
Chrysippus of Soli, 22, 23
Churchman, D., 18, 157
Ciccone, A. A., 181
Clance, P. R., 149
Clandinin, D. J., 92, 93, 100, 159, 162
Clarke, C. A., 164
Clegg, S., vii, ix, xiii, 19, 26, 46, 47, 48, 54, 171
close reading, xii, 184–187
Coates, H., 26
Coffey, M., 78

Cohen, L., 160
collegiality, 27, 28, 30n; see also communities of practice
Collins, Brigid, x, xii, 166, 170
communities of practice, 11–13, 27, 28, 30n, 47, 85–88
community outreach programmes, 18, 19
conduct of concern, 77–88
confessions, 181–192
confidence, 145, 148–151
Connelly, F. M., 92, 93, 100
continuing professional development, 175, 176
'cool regard' (*oikeōisis*), 23, 27, 28
Cooper, A., 79
Cooper, C. L., 112n
corporate identity, 50; see also institutional culture
cosmopolitanism, 20
Cranton, P., 175, 176
creativity, x, xii, 38, 39, 105–111, 112n, 114n, 151, 152, 157–166
critical incidents, 181–192
Cunningham, Catriona, x, xii
curiosity, xi, 33–42, 172, 173
curriculum, and academic values, 3–13, 33–42, 172, 173
Cuthill, P., 199
Cynicism, 21, 22, 24–28, 29n

D
Dadaism, 113n
data analysis, 64
Davies, B., 49, 52
Dawson, J., 67
Day, C., 92, 93
de Boer, H., 66, 68
Dear Committee Members (Schumacher), 158
Dearing Report (NCIHE, 1997), 196
Debord, G., 113n
Deci, E. L., 4, 5, 12

Decramer, A., 113n
Deem, R., 113n
DEEWR 196
Deleuze, G., 135
Delgado, R., 113n
democracy, 20
demoralisation, viii, ix
Dempster, S., 189
depression, 106–108, 112n
dérive, 108–110, 113n, 114n
Desmond, W., 21
Dewey, A., 173
dialectics, 37–42, 43n
diatribes, 21, 22
Dickinson, Emily, 169
Dinerstein, A. C., 39
Diogenes Laertius, 22, 29n
Diogenes of Sinope, 21
discourse, 45–55
discrimination, 65, 66, 68–71, 188, 189
discursive psychology, viii, 45–55
Dobbie, D., 62
doctoral students, xi, xii, 117–140
    induction of, 117–127
    negotiation of identity, 129–140
Doughney, J., 71
Doyle, J., 199
Dua, J., 112n
Dunning, D., 52

E
ecology metaphor, 4, 6–11
ecosystems, definition, 14n
Edley, N., 49
Edwards, D., 45, 51
Eisner, E. W., 157, 160, 162, 165, 166, 170, 172, 173
Elbaz-Luwisch, F., 162
Elbow, P., 140n, 141n
Elizabeth, V., 117, 118
Ellis, C., 111, 114n
Ellis, R. J., 191
Ellis, Sam, x, xii

embodiment, 23, 24
emotion, 23, 24, 27, 28, 33–42, 43n, 61–72, 92–101, 129–140, 159–162, 166
   and artistry, 172, 173
   confidence, 145, 148–151
   depression, 106–108, 112n
   fear and stress, 34–39, 117–127, 181, 182, 184–192
   love, 40–42, 43n, 65
   and writing, 143–153
Enders, J., 66, 68
Epictetus, 22, 23, 25, 28, 29n
Epicureanism, 23–26, 28
Epicurus, 23, 24
Epley, N., 52
essentialism, 46, 53
ethnographic fiction, 118–127
eudaimonia, 25, 29n
eupatheiai, 23, 27
evaluation, 67–72
Ewick, P., 111n, 112n
expert knowledge, 85, 86, 95, 96
expressive therapies, 175
extrinsic motivation, 12

F
Fanghanel, J., 48
fast writing, 140n, 141n
fear, 34–39, 117–127, 181, 182, 184–192
Ferguson, Pip, xi
finance, 61, 62, 66, 67
flexians, 19
Foucault, M., 42, 61, 72, 78, 139, 182
Fowler, J., 93–95, 100
Frank, A., 113n
Frankfurt School, 33
Fredman, N., 71
Freire, P., 33, 38, 41, 42, 43n
Freud, S., 38
Friedman, L. J., 43n
Fromm, E., 33–42
funding, 61, 62, 66, 67

G
Gabriel, Y., 160
Gardiner, D., 79
Gaughan, M., 27
GCert, impact on teaching practice, 77–88
Gecas, V., 52
Geiger, D., 160
Gergen, K. J., 48
Gibbons, M., 77
Gibbs, G., 78
Gill, R., 46, 65, 117, 118
Gillespie, N. A., 112n
globalisation, 17–20, 28, 34, 61, 62, 112n, 113n
Goedegebuure, L., 26
Goffman, E., 45
Golde, C., 198–200
Gonçalves, M., 49, 50
Gordon, G., 18, 26
Gornall, L., 72
Gosling, J., 158
Goulet-Cazé, M.-O., 21, 25, 29n
Gourlay, L., 182–184, 187, 191
governmentality, 78, 79
Grant, Barbara, ix, xi, xii, 117, 118
Gray, R., 118
Great Britain, viii, ix, 18, 62, 169–172, 176–177
Greek philosophy, 19–28, 29n
Greene, M., 173
Grisoni, L., 170
Grosz, E., 134, 135
Gurney, R. M., 6
Gysin, Brion, 170

H
Haamer, A., 48
Hager, P., 160

Haggis, T., 77
Hall, S., 140
happiness, 23–25, 29n
Haque, E., 65, 73n
Harley, S., 18
Harré, R., 46, 49, 52
Harris, S., 27
Harvey, L., 61
hedonism, 24
Heidegger, M., 10
Hellenistic philosophy, 19–28, 29n
Henkel, M., 18, 19, 28, 47, 158, 171
Heritage, J., 54
Herrington, A., 182
Herrington, J., 182
Hey, V., 72
Higher Education Academy (UK), 4, 169, 171
Higher Education Quality Council of Ontario (HEQCO), 63
higher education systems, viii, ix, xi
   audit culture, viii, 17–19, 61–63, 66–72, 73n, 113n, 171, 172, 196, 197
   and discrimination, 65, 66, 68–71, 188, 189
   as ecologies, 4, 6–11
   funding, 61, 62, 66, 67
   globalisation, 19, 20, 34, 35, 112n, 113n
   and the knowledge economy, 17, 18, 36–42, 112n, 113n
Hillyard, S., 113n
Himmelfarb, G., 4
Hirshfield, L., 71
Ho, A., 78
Hoad, T. F., 34
Holloway, J., 42
Holowchak, M. A., 23
hooks, b., 43n
Horney, M. H., 41
Howarth, C., 46
Hughes, Langston, 170

Hussey, J., 162
Huston, N., 183, 188
hybrid identities, 151–153, 197, 198

I
ICT (information and communications technology), 17, 18
ideal types, 37
identity maps, 162–165
identity positioning, 50–55, 81–88
Illich, I., 4
images, 187–191
Imes, S. A., 149
imposter syndrome, 145, 148–150
information and communications technology (ICT), 17, 18
Ingram, Toni, ix, xi, xii
institutional culture, viii, ix, xi, xii, 7–11
   academic workgroups, 77–88
   audit culture, viii, 17, 18, 61–63, 66–72, 73n, 113n, 171, 172, 196, 197
   discrimination, 62, 65, 66, 68–71, 188, 189
   mission statements, 18
   and writing for publication, 148, 149
interdisciplinarity, 77, 191, 192
interviews, 63–72, 78, 93, 94, 145, 146
intrinsic motivation, 12, 33–42
Iqbal, I., 68
Irvine, W. B., 21–25
Irwin, T., 24
island maps (identity maps), 162–165
Ivanic, R., 151

J
Jackson, C., 189
Jackson, N., 4, 7–10
Jago, B. J., 106, 112n
Jawitz, J., 47
Jenks, C., 114n
job satisfaction, 61–72
job security, 62, 63, 65, 66, 72n, 73n

Johnson, M., 93, 159, 161, 163
Jones, A., 187
Jones, G. A., 62, 64, 71
Joseph, T., 71

K
Kahn, P., 47
Kamler, B., ix, 143
Kandlbinder, P., 79
Karm, M., 48, 51
Kearns, H., 145, 149, 150
Kelly, M., 78
King, Virginia, x, xii, 159, 162–164, 166
Kinman, G., 112n
Kligyte, Giedre xi
Knight, P. T., 77
Knights, D., 164
knowledge, 85–88
  expert knowledge, 85, 86, 95, 96
  'pathic' knowledge, 112n
  and values, 5, 6, 17, 18, 172, 173
knowledge economy, 17, 18, 36–42, 112n, 113n
Knowles, M., 159
Kreber, C., 77

L
"laddism", 189
Lakoff, G., 93, 159, 161, 163
Land, R., x, 190
language, and identity, 52–54
Lave, J., 45, 47, 49
Lawler, S., vii
Le Roux, C., 159
leadership, 81, 82, 86, 87
Leavy, P., 162, 163, 165, 174
lectures, 85
Lefevere, A., 183
Leggo, C., 112n
Leišyte, L., 66, 68
Leitch, R., 92, 93
Leitch Review of Skills, 7
Lepp, L., 48

Leslie, L. L., 112n
Letiche, H., 160
Levinas, E., 6
Li, S., 112n
Liefbroer, A. C., 24
Linkon, S. L., 182
Loads, Daphne, x, xii, 166, 178, 182, 188
Lombardi, M., 182
Long, A. A., 21–23, 25, 28, 29n
love, 40–42, 43n, 65, 66
Lucas, L., 51
Lucky Jim (Amis), 158
Lueckenhausen, G., 93
Lynch, K., 113n
Lyon, M. M., 34
Lyons, M., 196

M
Maccoby, M., 35, 36
MacCunn, J., 25
Macfarlane, B., 182–184, 187, 191, 196
MacIntosh, P., 173
Mackie, D. M., 52
managerialism, 61, 62, 66, 67
Manen, M. van; see van Manen, M.
Manion, L., 160
Marcus Aurelius, 22
marketing character orientation, 37–39, 42
Marková, I., 46
Mårtensson, K., 77, 88
Martin, E., 93
Marx, Karl, 34–38, 41, 42
Marxism xi, 33–42, 113n
Maybin, J., 144
McAlpine, L., 48, 51, 64
McKinney, K., 181
McLaughlin, N., 33, 43n
McLean, Jan, xi
McLean, M., 45
McLean, Neil, viii, xi, 12, 52
McMahon, D. A., 29n

Mead, G. H., 49
Mendoza, P., 72
Merlan, P., 19
metanoia, 181–192; see also transformative learning
metaphor, x, 4, 6–11, 48, 98–100, 114n, 129–140, 157–166, 175, 184–192, 195
Meyer, J., 190
Mezirow, J., 173, 176
Mitchell, Catherine ix, xi, xii
Moon, J., 93–95, 100
Moon, R., 159
Moore, S. M., 6
Morley, L., 17, 61, 71
Morrison, K., 160
Morrison, T., 143
Morrs, J. R., 35
Most, G. W., 22
motivation, 12, 33–42, 87
multiple identities, 47, 48, 151–153

N
Naidoo, R., 113n
narrative analysis, viii, xi, xii, 48, 51–55, 64, 78–88, 91, 93–101, 129, 130, 139, 140, 160–166, 182–192
NCIHE 196
Neame, Charles, viii, xi, 10
Neary, M., 39
necrophilia, 38, 39
negative visualisation, 25
Nehemas, A., 29n
neoliberalism, 34–39, 112n, 113n
Neves, T., 114n
New Zealand, viii, 62
Newson, J., 63
Nöbauer, H., 117
non-academic staff; see blended professionals
Nowotny, H., 77
Nussbaum, M., 143

O
O'Brien, A., 158
Ochberg, R. L., 51
oikeōisis, 23, 27, 28
Okai, Edward, ix, xi, xii
Ollman, B., 37–39
Onsman, A., 79
Ontario higher education system, 63–72
outreach programmes, 18, 19
Oxford English Dictionary, 8

P
para-academics, 196, 197
Pauwels, L., 162, 165, 166
peer reviews, 72, 145, 152
Pelias, R., 118
performance reviews, 67–72
performativity, viii, xi, xii, 5, 17–19, 61–72, 113n, 171, 172, 182, 196, 197
Perry, W., 6, 7
personal development, 6–11, 94, 95; see also professional development
personal portfolios, 91–101
Peseta, Tai, xi, 79
Petersen, E. Bendix; see Bendix Petersen, E.
philosophy, viii, xi, 4, 6–11, 17–28
  Cynicism, 21, 22, 24–28, 29n
  Epicureanism, 23–26, 28
  Stoicism, 22–28, 29n
Pitcher, R., 161
place to stand (*tūrangawaewae*), 91–101
Plato, 20, 21, 23, 29n
poesis, 13
poetry, 169, 170, 174, 175, 184–187
Pollard, L., 189
Polster, C., 63
Poon, T. S., 18
Poot, G., 24
portfolios, 91–101
positivism, 12

217

INDEX

Postgraduate Certificate in Tertiary Teaching, 91–101, 182
postgraduates, xi, xii, 117–140
  induction of, 117–127
  negotiation of identity, 129–140
Potter, J., 45, 51
Powell, K., 172
power relationships, ix, xi, 8–11, 78–82, 85–87, 113n
Prendergast, M., 112n
Price, Linda, viii, xi
primitivism, 21, 22
productive character orientation, 39–42
professional development, x, 157–166
  and academic writing, ix, xii, 18, 26, 67, 69, 143–153
  annual reviews, 69–72
  blended professionals, 18, 19, 26, 151–153, 196–198
  career progression, 7–11, 26–28
    tenure, 62, 63, 65, 66, 72n, 73n
  and identity formation, 4, 9, 11–13, 19, 23–28, 45–55, 91–101, 169–178
    critical incidents, 181–192
  peer reviews, 72, 145, 152
  student feedback, 68, 69, 96, 97, 189, 190
  supervisor identity, 138–140
  teaching, 77–88, 91–101
Professional Standards Framework (UK) 169, 171, 172, 176, 177
projective visualisation, 25
psychogeography, 114n
psychological needs, 4, 5, 12, 13, 35
publications ix, xii, 18, 26, 67, 69, 143–153

Q

qualifications, 77–88, 91–101, 182
qualitative data, analysis of, 51–55
quality assurance; see audit culture

R

racism, 68
RAE (Research Assessment Exercise), ix, 18, 144
Ramsden, P., 86–88
Randell-Moon, H., 117, 118
recognition, 144–146, 148, 149, 169–178
Reed, M., 113n
reflexivity, 26, 92–101, 157–166, 181–192
Remmik, M., 48, 51
Research Assessment Exercise/Research Excellence Framework (RAE/REF), ix, 18, 144
research grants, 68
research methodology
  arts-based methodologies, 174–176, 181–192
  discursive psychology, viii, 45–55
  ethnographic fiction, 118–127
  interdisciplinarity, 77, 191, 192
  interviews, 63–72, 78, 93, 94, 145, 146
  metaphor analysis, 157–166
  narrative analysis, viii, xi, xii, 48, 51–55, 64, 78–88, 91, 93–101, 129, 130, 139, 140, 160–166, 182–192
  sampling, 63, 64
  social character and ideal types, 36–42
  validity, 51–55
research questions, 18, 19, 183, 184
rhetoric, 20
Rhoades, G., 17, 18, 112n
Rich, A. N. M., 21, 22
Richardson, L., 112n, 118, 139, 140
Ricketts, C., 112n
Robinson, E. W., 20
Robinson, I., 62

Robinson, Susan R., viii, xi
Roggero, G., 36
Rollock, N., 113n
Ronai, C. R., 114n
Rose, M., 130, 137, 139
Rosenthal, D. A., 6
Rosenwald, G. C., 51
Rosetti-Ferreira, C., 51
Rowe, C., 21
Rowland, S., 19
Roxå, T., 77, 88
Ryan, R. M., 4, 5, 12

S
Said, E., 112n
Salgado, J., 49, 50
Salisbury, J., 72
Saltmarsh, S., 117, 118
Sameshima, S., 112n
Samuelowicz, K., 52
Savin-Baden, M., 145
Schmid, C., 12
Schmitt, R., 159, 162
Schofield, M., 21
scholarship, 11, 198, 199
Schön, D., 172
Schumacher, Julie, 158
Scott, P., 77
Seger, C. R., 52
self-authorship, 6
self-determination, 4, 11–13
self-presentation, 49–54, 81–88, 98–100
self-realisation, 49
self-sufficiency (*autarkeia*), 22, 24–26; see also autonomy
Serig, D., 160, 165
sexism, 62, 65–66, 68–71, 188, 189
Shanahan, T., 62, 63
Sharrock, G., 18
Shore, C., 195
Sidgwick, H., 29n

Silbey, S. S., 111n, 112n
Silva, A., 51
Silverstone, L., 175
Sims, P., 175
simultaneity, 49, 50
Sitwell, Edith, 136, 137
Slaughter, S., 112n
Smart, F., 174, 175, 191
Smith, C., 159
Smith, E., R., 52
Smith, Jan, xi
Smith, K., 19
Smolders, C., 113n
Smyth, E., 69, 72
social character, 36–42
social justice, 173
Socrates, 20, 21, 23, 29n
Sophists, 20, 29n
Sparkes, A., 118
Spiller, Dorothy, xi
Spry, T., 114n
staff x, xii
   blended professionals, 18, 19, 26
   career progression, 7–11, 26–28
      tenure, 62, 63, 65, 66, 72n, 73n
   work-life balance, 26, 27, 112n, 146–149, 153, 196
staff evaluation, 67–72
   annual reviews, 69–72
   peer reviews, 72, 145, 152
   student feedback, 68, 69, 96, 97, 189, 190
Stensaker, B., 61
Stephens, W. O., 19, 22, 23, 25, 29n
Stets, J. E., 46
Stevenson, J., 46, 54
steward-apprentice relationship, 8–11
stewardship, 199, 200
Stewart, M., 84
Stoicism, 22–28, 29n
Stokoe, E., 45, 49, 50
Stoncel, D., 84

Stough, C., 112n
Strathern, M., vii
stress, 117–127, 181, 182, 184–192
Strober, M., 181
student experience
   and academic values, 4, 7–11, 33–42
   doctoral students, 117–140
   relationship with supervisors, xi, xii, 129–140
   undergraduates, viii, xi, 33–42
student feedback, 68, 69, 96, 97, 189, 190
supercomplexity, 9
supervisors, xi, xii, 129–140
   co-supervisors, 138, 139
support, 148, 149
surprise, 172, 173; see also curiosity
'Surprising Spaces' (workshop), 169, 170, 176–178
Surrealism, 113n
Sutton, Paul, viii, xi
Swift, G., 34, 43n

T
Tajfel, H., 52
Taylor, P. G., 158
Taylor, S., 51
teaching, 91–101, 169–178, 181–192
   academic workgroups, 77–88
   dialectics, 37–42, 43n
   evaluation of, 68, 69
   negotiation of identity, xi, 47–54, 181, 182
   student feedback, 68, 69
   technology-enhanced methods, 17, 18
teaching and learning regimes (TLRs), 79, 80
teamwork, 77–88
tenure, 62, 63, 65, 66, 72n, 73n
theories, vii, viii, 3–55, 158, 159, 170–172, 196–200

"third space" professionals, 18, 19, 26, 151–153, 197, 198
Thomson, P., ix, 143
Tierney, W., 71, 118
time management, 146–148
Topping, M. E. H., 149
trajectory metaphor, 4, 6–10, 48
transformative learning, 3, 5–13, 42, 173, 176, 181–192, 199
Trapp, M., 21
travel metaphor, 98, 99
Trowler, P., 77, 79, 80, 181
Tsoukas, H., 17, 18
Tuchman, G., 72
tūrangawaewae (place to stand), 91–101
Turner, G., 64
Turner, V., 190
Tytherleigh, M. Y., 112n
Tzara, Tristan, 170

U
undergraduates, viii, xi, 33–42
United Kingdom (UK), viii, ix, 18, 62, 169–172, 176, 177
University and College Union (UK), 105, 112n
University of Colorado, 7
Upitis, R., 176

V
Valsiner, J., 48, 49
values, viii, ix, xi, 3–42, 172, 173
   autonomy, 12, 13, 22, 24–28, 62, 65, 66, 71, 72, 170, 171, 176
   and identity formation, 4, 9, 11–13, 19, 23–28, 158, 159, 169–178
   and performativity, 67–72
   and social character, 36–42
van Manen, M., 112n
Venuti, L., 183
Vincent, L., 159
Vygotsky, L. S., 49

W

Walker, G. E., 198, 199
Walsh, M., 112n
Ward, G. R., 149
Wardhaugh, R., 53
Warren, D., 173
Warren, Simon, ix, xi, 105–111, 118
Watkins, D., 78
Watson, D., viii, xiii
Watson, T., 170, 171
Webb, C., 112n
Webber, Michelle, xi, 65, 66, 69, 71, 72, 73n
Weber, M., 37
Weinrib, J., 62, 64
Weller, S., 181, 188
Wenger, E., 45, 47, 49
Wetherell, M., 49, 51–53
Whitchurch, C., 18, 26, 28, 197, 198
Whynot, C., 175
Widdicombe, S., 45, 49, 52
Wilkesmann, U., 12
Williams, J., 41
Winefield, A. H., 112n
Winter, R., 18
Wisker, Gina, ix, xii, 144, 145
Woelert, P., 71
Wolff, K. H., 182

women, and academic culture, 62, 65, 66, 68–71
workgroups, 77–88
work-life balance, 26, 27, 112n, 146–149, 153, 196
Wray, S., 112n
writing, viii, ix, 67, 143–153
    autoethnographic writing, xi, xii, 105–111, 112n, 114n, 117–127, 129–140
    fast writing, 140n, 141n
    peer review, 72, 145, 152
    publications, ix, xii, 18, 26, 67, 69, 143–153

X

Xenophon, 20, 21
Xu, Linlin, ix, xi, xii

Y

Yates, L., 71
Yates, S. J., 51
Ylijoki, O. H., 72

Z

Zembylas, M., 92
Zeno of Citium, 22, 23